Fieldwork in Social Work

M. Rezaul Islam

Fieldwork in Social Work

A Practical Guide

Springer

M. Rezaul Islam
Institute of Social Welfare and Research
University of Dhaka
Dhaka, Bangladesh

ISBN 978-3-031-56682-0 ISBN 978-3-031-56683-7 (eBook)
https://doi.org/10.1007/978-3-031-56683-7

This Springer imprint is published by the registered company Springer Nature Switzerland AG
The registered company address is: Gewerbestrasse 11, 6330 Cham, Switzerland

Paper in this product is recyclable.

To the resilient spirits of the slum children at Agargaon, Dhaka, whose strength and resilience left an indelible mark on my heart during my 60-day Master's fieldwork experience with Dhaka Ahsania Mission. Your stories, laughter, and challenges have become an enduring source of inspiration, shaping the core of this book. May your dreams and aspirations soar, and may the pages within these covers echo the echoes of your voices. Your vibrant existence and unwavering spirit have illuminated the path of social work, reminding us of all the profound impact it can have on individual lives and communities. This book is dedicated to you, with gratitude for the profound lessons you shared and a commitment to fostering positive change in the lives of those often marginalized and unheard.

Foreword

Professor Islam provides in this book a comprehensive analysis for modern times of fieldwork practice education in social work. Practising social work relies on responsiveness to the diverse human condition and its human, social and spiritual values.

To develop, to help means more than acquiring knowledge. It requires being part of people's lives, being among people in their communities, families, schools, workplaces. Learners taking up professional responsibilities need to be participants in their field of practice. Excellent performance in social work draws on excellent experience in the network of agencies and practitioners that are the context of authentic practice.

Fieldwork engages practitioners directly, from the start of our careers, in the ferment, the potential and the tensions of human lives, in social relations and social structures. It is our first step forward to pursue our commitment to act, with fear and hope, to achieve human flourishing. By developing our knowledge through experience, we can research the prospect of a better life to enrich our communities and societies.

Fieldwork education, therefore, has been an integral part of personal development in social work since its earliest days. Practitioners visiting people struggling with poverty in the slum housing of London in the 1870s were the earliest sources of practice ideas in social work. Detailed regular reporting and discussion developed attitudes, skills and commitment to helping people change their lives, the earliest form of fieldwork education. It was essential to the innovation of Octavia Hill in developing her ideas of social work practice. In one of her letters, she argued that it developed '...knowledge of the passions, hopes, and history of people...how to move, touch and reach them' (quoted by Richmond, 1917, p. 30).

Charlotte Towle (1954), an American social work educator influential in the mid-twentieth century, argued that social work is an exemplar of the importance of the fieldwork component of all professional education. This is because capability and skill in practice must be integrated through fieldwork with social science knowledge.

Dame Eileen Younghusband (1978) described the struggle of British social workers in the 1960s to focus fieldwork education on developing the integration of knowledge and practice skills rather than just observing agency procedures.

Follow up this historic tradition, by using this book in the best way possible, to learn by practising towards a flourishing human social future.

Emeritus Professor
Manchester Metropolitan University
Manchester, UK

Malcolm Payne

References

Richmond, M. E. (1917). *Social diagnosis*. Free Press.

Towle, C. (1954). *The learner in education for the professions, as seen in education for social work*. University of Chicago Press.

Younghusband, E. (1978). *Social work in Britain: 1950–1975: A follow-up study* (vol. 2, pp. 61–74). Allen and Unwin.

Preface

Welcome to the pages of *Fieldwork in Social Work: A Practical Guide*. This book is a dedicated exploration of the dynamic landscape of social work, crafted to illuminate the transformative journey undertaken by social work students, practitioners, and academics. As you delve into these pages, you will embark on a comprehensive expedition that spans the vast realm of fieldwork experiences, ethical dilemmas, technological advancements, and the perpetual evolution of social work practice.

Coverage

At its heart, this guide encompasses a panoramic view of fieldwork practices in the realm of social work. It unfurls an intricate tapestry of insights, offering a wealth of information that spans the entire spectrum of instructions and guidelines for navigating the practical challenges of the field. From in-depth explorations of field placements within hospital settings to the intricacies of navigating ethical considerations, this book leaves no stone unturned. It takes you by the hand and guides you through the labyrinth of reflective practice, unveiling the transformative power it holds. With a visionary outlook, this guide casts its gaze toward the horizon of social work's future, where technological innovations are seamlessly integrated into the fabric of compassionate practice.

Readers

Our aim in creating this guide was to offer a valuable resource that speaks to a diverse audience within the social work community. For students entering the field of social work, this book serves as a guiding light, bridging their academic studies with the complexities of real-world practice. Academics will uncover a wealth of insights to enhance their teaching methods, providing students with a nuanced comprehension of the profession. Agency-level supervisors and experienced social work practitioners will find a plethora of new perspectives and practical strategies for supervising fieldwork students, along with reflective wisdom to elevate their practice and increase their impact within the communities they serve.

Importance of This Book

The importance of this book lies in its ability to bridge the gap between theory and practice in the realm of social work. As the profession continues to evolve and respond to the changing needs of society, the value of this guide becomes more evident. It serves as a beacon of knowledge, offering practical solutions and strategic insights to address the challenges faced by social work professionals in today's complex world. With empathy, advocacy, and social change as its foundation, this guide speaks to the heart of the social work profession, making it an indispensable tool for anyone who seeks to create positive change in the lives of others.

As you embark on this literary journey, we invite you to immerse yourself in the rich tapestry of experiences, knowledge, and transformative potential that *Fieldwork in Social Work: A Practical Guide* has to offer. May these pages inspire and empower you on your unique path within the realm of social work.

Chapter Outlines

Chapter 1—Introduction to Social Work—provides an in-depth exploration of the meanings of social work, delving into its scope, principles, and professional code of ethics. It introduces the micro, mezzo, and macro levels of social work, highlighting the diverse divisions and differences within the field. The chapter discusses various theories of social work, emphasizing its role as a bridge between theory and practice. Furthermore, it explores social work as a profession, detailing the professional behaviors, traits, and roles expected of social workers.

Focusing on fieldwork, Chap. 2—Introduction to Fieldwork in Social Work—elucidates the understanding of fieldwork in social work and delineates different types of fieldwork practices. It underscores the importance of fieldwork in social work, emphasizing the EARIS formula for social work students preparing for field practice. The chapter also addresses the social and mental preparation necessary for effective fieldwork engagement.

Chapter 3—Preparing for Fieldwork in Social Work—guides readers through the preparation phase for fieldwork, emphasizing the significance of setting clear objectives and identifying personal learning goals. It discusses ethical considerations and principles, helping social work students navigate socioeconomic, cultural, and psychological issues addressed by fieldwork agencies. The chapter also introduces the function and challenges associated with fieldwork agencies.

Delving into the practical aspects, Chap. 4—Field Assignments and Duties in Social Work Field Practice—explores the foundations of field assignments, diverse duties, and the roles and responsibilities expected in the field. It sheds light on effective fieldwork documentation, ethical dimensions, supervision, adaptability, client-centered approaches, innovation, and technology in field assignments. The global perspectives on social work assignments are also discussed.

Focusing on cultural sensitivity, Chap. 5—Culturally Responsive Diversity in Social Work Field Practice—addresses the importance of understanding cultural nuances in field practice. It explores strategies for addressing intersectionality, fostering inclusivity, and integrating anti-oppressive practices. The chapter emphasizes enhancing cross-cultural communication skills, evaluating personal biases, collaborating with diverse stakeholders, and navigating ethical challenges in cross-cultural settings.

Chapter 6—Developing Professional Skills in Social Work Field Practice—lays the foundation for professional skills, covering communication, relationship building, assessment, intervention planning, crisis intervention, conflict resolution, cultural competence, diversity, advocacy, social justice, case management, documentation, supervision, and professional development.

Focusing on agency-level practice, Chap. 7: Assessing and Planning for Agency-Level Field Practice in Social Work—explores agency assessment, needs assessment, strategic planning, client-centered approaches, cultural competence, diversity integration, and evaluation for continuous improvement.

Chapter 8—Implementation and Intervention in Field Practice at the Agency Level—guides readers through tailoring interventions to client needs, collaborative goal setting, utilizing evidence-based practices, addressing systemic factors, adopting a case management model, and monitoring progress in agency-level field practice.

Offering insights into data collection, Chap. 9—Data Collection for Field Reports in Social Work Practice—covers qualitative and quantitative techniques, integrating mixed-methods approaches, ethical considerations, and utilizing technology for effective data collection in social work field practice.

Exploring various agency environments, specializations, and cultures, Chap. 10—Navigating Field Settings and Agency Dynamics—focuses on adapting to and understanding unique agency dynamics and structures. It introduces the application of SWOT analysis for effective fieldwork situations, providing examples and insights.

Chapter 11—Working Within Systems: Applications of Assessment Planning Interventions—details engagement with clients, families, groups, communities, policy assessment, political systems, and structures. It includes practical examples like the structure of a case record, writing referral and termination letters, collaborating within multidisciplinary teams, and navigating bureaucracy.

Covering the theoretical foundations, roles, responsibilities, techniques, and approaches in fieldwork supervision, Chap. 12—Supervision of Fieldwork Students—includes a template for supervision, cultural competence, addressing challenges, and evaluation in supervision. It also explores professional development for supervisors, case studies, and emerging trends.

Chapter 13—Challenges and Opportunities in Fieldwork Practice—delves into the challenges of ethical dilemmas, personal boundaries, emotional well-being, cultural diversity, systemic barriers, client resistance, supervisory challenges, and opportunities for students. It explores reflective practices, technology, and resilience in overcoming challenges, considering global perspectives and innovative solutions.

Detailing the concept, objectives, characteristics, and contents of fieldwork reports, Chap. 14: Fieldwork Report Writing Format—provides an example to guide students in producing effective reports.

Exploring reflective practice in the agency context, Chap. 15: Reflective Practice and Learning in Fieldwork—integrates reflective practices into organizational culture, discusses structural mechanisms for reflective learning, and evaluates outcomes. It addresses challenges and strategies for overcoming barriers.

Chapter 16—Concluding and Future Directions in Social Work Field Practice—covers transitioning out-of-field placement, celebrating achievements, embracing technological advancements, and adapting to evolving societal needs and challenges in social work field practice. It encourages an exploration of future directions and considerations for the field.

Dhaka, Bangladesh M. Rezaul Islam

Acknowledgments

The completion of this book has been a gratifying journey, one that would not have been possible without the involvement, encouragement, and support of various individuals whom I wish to acknowledge with sincere gratitude. My deepest appreciation goes to the social work educators, practitioners, and professionals who generously shared their insights and experiences, enriching the content of this book with practical wisdom and real-world perspectives.

I extend my heartfelt thanks to the students and fieldwork practitioners who candidly shared their stories and challenges, providing authenticity and depth to the narratives woven throughout these pages. Your willingness to contribute has truly shaped this resource.

A special word of thanks to the special people who make valuable opinions, time, and expertise to provide invaluable feedback, ensuring the accuracy, relevance, and quality of the material presented here. To the editorial and production teams, your meticulous efforts in refining and presenting this work are deeply appreciated. Your dedication has transformed raw ideas into a cohesive and informative book.

I am grateful to my family, friends, and colleagues for their unwavering encouragement and understanding during the creation of this book. Your support sustained me through the process, and I am truly fortunate to have you in my corner.

To the readers of this book, thank you for engaging with the material and for your commitment to the field of social work. I hope that this book serves as a valuable resource on your journey of learning and professional growth.

This endeavor stands as a testament to the collaborative spirit of many who believe in the significance of social work. As I reflect on the completion of this work, I am energized to continue contributing to the advancement of the field and the empowerment of those who dedicate themselves to making positive changes in the lives of individuals and communities.

About This Book

Fieldwork in Social Work: A Practical Guide is a comprehensive resource tailored for undergraduate and graduate social work students, offering essential insights and tools to navigate the intricate landscape of fieldwork placements. Whether initiating their fieldwork journey or actively engaged in practical experiences, students find a trustworthy companion in this guide, which spans foundational principles to advanced topics such as agency-level interventions, data collection techniques, and challenges in the field. Emphasizing cultural competence and diversity, the guide explores strategies for fostering inclusive interventions, reflecting the contemporary realities of globalized social work practice. With its integration of theoretical foundations and practical applications, the inclusion of technology and ethical considerations, and insights into emerging trends, the guide serves not only as an educational tool but as an inspirational source for social work educators and practitioners seeking a deeper understanding of the field's challenges and opportunities.

Contents

List of Figures

List of Tables

About the Author

M. Rezaul Islam, PhD an esteemed academic, currently serves as a Professor of Social Work at the Institute of Social Welfare and Research, University of Dhaka, Bangladesh. With a rich academic journey that includes an MSW and a PhD from the University of Nottingham, UK, Dr. Islam brings over 27 years of diverse experience in teaching, research, and global collaborative initiatives. His expertise transcends disciplinary boundaries, enabling him to unravel complex socio-political dynamics. Dr. Islam has been recognized as one of the top 2% of scientists globally. In 2018, he was honored with the UGC Gold Medal for publishing a high-impact journal article. Dr. Islam has contributed significantly to various universities worldwide, including the University of Malaya, the University of Johannesburg, Universiti Sains Malaysia, and the BRAC Institute of Governance and Development (BIGD). His extensive scholarship covers social work, community development, climate change and disasters, and migration studies, reflected in 120 impactful journal articles, 45 insightful book chapters, and 15 meticulously authored and edited books. Dr. Islam's research spans various topics, such as climate change, migration, and social inequality, with a specific focus on the contexts of South Asia and the Arab world. Advocating for social justice and empowerment, he addresses challenges faced by marginalized communities and champions research-informed solutions. As a doctoral supervisor, Dr. Islam plays a pivotal role in guiding impactful research endeavors, leaving an enduring mark on the advancement of knowledge in these vital domains. He currently serves as a Member of the International Advisory Board of the *Community Development Journal* (Oxford University Press) and as an editorial board member of three journals: *Asian Social Work and Policy Review* (Wiley), *Local Development & Society* (Taylor & Francis), and *International Journal of Community Well-Being* (Springer).

Chapter 1
Introduction to Social Work

Learning Objectives
After reading this chapter, you will be able to:

- Define the diverse meanings associated with social work
- Explore the broad scope of social work practice at micro, mezzo, and macro levels
- Comprehend the guiding principles and ethical considerations in social work
- Distinguish between micro, mezzo, and macro levels of practice
- Recognize the diverse divisions and differences within social work
- Understand the major theories underpinning social work practice
- Appreciate social work as a recognized and vital profession
- Connect the theoretical concepts of social work to practical application in real-world scenarios

1.1 Meanings of Social Work

Social work encompasses a multifaceted profession dedicated to enhancing the well-being and quality of life for individuals, families, groups, and communities (Adams et al., 2017). At its core, social work is a field that seeks to address and alleviate social issues, inequalities, and injustices. The profession operates within a framework of values such as social justice, human rights, and the dignity and worth of every person. Social workers engage in a diverse range of activities, including but not limited to counseling, advocacy, community organizing, and policy analysis. They aim to empower individuals and communities to overcome challenges and obstacles, promoting positive change and social cohesion. Social work operates in various settings, including healthcare, education, government agencies, and non-profit organizations.

M. R. Islam, *Fieldwork in Social Work*,
https://doi.org/10.1007/978-3-031-56683-7_1

One of the distinguishing features of social work is its commitment to addressing systemic issues that contribute to social problems. Social workers strive not only to alleviate immediate challenges but also to advocate for broader social change. Through interventions at the micro, mezzo, and macro levels, social work seeks to create a more just and equitable society. Social work is a profession deeply rooted in compassion, empathy, and a commitment to social justice (Reisch & Garvin, 2016). It involves a dynamic and challenging set of roles aimed at improving the lives of individuals and communities while advocating for systemic change to create a fair and inclusive society.

1.2 Scope of Social Work

The scope of social work is vast and encompasses a broad range of activities aimed at addressing social issues, promoting well-being, and fostering positive social change. Key aspects of the scope of social work include (Fig. 1.1):

Individual and Family Support: Individual and family support stands as a pivotal component within the expansive scope of social work, embodying the profession's commitment to fostering the well-being of individuals and families facing diverse challenges. Social workers operating in this domain provide empathetic counseling, practical assistance, and essential resources to address a spectrum of issues, including mental health struggles, substance abuse, domestic violence, and familial conflicts. Grounded in the principles of empowerment and resilience, social workers collaborate with clients to navigate complex life circumstances, promoting coping strategies and facilitating access to necessary services. This facet of social work involves creating a safe space for individuals and families to share their concerns, fostering a therapeutic alliance that facilitates positive change. Through a

Fig. 1.1 Scope of social work. (Source: Author)

strengths-based approach, social workers aim to enhance the overall functioning and quality of life for those they serve, recognizing the interconnectedness of individual well-being and the health of family systems. As advocates for vulnerable populations, social workers within the realm of Individual and Family Support contribute to the restoration of stability, the strengthening of relationships, and the promotion of holistic resilience in the face of life's challenges.

Community Development: Community development in social work encompasses a dynamic and participatory process aimed at improving the overall well-being and quality of life within a specific geographic or social community. This multifaceted approach involves collaboration between community members, social workers, and various stakeholders to identify, prioritize, and address local needs and challenges. Social workers engaged in community development work strive to empower residents, enhance social capital, and build sustainable solutions that promote social justice and equity. Through methods such as community organizing, capacity building, and advocacy, social workers facilitate the mobilization of resources, foster community engagement, and advocate for policies that positively impact the collective welfare of the community. This scope of social work emphasizes the importance of grassroots initiatives, cultural competence, and the recognition of diverse perspectives to create inclusive and thriving communities.

Advocacy and Social Justice: Advocacy and social justice represent fundamental pillars within the scope of social work, embodying the profession's commitment to challenging systemic inequalities and promoting equitable outcomes for individuals and communities. Social workers engaged in advocacy strive to amplify the voices of marginalized populations, address discriminatory practices, and influence policies that perpetuate social injustice. This scope encompasses a range of activities, including legislative advocacy, community mobilization, and public awareness campaigns, all geared toward dismantling barriers and fostering inclusive environments. Social workers advocate for human rights, fair access to resources, and policies that address the root causes of societal challenges. By embracing advocacy and social justice, social workers contribute to creating a more just and compassionate society where every individual, regardless of background or circumstance, can access opportunities for growth, development, and well-being.

Healthcare and Medical Social Work: Healthcare and medical social work constitute a vital dimension within the expansive scope of social work, focusing on the intersection of health, well-being, and social factors. Social workers in healthcare settings play pivotal roles in facilitating the psychosocial aspects of patient care, collaborating with interdisciplinary teams to address the complex challenges individuals face due to illness or medical conditions. This scope involves providing emotional support, counseling, and practical assistance to patients and their families, navigating the healthcare system, and advocating for their rights. Medical social workers also engage in healthcare policy advocacy, aiming to improve healthcare delivery, accessibility, and equity. By integrating the principles of social work into healthcare, professionals in this field contribute to holistic patient care, emphasizing the interconnectedness of physical, social, and emotional dimensions in the pursuit of optimal health outcomes and quality of life.

Education: In the realm of social work, education stands as a significant and multifaceted scope, encompassing various dimensions that contribute to individual and societal well-being. Social workers engaged in the field of education operate at different levels, from early childhood education to higher education institutions. They play pivotal roles in addressing the diverse needs of students, families, and educational communities. This scope involves supporting students facing challenges, promoting inclusive and equitable educational environments, addressing issues related to bullying or discrimination, and collaborating with educators, administrators, and families to enhance the overall educational experience. Social workers in education also advocate for systemic changes, ensuring policies and practices prioritize the welfare and development of all learners. The focus extends beyond academic success to encompass the social and emotional aspects of students' lives, fostering environments that nurture growth, resilience, and lifelong learning.

Policy Analysis and Development: Policy analysis and development represent a crucial scope within the field of social work, where professionals engage in the examination, formulation, and advocacy of policies aimed at creating positive social change. Social workers involved in policy analysis navigate the complexities of social issues, evaluate existing policies, and propose innovative solutions to address systemic challenges. They collaborate with governmental bodies, nonprofit organizations, and community stakeholders to shape policies that promote social justice, equity, and the well-being of diverse populations. This scope involves a comprehensive understanding of social problems, the legislative process, and the impact of policies on individuals and communities. Social workers in policy analysis actively contribute to shaping laws and regulations, advocating for marginalized groups, and striving for a more just and inclusive society. Their work bridges the gap between research, practice, and advocacy, driving systemic changes that positively influence the lives of individuals and communities.

Gerontology and Aging Services: Gerontology and aging services represent a vital scope within the field of social work, focusing on the unique needs and challenges of the aging population. Social workers in this specialization play a crucial role in enhancing the quality of life for older adults and promoting their well-being. They engage in comprehensive assessments, address issues related to healthcare, housing, and social support, and advocate for policies that benefit older individuals. Gerontological social workers often collaborate with healthcare professionals, families, and community resources to provide holistic care and support for seniors. Their work includes addressing issues such as elder abuse, dementia care, end-of-life planning, and promoting social inclusion for older adults. By specializing in gerontology and aging services, social workers contribute to creating age-friendly environments and fostering dignified and fulfilling lives for older individuals in our communities.

Child Welfare: Child welfare is a critical and specialized area within social work that focuses on the well-being, safety, and development of children and families. Social workers in child welfare play multifaceted roles, including assessing and intervening in situations of child abuse and neglect, supporting families in crisis, and facilitating foster care and adoption processes when necessary. They collaborate with various stakeholders, such as child protective services, legal authorities, and community resources, to ensure the best interests of children are upheld. Child welfare social workers strive to create safe and nurturing environments for children, offering counseling, advocacy, and support services to families facing challenges. Their work is guided by principles of child protection, family preservation, and promoting healthy child development, contributing significantly to the broader mission of safeguarding the welfare of our youngest community members.

Crisis Intervention: Crisis intervention is a vital domain within social work that focuses on providing immediate and targeted support to individuals or communities facing acute and distressing situations. Social workers engaged in crisis intervention are trained to assess, de-escalate, and intervene during emergencies such as natural disasters, accidents, violence, or mental health crises. Their role involves offering emotional support, practical assistance, and connecting individuals with essential resources to navigate and cope with the immediate aftermath of a crisis. Crisis intervention social workers collaborate with emergency services, mental health professionals, and community organizations to ensure a coordinated and effective response. The goal is to stabilize individuals in crisis, address their immediate needs, and facilitate a pathway toward recovery and resilience. This specialized area of social work plays a crucial role in promoting community well-being and mitigating the adverse effects of sudden and challenging circumstances.

International Social Work: International social work is a multifaceted field within the broader discipline that extends the principles and practices of social work to a global context. Social workers engaging in international social work operate across borders and cultures, addressing complex issues such as poverty, inequality, human rights, and social justice on a global scale. This specialization involves collaborating with diverse communities, organizations, and governments to develop and implement strategies that enhance the well-being of individuals and populations worldwide. International social workers navigate cultural nuances, advocate for the rights of vulnerable populations, and contribute to the development of sustainable solutions in response to global challenges. Their roles may include humanitarian aid, capacity building, policy advocacy, and fostering cross-cultural understanding. International social work reflects a commitment to promoting social and economic justice on a global level, acknowledging the interconnectedness of social issues and the importance of collaborative efforts to create positive change.

The scope of social work is dynamic and responsive to evolving social challenges, reflecting a commitment to creating positive change at various levels of society. Social workers collaborate with diverse populations and engage in interdisciplinary efforts to address complex social issues effectively.

1.3 Social Work Principles and Professional Code of Ethics

Social work, as an applied social science, stands as a dynamic and compassionate profession dedicated to the enhancement of individual well-being, strengthening of families, supporting groups, and empowering entire communities (Berg-Weger, 2019). At its core, social work represents a systematic and organized initiative through agencies to address and ameliorate societal issues, advocating for positive change and justice. In this noble pursuit, social workers operate within a framework defined by fundamental principles and a robust professional code of ethics. The essence of social work lies in its commitment to service, embodying a mission to alleviate suffering, promote social justice, and enhance the overall quality of life for diverse populations. Whether intervening at the individual, family, group, or community level, social workers carry the responsibility of facilitating positive change and contributing to the betterment of society (Knight & Gitterman, 2018).

This professional and organized service, often initiated through agencies, operates within a framework defined by a set of core principles that guide the ethical conduct of social workers. These principles, rooted in a deep understanding of the inherent dignity of every individual, the importance of human relationships, and a dedication to social justice, shape the ethical landscape of social work practice. As social work is a profession deeply embedded in the ethos of service, social workers navigate their responsibilities with integrity, cultural competence, and a profound respect for the diverse backgrounds of those they serve. These principles, collectively forming the ethical compass of social work, ensure that practitioners engage in interventions that are not only effective but also aligned with the values of justice, respect, and empowerment.

For social work students aspiring to embark on their journey at the agency level, a thorough understanding of these core principles and the professional code of ethics is paramount (McAuliffe et al., 2023). Social work education serves as the foundation for cultivating the knowledge, skills, and ethical awareness necessary to navigate the complexities of real-world practice. The principles and code of ethics act as guiding lights, shaping the ethical decision-making processes of students as they prepare to take on responsibilities within agencies (Beckett et al., 2017). This section delves into an exploration of the core principles and the professional code of ethics that underpin social work practice. It serves as a vital resource for social work students, offering a comprehensive understanding of the ethical considerations and values that should inform their professional conduct. As students prepare to step into the diverse and challenging landscape of agency-level fieldwork, a solid grasp of these principles ensures they are well-equipped to uphold the highest standards of ethical practice and contribute meaningfully to the well-being of individuals and communities.

1.3.1 Core Principles of Social Work

To understand the foundational principles of social work, please see Fig. 1.2 for an illustrative representation of the core values and ethics that underpin the profession's practice.

Service: The primary mission of social work is to enhance the well-being of individuals and communities. Social workers are dedicated to providing competent and compassionate services to those in need, addressing both individual and societal challenges.

Social Justice: Social workers champion social justice by challenging systemic barriers, advocating for equitable distribution of resources, and promoting inclusivity. They strive to eliminate discrimination and work towards creating a fair and just society.

Dignity and Worth of the Person: Social workers respect the inherent dignity and worth of each individual. Regardless of background, identity, or circumstances, everyone is entitled to be treated with respect and compassion.

Importance of Human Relationships: Social work is founded on the recognition of the significance of human relationships. Building rapport, fostering connections, and understanding the dynamics of relationships are integral aspects of social work practice.

Integrity: Social workers uphold the highest standards of integrity, maintaining honesty and transparency in their interactions. They act with sincerity, building trust with clients and stakeholders.

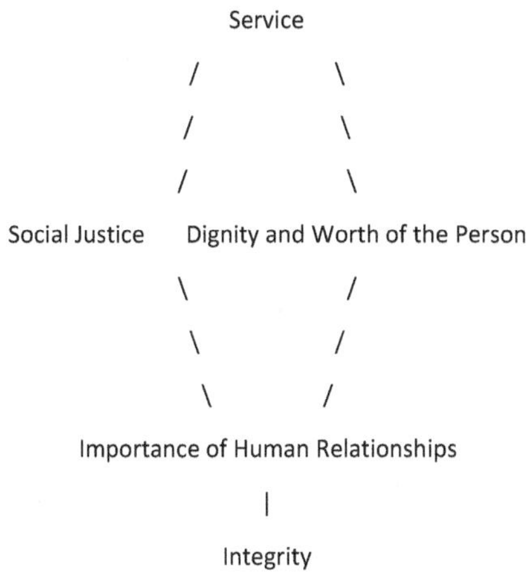

Fig. 1.2 Core principles of social work. (Source: Author)

1.3.2 Professional Code of Ethics

Confidentiality: Social workers adhere to strict standards of confidentiality, safeguarding the privacy of clients. Information shared during professional relationships is treated with the utmost discretion unless mandated otherwise by legal and ethical obligations.

Informed Consent: Social workers obtain informed consent from clients before initiating any interventions. This involves ensuring clients have a clear understanding of the nature, purpose, and potential risks and benefits of the services provided.

Cultural Competence: Social workers commit to cultural competence, recognizing and respecting the diverse backgrounds of clients. They strive to be aware of their own cultural biases and continually seek to enhance their cultural competence to provide effective and sensitive services.

Conflict of Interest: Social workers avoid conflicts of interest that may compromise their professional judgment. They are transparent about potential conflicts and take steps to address them to ensure the best interests of clients.

Professional Boundaries: Maintaining appropriate professional boundaries is crucial. Social workers establish and uphold clear boundaries to ensure a professional and ethical relationship with clients, avoiding dual relationships that could compromise objectivity.

Continuous Professional Development: Social workers engage in continuous learning and professional development to stay abreast of evolving practices, research, and ethical standards. This commitment to ongoing education enhances their competence and effectiveness.

Social work principles and ethics guide decision-making in complex situations. Practitioners often face dilemmas where they must balance competing values or navigate challenging ethical terrain. The principles and code of ethics provide a framework for ethical decision-making, helping practitioners uphold their commitment to service and justice. Social workers participate in regular supervision to discuss cases, ethical challenges, and personal and professional development. This accountability mechanism ensures that practitioners receive guidance, reflect on their practice, and address any ethical concerns in a supportive environment. Social work principles and the professional code of ethics serve as guiding lights for practitioners, shaping their values, decisions, and interactions. Grounded in the commitment to service, justice, and the dignity of individuals, these principles underscore the importance of ethical and compassionate practice in the field of social work.

1.4 Micro, Mezzo, and Macro Levels Social Work

Micro, mezzo, and macro levels in social work represent different scales of intervention and analysis within the field, each focusing on specific aspects of individuals, families, groups, communities, and societies (Hopps & Lowe, 2008; Mattocks,

2018). Understanding and applying interventions at these levels are integral to the comprehensive and systemic nature of social work practice.

Micro-level social work: Micro-level social work involves direct interactions with individuals and families, focusing on personal challenges, emotional well-being, and behavioral issues. Social workers at the micro level engage in therapeutic relationships and provide tailored interventions to address specific needs. For instance, a clinical social worker working at a counseling center might offer one-on-one therapy sessions to an individual dealing with anxiety. In this scenario, the social worker conducts assessments, develops personalized treatment plans, and employs therapeutic techniques to enhance the client's mental health. Micro-level social work is characterized by its intimate and individualized approach, aiming to empower individuals to cope with life's difficulties and improve their overall well-being. The impact of micro-level interventions is profound, as they directly influence the lives of individuals and contribute to the enhancement of their emotional and psychological resilience.

Mezzo-level social work: Mezzo-level social work operates on an intermediary scale, addressing the needs of smaller groups and communities. Social workers at the mezzo level work with organizations, schools, or local community groups, focusing on fostering positive relationships and facilitating communication. An example of mezzo-level social work could be a school social worker who collaborates with teachers, parents, and community organizations to create programs addressing bullying prevention. In this role, the social worker may organize workshops, mediate conflicts among students, and implement strategies to improve the overall social and emotional climate within the school community. Mezzo-level interventions have a broader reach than micro-level work, impacting not just individuals but the dynamics within a specific group or community, fostering social cohesion and collective well-being.

Macro-level social work: Macro-level social work involves addressing social issues and creating systemic change on a larger scale, often focusing on communities, organizations, and policies. Social workers at the macro level may engage in advocacy, research, and policy development to influence social structures and institutions. An example of macro-level social work could be a social worker working for a nonprofit organization that advocates for affordable housing policies. In this role, the social worker might engage with policymakers, conduct research on housing disparities, and mobilize community members to advocate for legislative changes that promote equitable access to housing. Macro-level interventions aim to bring about widespread social change, influencing policies and practices to create a more just and inclusive society.

1.5 Social Work-Diverse, Divisions, and Differences

1.5.1 Social Work Is a Diverse Discipline

Social work stands out as a diverse discipline through its engagement across a myriad of practice settings. Social workers operate in schools, healthcare institutions, government agencies, nonprofit organizations, and private practices, illustrating the field's adaptability in addressing a broad spectrum of social issues (Dominelli, 2010; Rogowski, 2020). This versatility reflects a commitment to meeting the unique needs of individuals and communities in diverse contexts.

In addition to diverse practice settings, social work encompasses various specialized areas of practice. Clinical social work focuses on mental health, medical social work intersects with healthcare, and school social work addresses challenges within educational environments. Specializations such as child welfare, gerontological social work, and macro social work further showcase the profession's ability to cater to the distinct needs of diverse populations.

Beyond varied practice and specialization, the diversity of social work is also expressed through its unwavering commitment to social justice. Social workers actively advocate for policy changes, engage in community organizing efforts, and work at the macro level to address systemic issues contributing to inequality. This commitment underscores the profession's role in challenging social injustices and promoting inclusivity, showcasing how social work extends beyond individual client interactions to effect broader societal change.

1.5.2 Social Work Divisions

Social work is a multifaceted profession with several divisions that cater to specific aspects of human needs and social issues (for details, please read Dominelli et al., 2002; Adams et al., 2017).

Clinical Social Work: Clinical social workers, often known as therapists or counselors, specialize in providing mental health services. They work with individuals, families, and groups to address various mental health challenges, emotional issues, and behavioral disorders. Clinical social workers utilize psychotherapeutic techniques, assessments, and interventions to help clients understand and manage their mental health conditions. Whether in private practice, hospitals, or mental health agencies, their primary focus is on improving clients' overall well-being.

Medical Social Work: In healthcare settings, medical social workers contribute to the holistic care of patients by addressing the psychosocial aspects of illness. They work closely with medical teams to assess the social and emotional factors affecting patients and their families. Medical social workers assist in coping with diagnoses, facilitate communication between patients and healthcare providers, and help navigate complex healthcare systems. Their role is pivotal in enhancing the quality of life for individuals facing health challenges.

School Social Work: School social workers operate within educational institutions, supporting students in overcoming social, emotional, and behavioral obstacles that may hinder academic success. They collaborate with teachers, parents, and administrators to create a positive and inclusive school environment. School social workers conduct assessments, provide counseling, and develop intervention plans to address students' individual needs. They play a vital role in promoting a conducive atmosphere for learning and personal development.

Macro Social Work: Macro social workers focus on creating systemic change to address social issues at a broader level. This involves policy advocacy, community organizing, and program development aimed at improving social conditions. Macro social workers engage with government agencies, nonprofit organizations, and community groups to influence policies and practices that contribute to social inequalities. Their work often revolves around addressing structural barriers and advocating for social justice on a large scale.

Gerontological Social Work: Gerontological social workers specialize in working with older adults, addressing issues related to aging, health, and quality of life. They provide support to seniors in navigating healthcare systems, adapting to changes in living arrangements, and coping with issues such as grief and loss.

Child Welfare Social Work: Social workers in child welfare focus on the protection and well-being of children. They may work for child protective services, advocating for the safety of at-risk children, and facilitating placements in foster care or adoptive homes. Child welfare social workers often collaborate with families to strengthen parenting skills and create safe environments for children.

Crisis Intervention Social Work: Crisis intervention social workers are trained to respond to immediate and acute situations, such as natural disasters, accidents, or traumatic events. They provide psychological first aid, emotional support, and resources to individuals and communities facing crises, helping them cope and recover.

International Social Work: Social workers engaged in international social work address global issues, including poverty, human rights, and humanitarian crises. They may work for international organizations, NGOs, or governmental agencies, focusing on social development, refugee assistance, and cross-cultural understanding.

Addictions Social Work: Social workers in the field of addictions assist individuals and families affected by substance abuse or behavioral addictions. They provide counseling, support group facilitation, and interventions to help clients overcome addiction and maintain recovery.

Forensic Social Work: Forensic social workers operate at the intersection of social work and the legal system. They may work in criminal justice settings, providing assessments, counseling, and support to individuals involved in legal processes, such as defendants, victims, or those within correctional facilities.

Military Social Work: Military social workers support active-duty service members, veterans, and their families. They address issues unique to military life, including deployment stress, post-traumatic stress disorder (PTSD), and family dynamics related to military service.

1.5.3 Differences in Social Work

The practice of social work is highly nuanced and context-dependent, varying significantly based on factors such as country, culture, legal frameworks, the nature of the problem, and the scope of the profession (for details, please read Dominelli et al., 2002; Adams et al., 2017). Here's an exploration of how these diverse elements influence the field of social work:

Country and Legal Frameworks: Social work is deeply influenced by the legal and policy frameworks of individual countries. The rights, responsibilities, and scope of social work practitioners may differ based on national laws and regulations. For example, the approach to child protection or mental health interventions may vary significantly between countries due to distinct legal mandates.

Cultural Context: Cultural considerations play a pivotal role in shaping social work practices. Social workers need to be culturally competent, understanding and respecting the diverse beliefs, values, and practices of the populations they serve. Cultural nuances influence communication styles, help-seeking behaviors, and the perception of social issues, requiring social workers to adapt their approaches accordingly.

Nature of the Problem: The nature of social issues and challenges varies widely, impacting the strategies employed by social workers. Whether addressing issues like poverty, substance abuse, domestic violence, or mental health, practitioners must tailor their interventions to the specific characteristics of the problem at hand. For instance, addressing homelessness requires different approaches than tackling educational disparities.

Scope of Social Work: Social work's scope encompasses a broad spectrum, ranging from micro-level interventions (individuals and families) to mezzo-level work (groups and communities) and macro-level initiatives (societal and systemic change). The scope may also extend to various specializations such as healthcare social work, school social work, and forensic social work, each demanding specialized knowledge and skills.

Global Variances: Social work is practiced globally, and while there are common principles, the application may differ based on global disparities in resources, socioeconomic conditions, and political landscapes. International social work involves addressing issues like migration, human rights, and global health, requiring an understanding of transnational challenges and collaboration with diverse communities.

Ethical Considerations: Ethical considerations in social work are universal and guided by principles like confidentiality, respect, and autonomy. However, the interpretation and application of ethical guidelines may be influenced by cultural norms and legal frameworks, necessitating a nuanced understanding of ethical dilemmas in different contexts.

In essence, social work's adaptability is its strength, allowing professionals to navigate the intricate interplay of cultural, legal, and contextual factors. Social workers must continuously engage in reflective practice, recognizing the dynamic nature of their profession and the need for context-specific interventions to promote positive change.

1.6 Theories of Social Work

Social work theories form the conceptual framework that guides social workers in understanding, analyzing, and intervening in diverse human situations. These theories are crucial tools for practitioners, providing a lens through which to interpret complex social issues and human behavior (for details, please read Hutchinson & Oltedal, 2014; Teater, 2019; Healy, 2022). Here, we delve into the multifaceted landscape of social work theories, recognizing their diverse perspectives and applications.

Micro-Level Theories: Micro-level theories focus on individual and interpersonal dynamics. Psychodynamic theories, rooted in the work of Freud, explore unconscious motivations and childhood experiences shaping behavior. Cognitive-behavioral theories emphasize the role of thoughts and behaviors in shaping emotional experiences. Humanistic theories, like person-centered therapy, underscore the importance of empathy and unconditional positive regard in fostering personal growth. At the micro level, social workers engage with individuals to address mental health challenges, trauma, and interpersonal relationships.

Mezzo-Level Theories: Mezzo-level theories operate at the intermediate level, examining group dynamics and relationships within communities. Systems theory, a cornerstone of mezzo-level practice, views individuals as part of larger social systems. Social exchange theory explores the dynamics of give-and-take within relationships. Mezzo-level social work involves working with families, small groups, and communities, addressing issues like family dynamics, group cohesion, and community development.

Macro-Level Theories: Macro-level theories zoom out to the societal and structural dimensions of human behavior. Structural-functionalism analyzes how social structures contribute to the stability of society. Conflict theory explores power imbalances and social inequalities. Feminist theories highlight gender-based oppression. Social workers engaged at the macro level aim to influence policy, advocate for social justice, and address systemic issues such as poverty, discrimination, and institutional barriers.

Eclectic Approaches: Many contemporary social workers adopt eclectic approaches, drawing on multiple theories to create a comprehensive understanding of human behavior. Eclecticism allows practitioners to tailor interventions to the unique needs of individuals and communities. Integrative approaches may blend elements of psychodynamic, cognitive-behavioral, and systems theories, providing a flexible toolkit for addressing diverse challenges.

Critical and Postmodern Perspectives: Critical theories in social work emphasize social justice, challenging power structures, and advocating for marginalized groups. Postmodern perspectives question grand narratives, recognizing diverse truths and perspectives. These frameworks encourage reflexivity, acknowledging the impact of language, culture, and societal norms on social work practice. Social workers embracing critical and postmodern theories aim to dismantle oppressive systems and amplify the voices of those on the margins.

The rich tapestry of social work theories offers practitioners a nuanced understanding of human behavior and social systems. The integration of micro, mezzo, and macro-level perspectives, along with eclectic and critical approaches, empowers social workers to navigate the intricate challenges of promoting individual well-being and societal transformation.

1.6.1 Social Work Theories, Models, and Approaches in Field Practice

The landscape of social work practice encompasses diverse and varied applications tailored to individuals, families, groups, and communities, varying from person to person, culture to culture, and country to country. To address this array of challenges, social workers employ an array of theories, approaches, and models that align with specific problems and requirements. Here is a brief description of some common approaches, models, and theories that social work employs:

- Systems Theory (Talcott Parsons, mid-twentieth century): Systems theory views individuals as interconnected systems that are influenced by their surroundings. Social workers applying this model analyze how changes in one part of the system impact the whole.
- Ecological Systems Theory (Germain & Gitterman, 1996): Building on systems theory, this perspective emphasizes the dynamic interaction between individuals and their environments. Germain and Gitterman's work highlights the importance of understanding individuals within the context of their ecological surroundings.
- Social Learning Theory (Bandura & Walters, 1977): Albert Bandura's theory underscores the role of observational learning and modeling in shaping behavior. It suggests that people learn by observing the actions and consequences of others.
- Cognitive-Behavioral Theory (Beck, 1967): Aaron Beck's theory focuses on the interplay between thoughts, emotions, and behaviors. It posits that cognitive patterns influence emotional responses and behaviors and seek to modify negative thought patterns to improve well-being.
- Person-Centered Theory (Rogers, 1959 in Rogers, 2013): Carl Rogers' theory emphasizes the therapeutic relationship and the creation of a nonjudgmental and empathetic environment for clients. It highlights the role of unconditional positive regard in facilitating personal growth.
- Psychodynamic Theory (Freud, 1895–1939): Sigmund Freud's theory delves into the unconscious mind and the influence of early experiences on personality

development and behavior. It emphasizes the role of the subconscious and unresolved conflicts (Borch-Jacobsen & Shamdasani, 2011).

- Structural Theory (Minuchin, 1974): Salvador Minuchin's theory focuses on family dynamics and patterns of interaction. It explores how family structures and hierarchies impact individual behaviors and well-being.
- Feminist Theory (Various Contributors): Emerging from various feminist scholars, this theory critiques social inequalities and oppression, especially concerning gender. It seeks to challenge patriarchal norms and empower marginalized groups.
- Critical Theory (Mullaly, 2007): Mullaly's perspective examines the impact of social structures, power dynamics, and inequalities on individual and societal well-being. It advocates for social justice, equity, and the transformation of unjust systems.
- Empowerment Theory (Rappaport, 1981): Developed by Julian Rappaport, this theory emphasizes the importance of empowering individuals and communities to take control of their own lives and circumstances.
- Strengths-Based Theory (Saleebey, 1996): This approach focuses on clients' strengths and resources rather than their deficits. It encourages social workers to identify and utilize clients' capabilities to address challenges.
- Trauma-Informed Theory (Herman, 2015): Judith Herman's theory addresses the impact of trauma on individuals and emphasizes the importance of understanding and supporting individuals who have experienced trauma.
- Attachment Theory (Bowlby, 1969): John Bowlby's theory explores the significance of early attachments in shaping emotional and psychological development. It highlights the role of secure attachments in fostering healthy relationships.
- Narrative Theory (White & Epston, 1990s): Michael White and David Epston's theory views individuals as the authors of their narratives. It focuses on exploring and reshaping the stories people tell about themselves and their experiences (Begum, 2023).
- Relational Cultural Theory (Miller & Stiver, 1997): Jean Baker Miller and Irene Pierce Stiver's theory focuses on the significance of relationships in human development. It highlights the role of connectedness and mutual growth.
- Cultural Humility Theory (Tervalon & Murray-Garcia, 1998): Tervalon and Murray-García's theory emphasizes cultural humility and the importance of self-awareness, respectful communication, and collaborative learning when working with diverse populations.
- Resilience Theory (Various Contributors): Resilience theory explores individuals' ability to adapt, cope, and thrive in the face of adversity. It emphasizes protective factors that contribute to positive outcomes.
- Intersectionality Theory (Crenshaw, 1989): Kimberlé Crenshaw's theory examines how different aspects of an individual's identity (such as race, gender, and class) intersect and contribute to unique experiences of oppression and privilege.
- Human Rights Theory (Various Contributors): This theory centers on the recognition and protection of human rights as a foundational aspect of social work practice. It emphasizes advocacy for individuals' dignity and well-being.

- Person-in-Environment Model: Developed by Mary Ellen Richmond (late nineteenth century), the person-in-environment model underscores the reciprocal relationship between individuals and their social surroundings. It emphasizes the importance of assessing clients within their broader context.
- Strengths-Based Model: Coined by Albert Bandura and applied in social work by Charles Rapp and Richard Goscha (late twentieth century), the strengths-based model centers on identifying and leveraging clients' strengths, assets, and capabilities to drive positive change.
- Person-Centered Approach: Pioneered by Carl Rogers (mid-twentieth century), the person-centered approach prioritizes empathy, unconditional positive regard, and active listening. Social workers who adopt this approach create a safe space for clients to explore their emotions and concerns.
- Empowerment Approach: Influenced by Paulo Freire and Julian Rappaport, the empowerment approach emerged in the 1980s. It empowers clients to enhance their self-determination and confront systemic barriers that hinder their progress.
- Psychoanalytic Approach: Founded by Sigmund Freud and adapted for social work by Erik Erikson, the psychoanalytic approach delves into unconscious motivations and unresolved conflicts to comprehend and address clients' psychological challenges.
- Feminist Approach: Evolving from the feminist movement in the 1970s, the feminist approach addresses gender-based disparities and power imbalances. Social workers applying this approach advocate for gender equality and challenge societal norms that perpetuate inequality.

1.7 Social Work Is the Bridge Between Theory and Practice

Social work stands as a vital bridge between theoretical knowledge and practical application, embodying a dynamic interplay between academia and real-world scenarios (for details, please read Herie & Martin, 2002; Gray et al., 2009; Staempfli et al., 2012). This symbiotic relationship is fundamental to the profession, manifesting in several key dimensions.

Theoretical Foundations: Social work education provides a robust grounding in various theories that inform the understanding of human behavior, social structures, and societal challenges. From psychodynamic theories to systems perspectives, students acquire a diverse theoretical toolkit. This theoretical foundation serves as the compass guiding practitioners in comprehending the complexities of the human experience.

Application in Real-world Contexts: The essence of social work lies in its application in diverse and dynamic real-world contexts. Social workers navigate the intricate interplay between theory and practice, applying theoretical insights to address the multifaceted needs of individuals, families, groups, and communities. Theories are not abstract concepts but practical tools wielded to create positive change in the lives of those they serve.

Tailoring Interventions: The bridge between theory and practice enables social workers to tailor interventions based on the unique circumstances of each client or community. Drawing on theoretical frameworks, practitioners develop nuanced strategies that consider individual strengths, cultural nuances, and systemic influences. This adaptability is essential in addressing the diverse and evolving challenges encountered in the field.

Evidence-Informed Practice: Social work thrives on the integration of evidence-informed practice, aligning theoretical insights with empirical research. Practitioners continually engage with the latest research findings, allowing theory to evolve and adapt in response to emerging evidence. This commitment to evidence ensures that social work remains a dynamic and responsive profession, grounded in both theoretical wisdom and empirical rigor.

Reflective Practice: The bridge between theory and practice is traversed through reflective practice. Social workers engage in ongoing reflection, critically assessing the application of theory in various contexts. Reflection enhances professional growth, fostering an iterative process where theoretical understanding deepens through hands-on experience, and practical challenges inform the evolution of theoretical perspectives.

In essence, social work serves as a vital conduit where theoretical insights are translated into meaningful and transformative interventions. This dynamic interconnection between theory and practice propels the profession forward, ensuring that social workers are equipped with the knowledge, skills, and ethical foundations needed to navigate the complex terrain of human well-being and social justice.

1.8 Social Work as a Profession

Social work, as a dynamic and multifaceted profession, plays a pivotal role in addressing the diverse and complex challenges faced by individuals and communities (Adams et al., 2017; Dominelli, 2010). Rooted in principles of social justice, empowerment, and advocacy, social work encompasses a range of approaches aimed at enhancing the well-being of those in need. This noble profession operates on the frontlines of human struggles, intertwining compassion with a systematic understanding of societal structures. In exploring the key dimensions of social work, we delve into its holistic perspective, ethical foundations, trauma-informed practices, a proactive stance in prevention and intervention, and a global outlook fostering cultural competence. These defining features underscore the profession's commitment to navigating the intricate tapestry of human experiences with empathy, professionalism, and a profound dedication to positive change.

Professional Identity and Ethics: Social work, as a distinguished profession, is characterized by a strong professional identity and a commitment to ethical practice. Social workers adhere to a set of core values—such as service, social justice, dignity, and integrity—that form the ethical bedrock of the profession. This commitment shapes their interactions, decisions, and interventions, ensuring a principled approach to addressing societal challenges.

Education and Training: Becoming a social worker involves rigorous education and training. Professionals typically hold at least a bachelor's degree in social work (BSW) or a master's degree in social work (MSW). This academic foundation equips them with a comprehensive understanding of social work theories, methods, and ethical considerations. Continuous professional development is also emphasized, ensuring practitioners stay current with evolving societal needs and best practices.

Diverse Specializations: Social work encompasses a vast array of specializations, allowing professionals to tailor their expertise to specific areas of need. Whether working in healthcare, child welfare, mental health, or community development, social workers bring their skills and knowledge to diverse settings. This adaptability is a hallmark of the profession, reflecting its capacity to address a broad spectrum of individual and societal challenges.

Advocacy and Social Change: At its core, social work is a catalyst for advocacy and social change. Social workers play a pivotal role in identifying systemic injustices, advocating for marginalized populations, and contributing to policy development. The profession's commitment to social justice underscores its transformative impact on societal structures and policies, striving for a more equitable and inclusive world.

Client-Centered Practice: The essence of social work lies in client-centered practice. Social workers prioritize the well-being and empowerment of their clients, employing a strengths-based approach. Through active listening, empathy, and collaborative problem-solving, they build partnerships with individuals, families, and communities. This client-focused orientation distinguishes social work as a profession deeply rooted in human connection and the pursuit of positive social outcomes.

Holistic and Systemic Perspective: Social work adopts a holistic and systemic perspective, recognizing the interconnectedness of individuals with their environments. This approach considers not only individual challenges but also the broader societal, cultural, and economic factors influencing well-being. Social workers engage with clients on multiple levels, addressing both immediate concerns and systemic barriers to positive outcomes.

Confidentiality and Boundaries: Professional ethics in social work emphasize the importance of confidentiality and maintaining appropriate boundaries with clients. Social workers navigate complex interpersonal dynamics while upholding the privacy and dignity of those they serve. This commitment to ethical conduct contributes to the trust clients place in social workers as reliable and principled professionals.

Trauma-Informed Practice: Given the prevalence of trauma in individuals' lives, social work embraces a trauma-informed approach. Social workers are trained to recognize the impact of trauma on mental health and well-being. They create environments that foster safety, trust, and empowerment, understanding the sensitive nature of their clients' experiences and the need for trauma-sensitive interventions.

Prevention and Intervention: Social work is proactive in its orientation, emphasizing both prevention and intervention strategies. Professionals work to identify and address issues at early stages, aiming to prevent the escalation of challenges. Simultaneously, they are skilled in crisis intervention, providing support during times of acute need. This dual focus contributes to the profession's effectiveness in promoting long-term well-being.

Global Perspectives and Cultural Competence: In an increasingly interconnected world, social work embraces global perspectives and cultural competence. Social workers recognize the diversity of cultures, identities, and experiences within their practice. Cultural competence is integrated into training and practice, ensuring professionals are equipped to work effectively with individuals from various backgrounds and navigate cross-cultural complexities.

In essence, social work's multifaceted nature incorporates a holistic view, ethical considerations, trauma sensitivity, a balance of prevention and intervention, and a commitment to global and cultural competence. These facets collectively define social work as a dynamic and responsive profession dedicated to enhancing the lives of individuals and communities.

1.9 Professional Social Worker: Professional Behaviors, Traits, and Roles

Becoming a professional social worker involves a thoughtful and purposeful journey that integrates education, experience, and a commitment to serving communities (for details, please read Gann, 1979; Giurgiu & Marica, 2013; Freund et al., 2013). Here is a comprehensive guide on how to embark on the path of becoming a professional social worker:

Educational Foundation: Begin by acquiring the necessary education. A bachelor's degree in social work (BSW) serves as the foundational step, providing a broad understanding of social work principles. Pursuing a Master of Social Work (MSW) degree enhances specialized knowledge and opens doors to advanced roles and responsibilities.

Fieldwork and Internship: Practical experience is crucial. Engage in fieldwork and internships during your academic journey. This hands-on experience allows you to apply theoretical knowledge in real-world settings, honing your skills and understanding the complexities of social work practice.

Licensing and Certification: Check the licensing requirements in your region. Social workers often need to obtain a license to practice professionally. This may involve passing a licensure exam and fulfilling specific criteria related to education and supervised experience.

Specialization and Continuing Education: Social work offers diverse specializations such as clinical, school, medical, or macro-level practice. Choose an area that aligns with your passion and interests. Pursue continuing education to stay updated on evolving practices and methodologies.

Networking and Professional Associations: Connect with professionals in the field. Joining social work associations provides networking opportunities, access to resources, and a platform for staying informed about industry trends and advocacy efforts.

Ethical Standards and Cultural Competence: Adhere to ethical standards and principles integral to social work. Develop cultural competence to work effectively with diverse populations, respecting individual differences and promoting inclusivity.

Supervision and Mentorship: Seek supervision and mentorship throughout your career. Experienced professionals can provide valuable insights, guidance, and support as you navigate the challenges and rewards of social work practice.

Advocacy and Social Justice: Embrace the role of advocate for social justice. Understand the systemic issues affecting vulnerable populations and actively contribute to initiatives that promote positive social change.

Self-Care and Professional Development: Social work can be emotionally demanding. Prioritize self-care to maintain personal well-being. Engage in continuous professional development to enhance your skills and stay abreast of innovations in the field.

Job Search and Career Development: Begin your job search with a well-crafted resume and cover letter. Leverage your network and utilize online platforms to explore job opportunities. Consider career development opportunities for long-term growth.

Embarking on a career in social work requires a commitment to lifelong learning, empathy, and a genuine desire to make a positive impact on individuals and communities. By following these steps, aspiring social workers can navigate the path toward becoming skilled, ethical, and compassionate professionals.

1.9.1 Professional Behaviors

Ethical Conduct: Professional social workers adhere to the highest ethical standards, upholding the principles of confidentiality, informed consent, and professional integrity. Ethical conduct forms the bedrock of trust between social workers and their clients, ensuring the profession's credibility and commitment to ethical practice.

Empathy and Compassion: Central to professional behavior in social work is the demonstration of empathy and compassion. Social workers must connect with clients on an emotional level, showing understanding, sensitivity, and genuine care. These qualities create a supportive environment and enhance the therapeutic relationship.

Cultural Competence: Professional social workers actively engage in ongoing learning to enhance their cultural competence. This involves understanding and respecting the diverse backgrounds, beliefs, and values of clients. Cultural competence ensures that social workers can effectively navigate and address the unique challenges faced by individuals from different cultures.

Effective Communication: Clear and effective communication is a fundamental aspect of professional behavior. Social workers must convey information in a manner that is easily understood by clients and other stakeholders. Both verbal and written communication skills are essential for maintaining transparency and fostering collaboration.

Professional Boundaries: Maintaining professional boundaries is critical in social work practice. Social workers establish and maintain appropriate boundaries with clients to ensure ethical practice. This involves managing issues related to self-disclosure, maintaining confidentiality, and avoiding conflicts of interest.

Advocacy and Social Justice: Professional social workers advocate for social justice and work to address systemic issues contributing to inequality. Advocacy involves speaking up for the rights of marginalized populations and influencing policies that promote fairness and equity. By actively engaging in advocacy efforts, social workers contribute to broader social change.

Critical Thinking and Problem-Solving: Professional behavior in social work includes the ability to think critically and solve problems effectively. Social workers analyze complex situations, assess client needs, and develop interventions that address the root causes of problems. Critical thinking skills are essential for providing high-quality and individualized services.

Professional Development: Engaging in continuous professional development is a hallmark of responsible social work practice. Social workers stay updated on the latest research, interventions, and ethical guidelines. This commitment to ongoing learning ensures that professionals provide services that align with current best practices and standards.

Collaboration and Teamwork: Social work often involves collaboration with interdisciplinary teams. Professional social workers work alongside professionals from various fields to provide comprehensive and holistic support to clients. Effective collaboration enhances the overall impact of social work interventions.

Self-Reflection and Supervision: Professional behavior includes a commitment to self-reflection and seeking supervision. Social workers regularly reflect on their values, biases, and reactions to ensure ethical and culturally sensitive practice. Supervision provides a structured space for discussing challenging cases, receiving feedback, and prioritizing personal well-being.

Professional behaviors in social work encompass ethical conduct, empathy, cultural competence, effective communication, maintaining professional boundaries, advocacy for social justice, critical thinking, continuous professional development, collaboration, and a commitment to self-reflection and supervision. These behaviors collectively contribute to the ethical, effective, and client-centered practice of social work professionals.

1.9.2 Professional Traits

Empathy: Empathy is a foundational trait for professional social workers. It involves the ability to understand and share the feelings of clients, demonstrating a genuine concern for their well-being. Social workers with a high level of empathy can establish meaningful connections, fostering trust and rapport with those they serve.

Resilience: Resilience is a crucial trait for social workers who often navigate challenging and emotionally demanding situations. The ability to bounce back from setbacks, cope with stress, and maintain a positive outlook is essential for sustaining a long and impactful career in social work.

Cultural Sensitivity: Cultural sensitivity is a trait that allows social workers to interact effectively with individuals from diverse backgrounds. Being aware of and respecting cultural differences enables social workers to provide culturally competent and inclusive services, acknowledging the uniqueness of each client.

Flexibility: Given the dynamic nature of social work, flexibility is a valuable trait. Social workers must adapt to evolving situations, navigate unexpected challenges, and adjust their approaches to best meet the needs of clients. Flexibility ensures responsiveness and effectiveness in a constantly changing environment.

Patience: Patience is a virtue in social work, as meaningful change often takes time. Social workers with patience can provide consistent support, guide clients through their challenges, and celebrate incremental progress. This trait contributes to the overall resilience and perseverance of the social worker.

Open-mindedness: Open-mindedness involves a willingness to consider diverse perspectives and ideas without judgment. Social workers with this trait can approach situations with curiosity and a nonjudgmental attitude, fostering an environment where clients feel heard and accepted.

Communication Skills: Effective communication is a fundamental trait for social workers. This includes the ability to express ideas clearly, actively listen to clients, and navigate difficult conversations. Strong communication skills enhance the therapeutic relationship and contribute to successful interventions.

Empowerment Orientation: Social workers with an empowerment orientation believe in the inherent strengths and capabilities of their clients. This trait involves encouraging and supporting clients to identify and utilize their strengths, fostering a sense of self-efficacy and empowerment.

Adaptability: Similar to flexibility, adaptability is the ability to adjust to new circumstances and challenges. Social workers who are adaptable can navigate unexpected situations, embrace change, and continue to provide effective services even in dynamic and uncertain environments.

Reflective Practice: Reflective practice is a trait that involves regularly examining one's actions, values, and decisions. Social workers who engage in reflective practice can learn from their experiences, identify areas for improvement, and continuously enhance their professional skills and effectiveness.

These professional traits collectively contribute to the success of social workers in their roles. Empathy, resilience, cultural sensitivity, flexibility, patience, open-mindedness, communication skills, empowerment orientation, adaptability, and reflective practice are integral to providing ethical, client-centered, and impactful social work services.

1.9.3 Professional Roles

Advocate: One of the primary roles of a professional social worker is that of an advocate. Social workers advocate for the rights and well-being of their clients, working to ensure they have access to necessary resources, services, and opportunities. Advocacy may involve addressing systemic issues contributing to social injustices and promoting social change.

Counselor: Social workers often take on the role of a counselor, providing emotional support and guidance to individuals and families facing challenges. Counseling involves helping clients explore their feelings, cope with difficulties, and develop strategies for positive change.

Case Manager: In the role of a case manager, social workers coordinate and manage the services and resources needed to support clients. This may include collaborating with various agencies, organizing care plans, and ensuring that clients receive comprehensive and integrated support.

Mediator: Social workers act as mediators in situations where conflicts arise, working to facilitate communication and resolution. Whether within families, communities, or organizations, social workers help parties find common ground and work towards mutually beneficial solutions.

Educator: Educational roles are common in social work, involving the provision of information and resources to clients and communities. Social workers may educate clients about available services, teach coping skills, and conduct workshops on topics such as parenting, mental health, or substance abuse prevention.

Researcher: Social workers contribute to the field's knowledge base by engaging in research. Research-oriented roles involve studying social issues, evaluating intervention strategies, and generating evidence to inform effective social work practices. Research can influence policy changes and enhance the overall effectiveness of social work interventions.

Facilitator: As facilitators, social workers organize and lead group sessions or support groups. This role involves creating a safe and supportive environment for individuals with shared experiences to connect, share insights, and work towards common goals.

Supervisor: Experienced social workers often take on supervisory roles, overseeing the work of less experienced practitioners or students. Supervision involves providing guidance, feedback, and support to ensure ethical and effective social work practice.

Community Organizer: Social workers engage in community organizing to address broader social issues and empower communities. This role involves mobilizing community members, advocating for social change, and facilitating collaborative efforts to improve overall community well-being.

Policy Analyst: In the realm of macro social work, social workers may take on roles as policy analysts. This involves examining existing social policies, identifying areas for improvement, and advocating for policy changes that better address the needs of vulnerable populations.

Coordinator: Coordinating services and resources is a common role for social workers, particularly in settings with multiple service providers. Social workers in this role ensure that clients receive comprehensive and cohesive support by connecting them with various services and coordinating care plans.

These professional roles collectively contribute to the multifaceted nature of social work. Whether advocating for clients' rights, providing counseling, conducting research, or organizing communities, social workers play diverse and crucial roles in promoting social justice, well-being, and positive change.

Review Questions

1. What are the key meanings associated with social work, and how do they contribute to the profession's identity?
2. How does the scope of social work extend across micro, mezzo, and macro levels of practice, and what distinguishes each level?
3. Discuss the importance of ethical considerations and principles in social work, providing examples of their application.
4. Explore the diverse divisions and differences within social work, considering the specialized areas of practice.
5. How do major social work theories contribute to understanding and addressing various social issues and challenges?
6. Reflect on the significance of social work as a recognized and vital profession, considering its impact on individuals and communities.
7. Differentiate between micro, mezzo, and macro levels of social work practice, providing examples for each.
8. How can theoretical concepts in social work be translated into practical applications to address real-world challenges?

Multiple Choice Questions

1. What is the primary focus of social work at the micro level?

   (a) Individual clients
   (b) Community advocacy
   (c) National policy analysis
   (d) Global social justice initiatives

2. In the context of social work principles, which of the following best reflects the concept of self-determination?
   (a) Imposing decisions on clients
   (b) Respecting clients' autonomy and choices
   (c) Advocating for clients without their input
   (d) Limiting clients' access to information
3. Which of the following is an example of mezzo-level social work practice?
   (a) Providing counseling to an individual client
   (b) Advocating for policy changes at the national level
   (c) Facilitating support groups for families
   (d) Conducting research on global social issues
4. How do social work theories contribute to the profession?
   (a) They are irrelevant to practical applications.
   (b) They provide a historical perspective only.
   (c) They guide understanding and intervention in social issues.
   (d) They focus solely on individual psychology.
5. What role does social work play as a bridge between theory and practice?
   (a) It separates theory from practical applications.
   (b) It ignores theoretical foundations in practice.
   (c) It dismisses the relevance of theory in the field.
   (d) It integrates theoretical knowledge into practical interventions.

References

Adams, R., Dominelli, L., & Payne, M. (2017). *Social work: Themes, issues and critical debates*. Bloomsbury Publishing.

Bandura, A., & Walters, R. H. (1977). *Social learning theory* (Vol. 1). Prentice Hall.

Beck, A. T. (1967). *Depression: Clinical, experimental, and theoretical aspects*. Hoeber.

Beckett, C., Maynard, A., & Jordan, P. (2023). What are values and ethics?. In Cree, V. E., & McCulloch, T. (Eds.). *Social work: a reader* (pp. 170–176). Routledge.

Begum, A. (2023). The multi-layers of attachment. *Attachment, 17*(2), 8–12.

Berg-Weger, M. (2019). *Social work and social welfare: An invitation*. Routledge.

Borch-Jacobsen, M., & Shamdasani, S. (2011). *The Freud files: An inquiry into the history of psychoanalysis*. Cambridge University Press.

Bowlby, J. (1969). *Attachment and loss* (Vol. 1. Attachment). Basic Books.

Crenshaw, K. (1989). *Demarginalizing the Intersection of Race and Sex: A Black Feminist Critique of Antidiscrimination Doctrine*, Feminist Theory and Antiracist Politics, University of Chicago Legal Forum, 14: 538–54.

Dominelli, L. (2010). Social work in a globalizing world. *Polity*.

Dominelli, L., Dominelli, L., & Campling, J. (2002). *Oppression, social divisions and identity* (pp. 37–58). Anti-oppressive social work theory and practice.

Freund, A., Blit-Cohen, E., Cohen, A., & Dehan, N. (2013). Professional commitment in novice social work students: Socio-demographic characteristics, motives and perceptions of the profession. *Social Work Education, 32*(7), 867–887.

Gann, M. L. (1979). *The role of personality factors and job characteristics in burnout: A study of social service workers*. University of California.

Germain, C. B., & Gitterman, A. (1996). *The life model of social work practice*. Columbia University Press.

Giurgiu, L. R., & Marica, M. A. (2013). Professional values in social work students and mid-career practitioners: A comparative study. *Procedia-Social and Behavioral Sciences, 76*, 372–377.

Gray, M., Plath, D., & Webb, S. (2009). *Evidence-based social work: A critical stance*. Routledge.

Healy, K. (2022). *Social work theories in context: Creating frameworks for practice*. Bloomsbury Publishing.

Herie, M., & Martin, G. W. (2002). Knowledge diffusion in social work: A new approach to bridging the gap. *Social Work, 47*(1), 85–95.

Herman, J. L. (2015). *Trauma and recovery: The aftermath of violence—From domestic abuse to political terror*. Hachette.

Hopps, J. G., & Lowe, T. B. (2008). The scope of social work practice. In K. M. Sowers, C. N. Dulmus, & B. W. White (Eds.), *Comprehensive Handbook of Social Work and Social Welfare, The Profession of Social Work* (Vol. 1, pp. 37–64). Wiley.

Hutchinson, G. S., & Oltedal, S. (2014). *Five theories in social work*. Universitetet i Nordland.

Knight, C., & Gitterman, A. (2018). Merging micro and macro intervention: Social work practice with groups in the community. *Journal of Social Work Education, 54*(1), 3–17.

Mattocks, N. O. (2018). Social action among social work practitioners: Examining the micro–macro divide. *Social Work, 63*(1), 7–16.

McAuliffe, D., Boddy, J., & Chenoweth, L. (2023). *The road to social work and human service practice*. Cengage AU.

Mullaly, B. (2007). *The new structural social work* (3rd ed.). Oxford University Press.

Miller, J. B., & Stiver, I. P. (1997). *The healing connection: How women form connections in therapy and in life*. Boston, MA: Beacon Press.

Minuchin, S. (1974). *Families and family therapy*. Cambridge, MA: Harvard University Press.

Rappaport, J. (1981). In praise of paradox: A social policy of empowerment over prevention. *American Journal of Community Psychology, 9*, 1–25.

Reisch, M., & Garvin, C. D. (2016). *Social work and social justice: Concepts, challenges, and strategies*. Oxford University Press.

Rogers, C. R. (2013). *A theory of therapy and personality change: As developed in the client-centered framework* (p. 341). Perspectives in Abnormal Behavior: Pergamon General Psychology Series.

Rogowski, S. (2020). *Social work: The rise and fall of a profession? 2E: The rise and fall of a profession?* Policy Press.

Saleebey, D. (1996). The strengths perspective in social work practice: Extensions and cautions. *Social Work, 41*(3), 296.

Staempfli, A., Kunz, R., & Tov, E. (2012). Creating a bridge between theory and practice: Working with key situations. *European Journal of Social Education, 22*(23), 60–78.

Teater, B. (2019). *An introduction to applying social work theories and methods 3e*. McGraw-Hill Education.

Tervalon, M., & Murray-Garcia, J. (1998). Cultural humility versus cultural competence: A critical distinction in defining physician training outcomes in multicultural education. *Journal of Health Care for the Poor and Underserved, 9*(2), 117–125.

White, M. & Epston, D. (1990). *Narrative means to therapeutic ends*. New York: Norton.

Chapter 2
Introduction to Fieldwork in Social Work

Learning Objectives
After reading this chapter, you will be able to:

- Define the importance of fieldwork in social work and its role in professional development
- Differentiate between various types of fieldwork in social work practice
- Recognize the significance of fieldwork for social work students and apply the EARIS formula
- Explore strategies for social and mental preparation before engaging in fieldwork
- Develop skills in setting clear objectives and aligning personal learning goals with broader educational and professional objectives

2.1 Understanding Fieldwork in Social Work

Fieldwork in social work is a cornerstone of professional development, providing students and aspiring practitioners with valuable hands-on experience in real-world settings (Ivry et al., 2005; Hay & O'Donoghue, 2009; Dhemba, 2012; DeGroot, 2019). This section discusses the fundamental importance of fieldwork, outlining its role in shaping social work practice and preparing individuals for the challenges and responsibilities they will encounter in their careers.

Fieldwork is an integral component of social work education that goes beyond classroom learning. It is a crucial phase in the development of students aspiring to become social workers. It enables students to apply their theoretical knowledge gained in the classroom to real-life scenarios, allowing them to assess and enhance their practical skills. Consequently, fieldwork practice serves as a preparation ground for students, equipping them to deliver direct intervention, support, and assistance in the lives of individuals (Baikady et al., 2022). It involves students

M. R. Islam, *Fieldwork in Social Work*,
https://doi.org/10.1007/978-3-031-56683-7_2

actively engaging with real-world scenarios, clients, and communities. This experiential learning allows them to witness the complexities and nuances of social work practice firsthand. Fieldwork is often conducted in various settings, such as community agencies, hospitals, schools, and government organizations. It is a structured and supervised experience that provides students with opportunities to apply theoretical knowledge to practical situations. Fieldwork in social work has some features:

Bridge Between Theory and Practice: Fieldwork serves as a bridge between the theories and concepts taught in classrooms and their practical application in real-life situations. While theories provide the groundwork for understanding human behavior, social systems, and interventions, fieldwork offers the chance to see how these theories play out in actual practice. It helps students connect abstract concepts to tangible outcomes and develop a deeper appreciation for the relevance of theory in guiding their actions.

Learning by Doing: The heart of fieldwork lies in the principle of learning by doing. This approach emphasizes active engagement and participation in the learning process. Through direct interactions with clients, students learn to navigate complex social issues, adapt to diverse situations, and make informed decisions. This practical experience enhances critical thinking, problem-solving, and decision-making skills, enabling students to become more effective and confident social work practitioners. Embrace the philosophy of "Learning by Doing," where an individual's openness to acquiring knowledge is seamlessly integrated with practical application (Smith et al., 2015). In this approach, understanding is gained through classroom learning, while hands-on training imparts the expertise required for active engagement. Aligned with this principle, each student participating in fieldwork is paired with a dedicated professional mentor. These mentors, similar to educators, play a pivotal role in not only transmitting theoretical concepts but also cultivating practical skills, values, and ethical principles essential for proficient social work practice.

Fieldwork as a Process: Fieldwork is not just a static experience; it's a dynamic and evolving process that unfolds over time. This section delves into the stages that make up the fieldwork process, highlighting how each stage contributes to the overall learning journey and professional growth of social work students.

Exploration: At the outset of fieldwork, students are presented with a unique opportunity for exploration. This stage involves immersing oneself in various practice settings, each with its challenges, client demographics, and systemic dynamics. Through this exploration, students gain exposure to the diverse landscape of social work practice, helping them identify their areas of interest and passion. Exploration extends beyond the surface level. Students engage with the broader community, familiarize themselves with the agencies they'll be working with, and observe the broader societal issues at play. This exploration phase is marked by curiosity, observation, and a willingness to step into the unknown.

Application: With a foundation of exploration, students transition to the application phase of fieldwork. Here, theoretical knowledge is put into action. Armed with a deeper understanding of their assigned agencies and the challenges clients face, students begin crafting interventions and strategies. This stage is marked by hands-on involvement and active participation. The application involves a blend of creativity and adaptability. Students experiment with various approaches, adjusting their methods based on real-time feedback and the evolving needs of their clients. This trial-and-error process not only builds practical skills but also nurtures resilience, which is essential in the ever-changing landscape of social work.

Reflection: Reflection is the heart of effective fieldwork (Pawar, 2017). This stage involves pausing to contemplate experiences, challenges, and interactions. Reflection offers a space to unpack emotions, decisions, and the impact of interventions. It's a self-reflective journey that goes beyond the surface and delves into the deeper layers of one's thoughts and responses. Through reflection, students develop a heightened awareness of their biases, assumptions, and strengths. This introspective practice encourages a constant dialogue with oneself, leading to personal growth, improved self-awareness, and enhanced cultural competence. By learning from both successes and setbacks, students become better equipped to adapt and adjust their approach in future interactions.

Feedback and Growth: Fieldwork is a collaborative process, and feedback plays a pivotal role in this collaboration. Supervisors, mentors, and instructors provide valuable insights and assessments of students' performance. This feedback serves as a mirror, offering an external perspective on their work and interactions. Receiving feedback requires openness and humility. Constructive feedback identifies areas for improvement, reinforces strengths, and supports ongoing learning. Students who actively seek and embrace feedback can refine their skills, address blind spots, and develop into more effective practitioners.

Integration and Synthesis: As students progress through the exploration, application, reflection, and feedback stages, they naturally engage in a process of integration and synthesis. The experiences, lessons, and insights gained from each stage combine to form a comprehensive understanding of social work practice. This synthesis phase is where the true value of fieldwork becomes evident. Students not only accumulate knowledge but also internalize it, transforming it into a part of their professional identity. This integrated knowledge serves as a foundation for future practice, enabling students to draw on their fieldwork experiences to make informed decisions and provide effective interventions.

The process of fieldwork is a dynamic journey encompassing exploration, application, reflection, and feedback. This process is not linear; rather, it is iterative, as each stage informs the others. Through this cyclical process, social work students gain valuable insights, refine their skills, and evolve into competent and compassionate practitioners.

2.2 Types of Fieldwork in Social Work Practice

Within the realm of social work field education, educators commonly employ two distinct approaches to field placements: block fieldwork and concurrent fieldwork (Dhemba, 2012; Sunirose, 2013; Singla, 2015). These methodologies offer students diverse avenues for gaining hands-on experience in the real world. The block fieldwork approach involves a deep dive into the field, where students immerse themselves fully in practical learning under the mentorship of seasoned social work professionals. Conversely, concurrent fieldwork divides students' time between classroom instruction and on-site fieldwork experiences, striking a balance between theoretical learning and practical application. Furthermore, the field practicum landscape in social work generally falls into two primary categories based on the nature of the experience and student involvement: concurrent and block placements.

2.2.1 Concurrent Fieldwork Placements

2.2.1.1 Definition

Concurrent fieldwork placement refers to a structured educational approach in social work in which students engage in practical learning experiences while simultaneously participating in classroom instruction. This approach ensures that students acquire theoretical knowledge alongside hands-on practice in real-world settings, offering a comprehensive and integrated learning experience. Students are typically assigned to concurrent fieldwork placements as an integral part of their social work education, especially in master's programs. This placement occurs concurrently with their academic coursework, allowing them to immediately apply classroom concepts to real-life situations.

2.2.1.2 Objectives and Importance of Concurrent Fieldwork

Concurrent fieldwork placements are designed to achieve several crucial objectives:

- Real-Life Application: By immersing students in real-world scenarios, concurrent fieldwork enables them to apply theories, methods, and skills learned in the classroom to authentic situations.
- Integration of Theory and Practice: This approach fosters the seamless integration of theoretical knowledge with practical application, enhancing students' ability to translate ideas into effective interventions.

- Holistic Learning: Students gain a holistic understanding of social work by engaging with clients, communities, and organizations, thereby fostering a well-rounded perspective of the profession.
- Skill Development: Practical experience hones students' social work skills, including assessment, intervention, communication, and collaboration.
- Cultural Competence: Students learn to work effectively with diverse populations, enhancing their cultural competence and adaptability.
- Self-Reflection: Concurrent fieldwork encourages self-reflection and self-awareness as students navigate real-world challenges and ethical dilemmas.

2.2.1.3 Advantages of Concurrent Fieldwork

- Immediate Application: Students apply classroom learning immediately in practical settings, reinforcing comprehension and skill acquisition.
- Realistic Exposure: Engagement in real-life scenarios enhances students' understanding of the complexities and dynamics of social work practice.
- Continuous Learning: The ongoing integration of theory and practice fosters a continuous learning cycle, refining students' professional growth.
- Adaptability: Exposure to diverse contexts and challenges cultivates adaptability, a vital skill for effective social work practice.
- Holistic Development: Concurrent fieldwork supports the development of well-rounded social work practitioners, equipped with both theoretical knowledge and practical competence.

2.2.1.4 Disadvantages of Concurrent Fieldwork

- Time Management: Balancing fieldwork with classroom commitments can be challenging, requiring disciplined time management skills.
- Reduced Immersion: The split between classroom and fieldwork may lead to less immersion in either environment compared to more focused approaches.
- Limited Reflection Time: The fast-paced nature of concurrent fieldwork might limit the time available for students to deeply reflect on their experiences.

Concurrent fieldwork placements offer a dynamic and integrated learning approach in social work education. This method equips students with the ability to seamlessly apply classroom knowledge to real-life situations, fostering well-rounded, culturally competent, and skillful social work practitioners.

2.2.2 *Block Fieldwork Placements*

2.2.2.1 Definition

Block fieldwork placement is a distinctive educational approach in social work where students undertake an intensive period of practical learning, concentrating solely on their internship after completing coursework. This approach provides students with a dedicated timeframe to immerse themselves in hands-on experience, applying their theoretical knowledge to real-world scenarios. Students are assigned to block fieldwork placements after they have completed their academic coursework. This allows them to transition seamlessly from classroom learning to a concentrated period of field-based education.

2.2.2.2 Objectives and Importance of Block Fieldwork

Block fieldwork placements are guided by the following key objectives:

- Focused Learning: Block placements offer students an uninterrupted period of immersive learning, enabling them to deeply engage with clients, interventions, and the nuances of social work practice.
- Application of Theory: This approach facilitates the direct application of theoretical concepts and skills learned in the classroom to real-world scenarios, reinforcing knowledge and competence.
- Client-Centered Focus: Students gain extended time to build relationships and work closely with clients, contributing to meaningful and comprehensive interventions.
- Mentorship Opportunities: The extended placement duration allows for stronger mentorship relationships with field instructors, providing guidance and insight throughout the internship.
- Skill Mastery: Block placements allow students to refine and master social work skills through continuous practice and reflection.

2.2.2.3 Advantages of Block Fieldwork

- Deep Immersion: The extended duration of block placements allows students to immerse themselves fully in practical experiences, fostering a deeper understanding of social work practice.
- Uninterrupted Focus: Students can focus solely on their internship without the distraction of coursework, enabling them to make the most of their field learning.
- Client Connection: The extended timeframe offers ample opportunities to develop meaningful relationships with clients, leading to more impactful interventions.

- Time for Reflection: The concentrated nature of block placements provides time for in-depth reflection on experiences, challenges, and growth.

2.2.2.4 Disadvantages of Block Fieldwork

- Theory-Practice Separation: Extended periods away from the classroom might lead to a disconnect between theoretical knowledge and practical application.
- Limited Flexibility: The block format might pose challenges for students who require flexibility in their schedules due to work or other commitments.
- Intensive Commitment: The intense nature of block placements requires students to manage their time and energy effectively to avoid burnout.

Block fieldwork placements offer a focused and immersive learning experience in social work education. This approach enables students to dive deeply into the practical application of their knowledge, build strong client relationships, and refine their skills. While block placements require careful time management and may necessitate adjustments for work-life balance, they provide a unique opportunity for students to undergo a concentrated period of transformative learning.

2.2.3 Differences Between Concurrent and Block Field Placements

Social work education offers two distinct approaches to field placements: concurrent and block field placements. These methodologies vary in their structure, learning outcomes, and overall experiences. Here are the key differences between these two types of field placements (Table 2.1).

Both concurrent and block field placements offer distinct advantages and challenges, catering to different learning styles and preferences. The choice between these two models depends on factors such as program curriculum, student commitments, and the desired depth of practical engagement.

2.3 Importance of Fieldwork in Social Work

Fieldwork stands as a cornerstone of social work education and practice, offering profound significance that goes beyond traditional classroom learning. Hamilton and Else (1983) describe it as a deliberately structured series of experiences taking place within a practical setting. Its purpose is to guide students from their initial levels of understanding, skills, and attitudes to levels associated with independent social work practice. Kaseke (1986) also notes that fieldwork serves as a means of socialization, as it readies the student for their forthcoming role as a social work

Table 2.1 Differences between concurrent and block field placements

Aspect	Concurrent field placements	Block field placements
Structure and duration	In concurrent placements, students divide their time between classroom instruction and fieldwork experiences. They typically spend two to three days per week at the agency while attending classes on the remaining days.	Block placements involve an intensive period of practical learning. Students concentrate solely on their internship after completing coursework, dedicating their full attention to hands-on experiences for an extended duration, often spanning one or more semesters.
Integration of theory	Concurrent placements emphasize the integration of classroom learning with practical application. Students have the opportunity to immediately apply theoretical concepts to real-world scenarios and vice versa.	Block placements focus on concentrated immersion in practical experiences. While there might be some reflection on theoretical knowledge, the primary emphasis is on the direct application of skills and concepts.
Time commitment	Students participating in concurrent placements need to manage their time effectively to balance both fieldwork and classroom commitments. These placements often require a consistent weekly schedule.	Block placements require an intensive commitment during the designated period. Students are fully engaged in the field and have a dedicated timeframe for practical experiences without the interruption of classroom obligations.
Depth of engagement	Concurrent placements offer consistent, ongoing engagement with clients, communities, and organizations. Students have the opportunity to establish rapport and build relationships over an extended period.	Block placements provide an opportunity for deeper immersion in the field during a concentrated timeframe. This intensity may lead to rapid skill development and more focused client interactions.
Flexibility	While providing opportunities for immediate application of knowledge, concurrent placements might be less flexible due to the ongoing commitments to both fieldwork and classes.	Block placements offer a concentrated period of immersion and may provide more flexibility in terms of scheduling and adapting to the internship environment.
Reflection and learning	These placements encourage ongoing reflection as students navigate both theoretical learning and practical application in parallel.	Block placements provide a unique opportunity for deeper reflection after intensive periods of hands-on experience, enabling students to process their learning in a more focused manner.
Client relationships	With ongoing interactions, concurrent placements allow students to build and maintain more prolonged client relationships, contributing to more comprehensive interventions.	While relationships can still be formed, the intensive nature of block placements might impact the duration and depth of client connections.

Source: Author

practitioner. He goes on to emphasize that a valuable fieldwork placement enriches the student's comprehension of the social work profession and the types of issues it tackles. Consequently, learning occurs on multiple fronts, encompassing intellectual, emotional, and practical dimensions. Moreover, fieldwork presents an opportunity to bridge the gap between theoretical knowledge and real-world societal demands. It allows students to actively take on the responsibility of addressing individual challenges. Consequently, when managed effectively, fieldwork becomes a crucial instrument for shaping a social work curriculum that is not only suitable but also adaptive to contemporary social development concerns (Dhemba, 2012). This section explores the multifaceted importance of fieldwork in shaping the development of social work students and equipping them with the skills and insights necessary for effective and impactful practice.

Holistic Learning: Fieldwork introduces students to the dynamic and intricate nature of social work practice. While classroom learning provides a foundational understanding of theories and concepts, fieldwork exposes students to the complexity of real-world situations. Clients' lives are shaped by a myriad of interrelated factors—from family dynamics to economic conditions to cultural influences. Engaging with these complexities encourages students to think holistically, viewing individuals and their challenges within the broader context of their lives.

Client-Centered Perspective: Direct interaction with clients allows students to witness the nuances of human experience. These interactions humanize the challenges faced by individuals and families, helping students recognize that each client's story is unique. This perspective fosters empathy and understanding, laying the groundwork for a client-centered approach. By tailoring interventions to meet the specific needs and strengths of each client, students are better positioned to effect positive change.

Ethical and Cultural Competence: Fieldwork serves as a crucible for ethical and cultural competence development. As students engage with clients from diverse backgrounds, they encounter ethical dilemmas and challenges that require thoughtful consideration. Negotiating these challenges hones their ability to make ethical decisions, navigate sensitive topics, and uphold the profession's ethical standards. Cultural competence is cultivated as students encounter individuals with varying cultural norms, beliefs, and traditions. The exposure to diverse perspectives fosters an appreciation for cultural differences and helps students develop the cultural sensitivity needed to establish effective rapport and tailor interventions that resonate with clients' values.

Building Relationships: Relationship-building is fundamental to social work practice, and fieldwork provides an opportunity to develop this critical skill. Students learn the art of communication, active listening, and empathy as they engage with clients and colleagues. Nurturing these skills is essential for forging strong alliances, which in turn enables effective collaboration and the implementation of successful interventions. Fieldwork also exposes students to interdisciplinary teamwork, where they collaborate with professionals from different fields. This experience prepares them for the collaborative nature of social work practice, where addressing complex issues often requires a collective effort.

Real-World Application: While theories and classroom discussions lay the groundwork, fieldwork is where knowledge transforms into practice. It bridges the gap between theory and reality, allowing students to test and apply theories in the context of actual client interactions. This transition from the theoretical to the practical is transformative, enhancing students' ability to adapt and problem-solve in real time. Fieldwork instills confidence in students as they witness the positive impact of their efforts. Seeing their interventions lead to meaningful change reinforces their sense of purpose and motivation to continue refining their skills.

Preparation for Professional Identity: Fieldwork not only imparts practical skills but also contributes to the formation of a professional identity. It instills the values, ethics, and principles that underpin the social work profession. Through exposure to the challenges and rewards of practice, students come to embody the empathy, resilience, and commitment that define effective social workers.

2.4 Social Work Students for Field Practice: EARIS Formula

Embarking on the transformative journey of field practice in social work, students play a pivotal role in societal betterment. The EARIS formula, where E signifies Exploration, becomes a guiding compass for engaged learning. This approach involves the intentional exploration of real-world scenarios, followed by the practical application of acquired knowledge and skills. The subsequent stages of Reflection, Integration, and Synthesizing form a cohesive process, fostering a deep understanding and mastery of social work principles. EARIS transcends its acronym, evolving into a dynamic methodology that empowers students to navigate the complexities of fieldwork with purpose and impact.

Doel et al. (2010) highlight that the two learning contexts for understanding social work practice, namely the classroom and fieldwork, should ideally be combined, harmonious, and in alignment with each other. They also emphasize that both social work students and agency supervisors face the challenge of translating this ideal into practice. Safari (1986) points out that during fieldwork, social work students engage with individuals in need, witnessing their challenges, reactions to these challenges, and their perspectives on social workers. In this context, students discover their capacity to assist. Through active observation, hands-on experience, and a sense of responsibility for helping individuals cope with their difficulties, social work students develop essential skills. Fieldwork is intentionally structured to offer students exposure and practical experience in the operations of social welfare agencies and the provision of social welfare services. Social work students benefit greatly from field practice in a social work agency due to several important reasons.

- Application of Theoretical Knowledge:
  - Field practice allows students to put the theories and concepts they learn in the classroom into action in real-world situations.
  - It provides a practical context to understand how these theories translate into effective interventions for clients.

- Bridge Between Theory and Practice:
  - Field practice bridges the gap between academic learning and hands-on application, helping students develop a comprehensive understanding of social work.
  - It enables students to see how their theoretical knowledge is directly relevant to helping individuals, families, and communities.
- Exposure to Diverse Challenges:
  - Working in a social work agency exposes students to the diverse challenges and needs faced by clients from various backgrounds.
  - This exposure enhances students' understanding of the complexities of people's lives and the social issues they encounter.
- Cultural Sensitivity and Empathy:
  - Interacting with clients from different cultures, backgrounds, and circumstances fosters cultural sensitivity and empathy.
  - This exposure is vital for developing the ability to communicate effectively and provide culturally appropriate support.
- Development of Professional Skills:
  - Field practice is a platform for students to develop essential professional skills such as effective communication, active listening, and problem-solving.
  - Skills like building rapport, managing conflicts, and adapting to diverse situations are cultivated through practical experience.
- Teamwork and Collaboration:
  - Social work often involves collaboration with colleagues, agencies, and other professionals. Field practice exposes students to the dynamics of teamwork.
  - Students learn how to work harmoniously within interdisciplinary teams to achieve the best outcomes for clients.
- Understanding Agency Dynamics:
  - Engaging with a social work agency provides students with insights into how agencies operate, their structure, and administrative procedures.
  - Students learn about case management, resource allocation, and the coordination of services to address clients' needs.
- Preparation for Real-world Challenges:
  - Field practice prepares students for the realities and challenges of the professional world, including ethical dilemmas and resource constraints.
  - It equips them with the ability to think critically and creatively to address complex client situations.

- Guided Learning and Feedback:
  - Supervision from experienced social workers offers a safe space for students to learn from their experiences, both successes and setbacks.
  - Constructive feedback from supervisors helps students refine their skills and approaches, promoting continuous improvement.
- Personal and Professional Growth:
  - Engaging in field practice encourages self-reflection and personal growth as students learn to navigate the emotional aspects of social work.
  - It fosters a commitment to lifelong learning, adaptability, and resilience in the face of challenges.

In essence, field practice in a social work agency is a pivotal component of a social work student‘s education. It cultivates a holistic understanding of social work, nurtures empathy and cultural competence, develops essential skills, and prepares students to be compassionate, effective, and socially responsible practitioners in their future careers.

The importance of fieldwork in social work education cannot be overstated. It is the crucible where theoretical knowledge transforms into practical wisdom, where empathy is nurtured, and where students emerge as well-rounded, culturally competent, and client-focused professionals. Through its experiential learning, fieldwork shapes the next generation of social work practitioners who will make meaningful contributions to the well-being of individuals and communities.

2.4.1 EARIS in Field Practice

Exploration, Application, Reflection, Integration, and Synthesis (EARIS) constitute a comprehensive framework that guides the field practice of social work, emphasizing a dynamic and iterative process.

Exploration: In the exploration phase, social work students embark on a journey of understanding diverse theoretical frameworks that underpin the profession. For instance, when dealing with issues of gender-based violence, a student may explore feminist theories to comprehend the root causes and dynamics. This stage involves delving into academic literature, participating in discussions, and attending workshops that expose students to the rich tapestry of social work theories.

Application: The application stage is where theoretical knowledge transitions into practical skills. Consider a student placed in a medical social work setting. Drawing from systems theory, they navigate the complex healthcare environment. This involves collaborating with medical professionals, advocating for patients' needs, and addressing psychosocial aspects of healthcare. The application goes beyond theoretical understanding, requiring adaptability and real-time problem-solving.

Reflection: Reflection is a cornerstone of professional growth in social work. A student engaged in a child welfare agency, for example, maintains reflective journals. These reflections provide a space for critical self-analysis, allowing the student to explore the impact of interventions, recognize personal biases, and refine their approaches. Reflection fosters self-awareness, a key competency in social work practice.

Integration: Integration involves connecting disparate pieces of knowledge gained from various sources. Imagine a student working in a school setting. They may integrate cognitive-behavioral theories when addressing behavioral issues among students. This phase requires the synthesis of micro-level interactions with mezzo-level systemic understanding, fostering a more holistic approach to social work practice.

Synthesis: The synthesis phase represents the pinnacle of learning in social work. For instance, a student engaged in macro-level social work might propose a community development project. By synthesizing knowledge acquired from micro and mezzo levels, they craft comprehensive solutions to address broader community issues. Synthesis reflects the ability to think critically, propose innovative solutions, and contribute meaningfully to the field.

2.5 Social and Mental Preparation for Fieldwork Practice

2.5.1 In General

Successfully engaging in fieldwork practice as a social work student requires more than just academic knowledge; it necessitates thorough social and mental preparation. This practice can function as a sort of social laboratory, where students learn to apply their theoretical knowledge and skills in practical, real-life social situations (Roy, 2017). This section discusses the crucial aspects of preparing oneself to navigate the complex and dynamic realm of fieldwork with effectiveness and confidence.

Understanding the Landscape: Before embarking on fieldwork, students must develop a comprehensive understanding of the social and cultural landscapes they will encounter. This involves familiarizing themselves with the communities, demographics, and prevalent issues within the field placement area. Gaining insights into the local customs, norms, and potential challenges enables students to approach their assignments with cultural sensitivity and awareness.

Managing Expectations: Fieldwork often presents unpredictable scenarios and demands that might differ from classroom simulations. Students should mentally prepare themselves for the unexpected, understanding that real-life situations can be nuanced and emotionally charged. This requires cultivating adaptability, resilience, and the ability to handle ambiguity while remaining focused on the objectives of the assignment.

Developing Self-Awareness: Effective social work practice demands self-awareness and introspection. Students must reflect on their values, biases, and assumptions that might influence their interactions with clients and the community. This self-awareness aids in maintaining professionalism, ensuring that personal beliefs do not hinder the provision of unbiased and client-centered services.

Building Emotional Resilience: Fieldwork can expose students to emotionally challenging situations, underscoring the significance of emotional resilience. Preparing mentally to encounter distressing narratives or witnessing difficult circumstances is essential. Strategies for self-care, coping mechanisms, and seeking support from supervisors or peers contribute to maintaining emotional well-being.

Communication and Relationship Skills: Engaging effectively with clients and stakeholders demands adept communication and relationship-building skills. Social work students should mentally prepare to actively listen, express empathy, and foster rapport with diverse individuals. Understanding the power dynamics inherent in client interactions helps ensure ethical and respectful communication.

Cultivating a Learning Mindset: Approaching fieldwork with a learning mindset is pivotal. Students should be open to gaining new insights, acknowledging that challenges and failures can provide valuable lessons. Embracing constructive feedback and utilizing it to enhance their practice fosters continuous growth.

Preparation for fieldwork practice extends beyond academic knowledge, encompassing social and mental readiness. As social work students embark on their journey in the field, equipping themselves with cultural sensitivity, adaptability, self-awareness, emotional resilience, and effective communication skills enhances their capacity to make meaningful contributions to the lives of those they serve.

2.5.2 *Coping Strategies for Challenging Situations: Addressing Fear and Emotional Responses*

Encountering distressing scenarios, such as witnessing a burnt patient in a burn hospital, can evoke strong emotional reactions among social work students during fieldwork. Implementing effective coping strategies is essential to manage these emotions and ensure the well-being of both students and clients. Here are some approaches to help students navigate such challenging situations:

Preparation and Education: Before entering the field, students can engage in thorough research and education about the specific contexts they might encounter. Understanding the conditions, challenges, and potential scenarios in advance can reduce the shock factor and provide a sense of preparedness.

Guided Exposure: Gradually exposing oneself to increasingly challenging situations can desensitize students over time. This approach involves starting with less distressing cases and progressively moving towards more intense scenarios, allowing students to build emotional resilience gradually.

Supervision and Reflection: Regular supervision sessions with experienced field instructors provide a safe space for students to discuss their emotions, fears, and concerns. Reflecting on their reactions and seeking guidance from mentors can help them process their emotions and receive guidance on managing difficult situations.

Emotional Resilience in Fieldwork: New social work students often encounter emotionally challenging situations in field settings, such as witnessing medical procedures or working with burn patients. Developing emotional resilience is key to coping effectively.

Supporting Student Well-Being: Ensuring the emotional well-being of social work students in field settings is vital. Supervisors and mentors should provide guidance and debriefing sessions to help them navigate emotionally demanding situations.

Self-Care Practices: Encouraging self-care routines is crucial. Engaging in activities that promote relaxation, such as meditation, exercise, and hobbies, can help students manage stress and emotional strain. Taking breaks and setting healthy boundaries also contribute to overall well-being.

Peer Support: Connecting with fellow students who are going through similar experiences can be comforting. Sharing feelings, discussing challenges, and seeking advice from peers can help students realize they are not alone in their emotional responses.

Professional Counseling: If emotions become overwhelming, seeking professional counseling or therapy can provide a confidential and supportive environment to process difficult feelings. A mental health professional can equip students with coping strategies tailored to their individual needs.

Mindfulness Techniques: Mindfulness practices, such as deep breathing, grounding exercises, and staying present in the moment, can help manage anxiety and fear. These techniques promote emotional regulation and prevent overwhelming emotional reactions.

Debriefing: After encountering distressing situations, debriefing with supervisors or peers can help students process their thoughts and emotions. Discussing what they witnessed, how it impacted them, and how they can cope moving forward promotes emotional release.

Positive Visualization: Encouraging students to visualize positive outcomes and successful interventions can mitigate feelings of helplessness. Imagining making a positive impact on the situation can provide a sense of empowerment.

Setting Limits: Students need to recognize their emotional boundaries and not force themselves into situations that could be detrimental to their mental well-being. If a situation is too distressing, it's acceptable to seek alternative tasks or assignments that align with their comfort level.

By integrating these coping strategies, students can better navigate emotionally challenging situations and foster their personal and professional growth during their fieldwork experience.

Review Questions

1. What is the significance of social and mental preparation before engaging in fieldwork?
2. How can the EARIS formula benefit social work students in preparing for field practice?
3. Why is setting clear objectives essential for effective fieldwork?
4. In what ways does fieldwork contribute to the overall development of social work students?
5. Explain the importance of ethical considerations and principles in the preparation phase of fieldwork.

Multiple Choice Questions

1. What is the significance of fieldwork in social work for professional development?
   (a) It is optional for social work students.
   (b) It has no impact on professional growth.
   (c) It is crucial for gaining practical experience and skills.
   (d) It is primarily for academic research.
2. How can the EARIS formula be applied in the context of fieldwork practice?
   (a) It guides social work students in preparing for fieldwork.
   (b) It is not applicable to social work.
   (c) It is a formula for personal fitness.
   (d) It is related to financial planning.
3. Why is social and mental preparation important before engaging in fieldwork?
   (a) It contributes to effective engagement and coping in fieldwork.
   (b) It has no impact on fieldwork outcomes.
   (c) It helps in avoiding fieldwork altogether.
   (d) It is only relevant for experienced social workers.
4. What role do clear objectives play in fieldwork?
   (a) They are unnecessary in social work.
   (b) They hinder the learning process.
   (c) They are only for academic purposes.
   (d) They provide a roadmap for effective fieldwork.

5. In what ways does fieldwork contribute to the overall development of social work students?
   (a) It has no impact on development.
   (b) It only focuses on theoretical knowledge.
   (c) It provides practical experience, skill development, and professional growth.
   (d) It is solely for academic credit.

References

Baikady, R., Nadesan, V., Sajid, S. M., & Islam, M. R. (2022). Introduction: New directions to field work education in social work: A global south perspective. In *The Routledge handbook of social work field education in the global south* (pp. 1–10). Routledge.

DeGroot, J. N. (2019). *Bachelor of social work students experiences: Understanding learning needs* (Doctoral dissertation, Capella University).

Dhemba, J. (2012). Fieldwork in social work education and training: issues and challenges in the case of Eastern and Southern Africa. *Social Work & Society, 10*(1), 1–16.

Doel, M., Shardlow, S. M., Shardlow, S., & Johnson, P. G. (2010). *Contemporary field social work: Integrating field and classroom experience.* .

Hamilton, N., & Else, J. F. (1983). *Designing field education: Philosophy, structure, and process.* Charles C. Thomas Publisher.

Hay, K., & O'Donoghue, K. (2009). Assessing social work field education: Towards standardising fieldwork assessment in New Zealand. *Social Work Education, 28*(1), 42–53.

Ivry, J., Lawrance, F. P., Damron-Rodriguez, J., & Robbins, V. C. (2005). Fieldwork rotation: A model for educating social work students for geriatric social work practice. *Journal of Social Work Education, 41*(3), 407–425.

Kaseke, E. (1986). The role of fieldwork in social work training. In *Social Development and Rural Fieldwork. Proceedings of a workshop held in Harare. Harare, Journal of Social Development in Africa* (pp. 52–62).

Pawar, M. (2017). Reflective learning and teaching in social work field education in international contexts. *The British Journal of Social Work, 47*(1), 198–218.

Roy, S. (2017). Field work practice in correctional settings: Indian social work perspective. *Global Journal of Archaeology and Anthropology, 2*(1), 001–008.

Safari, J. (1986, June). The role of fieldwork in the training of social workers for rural development in: Social development and rural fieldwork. In *Proceedings of a Workshop held* (Vol. 10, No. 14, pp. 74-80).

Singla, P. R. (2015). Fieldwork as signature pedagogy of social work education: As I see it. *Social Work Journal, 6*(1), 90–102.

Smith, D., Cleak, H., & Vreugdenhil, A. (2015). "What are they really doing?" An exploration of student learning activities in field placement. *Australian Social Work, 68*(4), 515–531.

Sunirose, I. P. (2013). Fieldwork in social work education: Challenges, issues and best practices. *Rajagiri Journal of Social Development, 5*(1), 48–56.

Chapter 3
Preparing for Fieldwork in Social Work

Learning Objectives
After reading this chapter, you will be able to:

- Understand the significance of setting clear objectives in social work fieldwork preparation.
- Identify and formulate personal learning goals aligned with fieldwork objectives.
- Demonstrate awareness of ethical considerations and principles guiding social work practice.
- Comprehend the diverse socioeconomic, cultural, and psychological challenges addressed by fieldwork agencies.
- Gain insight into the introduction, function, and challenges faced by social work agencies, laying the foundation for effective fieldwork engagement.

3.1 Setting Clear Objectives

As social work students embark on their fieldwork journey, setting clear objectives is an essential first step. This section delves into the significance of establishing well-defined goals and outlines the process of articulating objectives that guide and shape the fieldwork experience.

Understanding the Purpose of Objectives: Clear objectives provide a roadmap for both students and field instructors, outlining the intended outcomes of the fieldwork experience. Objectives serve as a foundation for planning, evaluating progress, and gauging the achievement of learning outcomes. By establishing objectives, students gain a sense of direction and purpose, ensuring that their fieldwork experience is focused and meaningful.

Aligning with Learning Goals: Setting objectives that align with personal learning goals is critical. Students should reflect on their strengths, areas for

M. R. Islam, *Fieldwork in Social Work*,
https://doi.org/10.1007/978-3-031-56683-7_3

improvement, and areas of interest within the field of social work. Whether the goal is to enhance communication skills, gain exposure to a specific population, or develop cultural competence, clear objectives help students customize their fieldwork experience to align with their individual learning needs.

SMART Objectives: An effective framework for setting objectives is the SMART criteria: Specific, Measurable, Achievable, Relevant, and Time-bound. Specific objectives define what will be achieved, measurable objectives provide a way to track progress, achievable objectives ensure feasibility, relevant objectives align with the broader learning goals, and time-bound objectives set a clear timeline for accomplishment. For example, a SMART objective might be: "By the end of the fieldwork period, I will demonstrate the ability to conduct a comprehensive client assessment, including gathering relevant information, identifying strengths and challenges, and formulating intervention plans."

Guiding Fieldwork Activities: Clear objectives act as a compass for planning fieldwork activities. Students and field instructors can design tasks, assignments, and interactions that directly contribute to the achievement of objectives. This intentional approach ensures that every experience during fieldwork is purposeful and contributes to the broader learning goals.

Enhancing Accountability: Objectives provide a basis for accountability. Both students and field instructors can track progress and assess whether the established objectives are being met. Regular check-ins and evaluations based on objectives encourage open communication and support the continuous improvement of fieldwork experiences.

Adapting and Evolving: While setting clear objectives is important, it's equally essential to recognize that objectives can evolve as the fieldwork experience unfolds. As students engage with clients, navigate challenges, and gain insights, their objectives may need adjustment to reflect new understandings or changing priorities. Flexibility in adapting objectives ensures that the fieldwork experience remains relevant and responsive to emerging learning needs.

Setting clear objectives is a foundational step in preparing for fieldwork. By defining specific, measurable, achievable, relevant, and time-bound objectives, students lay the groundwork for a focused and purposeful fieldwork experience. Objectives serve as guideposts, steering students toward their personal learning goals and enabling them to make the most of their journey toward becoming skilled and compassionate social work practitioners.

3.2 Identifying Personal Learning Goals

As social work students embark on their fieldwork journey, identifying personal learning goals becomes a pivotal step in ensuring a meaningful and transformative experience. This section explores the importance of setting individualized learning goals and provides insights into the process of identifying goals that align with one's aspirations and professional growth.

3.2.1 Defining Personal Learning Goals

Personal learning goals are specific objectives that students set for themselves to guide their fieldwork experience. These goals are tailored to individual strengths, areas for improvement, and areas of interest within the field of social work. Personal learning goals provide a framework for focusing efforts and shaping the trajectory of the fieldwork journey.

3.2.2 Benefits of Personalized Goals

- Customization: Personalized goals allow students to customize their fieldwork experience according to their unique needs and aspirations. This individualization ensures that the fieldwork journey is relevant and aligned with their professional development.
- Motivation: Goals provide students with a sense of purpose and motivation. When students see a clear connection between their actions in the field and their desired outcomes, they are more likely to remain engaged and committed to the process.
- Direction: Personal learning goals offer a sense of direction during fieldwork. They provide a roadmap for students to navigate various tasks, interactions, and challenges in ways that support their growth and development.

3.2.3 Process of Identifying Goals

- Self-Assessment: Begin by conducting a self-assessment of your skills, knowledge, and areas for improvement. Reflect on your strengths and the areas you wish to enhance during your fieldwork experience.
- Consider Interests: Think about your areas of interest within the field of social work. Do you have a particular passion for working with certain populations, addressing specific issues, or utilizing particular intervention methods?
- Learning Needs: Identify the learning needs that are relevant to your career goals. What skills or knowledge areas do you believe are essential for your future practice as a social worker?
- SMART Goals: Apply the SMART criteria (Specific, Measurable, Achievable, Relevant, Time-bound) to your learning goals. Ensure that each goal is well-defined, can be measured, is attainable within the scope of your fieldwork, aligns with your aspirations, and has a clear timeframe for achievement.

3.2.4 Example Learning Goals

- Specific: "Enhance my active listening skills during client interactions to foster better rapport and understanding."
- Measurable: "Conduct at least three comprehensive client assessments per week to practice applying assessment tools effectively."
- Achievable: "Develop proficiency in crisis intervention techniques by seeking guidance from experienced practitioners and attending relevant training sessions."
- Relevant: "Deepen my understanding of trauma-informed care through interactions with clients who have experienced trauma and by studying relevant literature."
- Time-bound: "Within the next three months, become proficient in using the agency's electronic client record system for accurate and timely documentation."

Identifying personal learning goals empowers social work students to take ownership of their fieldwork experience. By setting goals that align with their strengths, interests, and career aspirations, students can shape their fieldwork journey to maximize growth, enhance skills, and gain valuable insights that will serve them well in their future practice as dedicated and effective social work professionals.

3.3 Ethical Considerations and Principles

As social work students prepare to embark on their fieldwork experience, understanding and embracing ethical considerations and principles are essential foundations for professional practice. This section delves into the significance of ethical awareness in social work fieldwork and highlights key principles that guide ethical decision-making throughout the journey.

3.3.1 The Role of Ethical Considerations

Ethical considerations are the moral compass that guides social work practice. They provide a framework for making decisions that prioritize the well-being and rights of clients, communities, and society. In the context of fieldwork, ethical awareness helps students navigate complex situations, maintain professional boundaries, and uphold the values of the social work profession.

3.3.2 Global Social Work Statement of Ethical Principles

This Ethical Principles Statement functions as a comprehensive framework guiding social workers toward achieving the utmost standards of professional integrity. By embracing this Statement as social work professionals, instructors, learners, and researchers, we inherently pledge to uphold the fundamental values and principles underpinning the social work profession, as outlined within this very Statement. A variety of values and ethical principles shape our identity as social workers. This realization was acknowledged in 2014 by the International Federation of Social Workers (IFSW) and The International Association of Schools of Social Work within the global definition of social work. This definition is intricate, fostering regional and national interpretations.

All IFSW policies, including the definition of social work, stem from these ethical principles.

> Social work is a practice-based profession and an academic discipline that facilitates social change and development, social cohesion, and the empowerment and liberation of people. Principles of social justice, human rights, collective responsibility, and respect for diversities are central to social work. Underpinned by theories of social work, social sciences, humanities, and indigenous knowledge, social work engages people and structures to address life challenges and enhance wellbeing. (IFSW, 2018)

3.3.2.1 Ethical Principles

The Global Social Work Statement of Ethical Principles, as outlined by the International Federation of Social Workers (IFSW, 2018), emphasizes several key principles:

1. Acknowledgment of Human Dignity: Social workers commit to respecting the inherent dignity and worth of every individual and challenge any beliefs or actions that diminish this dignity.
2. Advocacy for Human Rights: Social workers advocate for the fundamental rights of all individuals, striving to balance conflicting rights and ensure equitable treatment.
3. Pursuit of Social Justice:

    - Confronting Discrimination: Social workers challenge discrimination based on factors like age, gender, race, and socioeconomic status.
    - Embracing Diversity: They promote inclusivity and respect for cultural and ethnic diversity.
    - Advocating for Resource Equity: Social workers advocate for fair distribution of resources and wealth.
    - Opposing Unjust Policies: They advocate for changes to oppressive or unfair policies and practices.

4. Support for Self-Determination: Social workers uphold individuals' rights to make their own decisions, provided they do not infringe on the rights of others.
5. Encouragement of Participation: Social workers empower individuals to participate fully in decisions and actions that affect their lives, fostering their self-esteem and capabilities.
6. Protection of Confidentiality and Privacy:
   - Respecting Privacy Rights: Social workers honor individuals' rights to confidentiality and privacy unless there is a risk of harm to themselves, or others, or statutory restrictions apply.
   - Informing Individuals: They communicate any limitations to confidentiality and privacy to individuals.
7. Treating People as Whole Persons: Social workers recognize and address the biological, psychological, social, and spiritual dimensions of people's lives, formulating holistic assessments and interventions with their full participation.
8. Ethical Use of Technology and Social Media: Social workers recognize the ethical implications of technology and social media in their practice, ensuring that digital interactions uphold privacy, confidentiality, and professional standards.
9. Professional Integrity: Social workers act with integrity, adhering to ethical codes, maintaining necessary qualifications, avoiding conflicts of interest, and ensuring accountability in their actions. They also prioritize self-care to maintain their well-being personally and professionally.

3.3.3 Applying Ethical Principles in Fieldwork

Informed Consent: Before engaging with clients, students should explain their roles, the purpose of their involvement, and the potential implications of their participation. Informed consent ensures that clients are aware of their rights and can make informed decisions.

Boundaries: Maintaining professional boundaries is essential to prevent conflicts of interest, dual relationships, and any potential harm to clients. Students should be vigilant about maintaining the appropriate boundaries between their personal lives and professional roles.

Conflicts of Interest: Students should recognize and address any conflicts of interest that might compromise their ability to provide unbiased and effective assistance to clients. Transparency and accountability are key in managing such situations.

Cultural Sensitivity: Understanding and respecting the cultural beliefs, practices, and values of clients is an ethical imperative. Students should approach each client with cultural humility and avoid imposing their cultural perspectives.

Ethical considerations and principles serve as the foundation of social work practice, and they are equally crucial in fieldwork experiences. By embracing ethical awareness and applying key principles, social work students can navigate the complexities of client interactions, decision-making, and maintaining professional integrity. This ethical foundation ensures that fieldwork contributes to the well-being of clients, promotes social justice, and upholds the highest standards of the social work profession.

3.4 Understanding the Socioeconomic, Cultural, and Psychological Problems Addressed by Fieldwork Agencies

As social work students prepare to embark on their fieldwork journey, gaining an in-depth understanding of the socioeconomic, cultural, and psychological problems that fieldwork agencies address is essential (Conners et al., 2019). This section explores the importance of comprehending the challenges faced by agencies and the communities they serve, as well as how students can engage meaningfully with these issues.

Socioeconomic Challenges: Fieldwork agencies often work with communities facing a range of socioeconomic challenges. These challenges may include poverty, unemployment, lack of access to education and healthcare, housing instability, and food insecurity. Understanding these challenges is crucial for students, as they need to grasp the systemic factors that contribute to clients' difficulties and advocate for resources and services that address these issues.

Cultural Considerations: Cultural competence is paramount in social work practice. Agencies serve diverse populations with varying cultural backgrounds, beliefs, and practices. Social work students must recognize the importance of cultural sensitivity, actively learn about the cultures they encounter, and adapt their approaches to best meet the needs of clients from different backgrounds.

Psychological and Mental Health Issues: Many individuals and families served by fieldwork agencies grapple with psychological and mental health challenges. These may include anxiety, depression, trauma, substance abuse, and more. Understanding the nuances of these issues is vital for students to provide appropriate interventions, offer empathetic support, and collaborate effectively with mental health professionals.

Engaging with Fieldwork Agencies: Agency Research: Before beginning fieldwork, conduct thorough research on the agencies you'll be working with. Understand their mission, client population, services offered, and the specific challenges they address.

Collaboration: Collaborate with agency staff to learn about the most pressing issues their clients face. Engage in open conversations to gain insights into the real-world experiences of individuals and families.

Listening to Clients: During interactions with clients, listen actively and empathetically to their stories. This will provide firsthand insights into the challenges they navigate daily and how the agency's services contribute to their well-being.

Cultural Humility: Approach each client with cultural humility, recognizing that their experiences and values may differ from your own. Seek to understand their perspectives and be willing to learn from their experiences.

Interdisciplinary Approach: Collaborate with professionals from various disciplines within the agency. Understand how social work intersects with fields such as healthcare, education, and mental health to provide comprehensive support.

Understanding the socioeconomic, cultural, and psychological challenges addressed by fieldwork agencies is essential for social work students. This awareness ensures that students engage meaningfully with the clients they serve and that their interventions are responsive to the diverse needs of the community. By recognizing the complexities of these challenges and tailoring their approach accordingly, students contribute to the broader mission of the agency and work towards positive change for individuals and communities in need.

3.5 Introduction, Function, and Challenges of Agencies

Before embarking on fieldwork, social work students need to familiarize themselves with the agencies they'll be working with. This section explores the significance of understanding the introduction, function, and challenges of these agencies, providing students with a comprehensive view of the environments in which they will be practicing.

Introduction to Agencies: Agencies play a pivotal role in addressing social issues and providing support to individuals, families, and communities. Understanding an agency's history, mission, and values provides context for the work being done. Familiarizing oneself with the agency's background allows students to align their efforts with its overarching goals and contribute effectively to its mission.

Function of Agencies: Agencies operate within specific sectors such as healthcare, education, child welfare, and more. Understanding the functions of these agencies—the services they offer, the client populations they serve, and the challenges they address—is crucial for social work students. This knowledge informs students' interactions with clients, the services they provide, and the resources they can connect clients to.

Challenges Faced by Agencies: Agencies often grapple with a range of challenges that can impact their ability to effectively serve their clients. These challenges may include limited funding, high caseloads, understaffing, bureaucratic hurdles, and navigating complex regulations (Dhemba, 2012). Recognizing these challenges helps students understand the broader context in which agencies operate and equips them to collaborate with agency staff in addressing these issues.

Engaging with Agencies: Agency Research: Conduct thorough research on the agencies you'll be working with. Understand their history, mission, and the specific services they provide to clients.

Observation: Spend time observing agency operations to gain insights into its daily functions, client interactions, and collaborative efforts among staff.

Staff Interviews: Engage in conversations with agency staff to learn about their roles, challenges, and the impact of their work. This insight provides a well-rounded perspective on the agency's dynamics.

Shadowing: If possible, engage in shadowing experiences with seasoned social workers and agency staff. This firsthand exposure provides valuable insights into the day-to-day operations of the agency.

Challenges Analysis: Reflect on the challenges the agency faces. Consider how these challenges might impact your fieldwork experience and explore ways you can contribute to addressing them.

In summary, gaining a comprehensive understanding of the introduction, function, and challenges of agencies is fundamental for social work students preparing for fieldwork. This knowledge enables students to engage thoughtfully and effectively with agency staff and clients, ensuring that their interventions are aligned with the agency's mission and responsive to the needs of the community. By immersing themselves in the agency's context, students become well-prepared to navigate the complexities of the fieldwork experience and make meaningful contributions to the agency's goals.

Review Questions

1. What is the importance of setting clear objectives in social work fieldwork preparation?
2. How can personal learning goals contribute to a meaningful fieldwork experience?
3. Discuss the ethical considerations and principles that guide social work practice in fieldwork settings.
4. In what ways do socioeconomic, cultural, and psychological factors impact the challenges addressed by fieldwork agencies?
5. Explain the significance of understanding the introduction, function, and challenges faced by social work agencies in preparing for fieldwork.

Multiple Choice Questions

1. What is the primary purpose of setting clear objectives in social work fieldwork preparation?

   (a) To guide and direct the fieldwork experience
   (b) To limit the scope of fieldwork
   (c) To enhance the challenges faced by agencies
   (d) To exclude personal learning goals

2. How do personal learning goals contribute to a meaningful fieldwork experience?

   (a) By restricting professional growth
   (b) By limiting adaptability in action
   (c) By fostering a more purposeful learning journey
   (d) By discouraging collaboration with diverse stakeholders

3. Which of the following is a crucial consideration in the ethical principles of social work fieldwork?

   (a) Ignoring the socioeconomic context
   (b) Avoiding cultural competence
   (c) Embracing discriminatory practices
   (d) Adhering to ethical standards and principles

4. In preparing for fieldwork, why is it important to understand the challenges faced by agencies?

   (a) To avoid collaboration with stakeholders
   (b) To limit adaptability in action
   (c) To foster a myopic approach
   (d) To navigate and address agency-specific issues

5. What role do the introduction, function, and challenges of social work agencies play in fieldwork preparation?

   (a) They have no impact on the fieldwork experience
   (b) They limit the adaptability of social work students
   (c) They provide insights into agency dynamics and structures
   (d) They discourage understanding the unique culture of agencies

References

Conners, B., Johnson, A., Duarte, J., Murriky, R., & Marks, K. (2019). Future directions of training and fieldwork in diversity issues in applied behavior analysis. *Behavior Analysis in Practice, 12*, 767–776.

Dhemba, J. (2012). Fieldwork in social work education and training: Issues and challenges in the case of Eastern and Southern Africa. *Social Work & Society, 10*(1), 1–16.

International Federation of Social Workers (IFSW) (2018). *Global social work statement of ethical principles*. https://www.ifsw.org/global-social-work-statement-of-ethical-principles/

Chapter 4
Field Assignments and Duties in Social Work Field Practice

Learning Objectives
After reading this chapter, you will be able to:

- Understand the foundational principles of field assignments in social work practice.
- Recognize and categorize diverse duties encountered in various fieldwork settings.
- Describe roles and responsibilities, considering ethical dimensions and client-centered approaches.
- Demonstrate proficiency in effective fieldwork documentation while adhering to ethical standards.
- Analyze and navigate ethical challenges in field practice, applying ethical principles.
- Recognize the significance of supervision and guidance in fieldwork for professional development.
- Develop adaptability skills to respond effectively to dynamic situations encountered during field assignments.
- Apply client-centered approaches, prioritizing client needs, preferences, and strengths in interventions.

4.1 Foundations of Field Assignments

In the realm of social work, establishing a robust foundation for field assignments is pivotal, in shaping the trajectory of practitioners' professional journeys. Serving as a cornerstone, this exploration provides an in-depth understanding of the indispensable elements that lay the groundwork for effective and impactful social work practice in the field (for details, please read LaPorte & Sweifach, 2011; Nuttman-Shwartz

M. R. Islam, *Fieldwork in Social Work*,
https://doi.org/10.1007/978-3-031-56683-7_4

& Berger, 2012; Bogo, 2015; Royse et al., 2016). From delving into the historical evolution of field assignments to grasping the fundamental principles guiding ethical decision-making, practitioners are equipped with a solid foundation as they embark on their fieldwork endeavors.

Tracing the Roots of Field Assignments: Delving into the historical evolution of field assignments offers practitioners invaluable insights into the roots and progression of social work practice. By scrutinizing past approaches and methodologies, social workers gain a deeper understanding of the foundations upon which contemporary field assignments are built. This historical context informs practitioners of the profession's evolution, fostering a sense of continuity and progression in their roles.

Grounding Practice in Social Work Theories: Foundational knowledge of social work theories is imperative for practitioners engaging in field assignments. Exploring key theoretical frameworks underpinning social work practice, including systems theory, ecological perspectives, and person-in-environment concepts, provides a theoretical lens for practitioners to analyze and address complex social issues within the context of their assignments.

Navigating the Moral Landscape: Ethical considerations form the bedrock of social work practice. The exploration of ethical principles and codes of conduct guiding practitioners in their field assignments emphasizes the importance of maintaining confidentiality, respecting autonomy, and upholding social justice, equipping social workers with the ethical compass necessary to navigate the moral landscape of their assignments.

Embracing Diversity in Fieldwork: Acknowledging and embracing cultural diversity is fundamental to effective social work practice. The emphasis on cultural competence in field assignments recognizes the unique cultural contexts within which practitioners operate. By fostering an understanding of diverse backgrounds, social workers approach their assignments with sensitivity and adaptability, enhancing the quality of their interventions.

Building Alliances for Impactful Fieldwork: The establishment of collaborative partnerships stands as a key pillar in successful social work assignments. The exploration of the importance of building alliances with community organizations, governmental agencies, and other stakeholders allows social workers to leverage collective resources and expertise, addressing complex social issues and achieving sustainable impact in the communities they serve.

Cultivating Personal Growth: The exploration delves into the development of a professional identity and the role of self-reflection in social work practice. Understanding one's values, biases, and personal strengths is crucial for effective engagement in field assignments. Encouraging practitioners to engage in continuous self-reflection fosters personal growth and enhances their capacity to navigate the complexities of their assignments.

"Foundations of Field Assignments" serves as an essential primer for social work practitioners, offering a comprehensive exploration of the historical, theoretical, ethical, and cultural underpinnings of their fieldwork. Grasping these foundational elements equips practitioners with the knowledge and mindset needed to embark on impactful and ethical social work practice in the diverse and dynamic settings where field assignments take place.

4.2 Diverse Duties

In the expansive landscape of social work, practitioners encounter a diverse spectrum of duties that demand adaptability, empathy, and a nuanced understanding of human experiences. This section delves into the myriad roles and responsibilities social workers undertake, highlighting the varied contexts and challenges they navigate while addressing the multifaceted needs of individuals, families, and communities.

Macro, Mezzo, and Micro Roles: Social workers operate at different levels: macro (influencing large-scale systems), mezzo (working with groups and communities), and micro (individual interventions). Balancing these roles requires an understanding of how they intersect and impact each other, ensuring a comprehensive approach to addressing social issues.

Advocacy and Activism: This duty involves actively supporting and championing the rights of marginalized individuals and communities. Social workers engage in advocacy and activism to influence policies, challenge systemic inequalities, and promote social justice. They serve as voices for those who may not have the power to advocate for themselves.

Case Management and Intervention: Involves creating and implementing plans to address the specific needs of individuals. This duty includes assessing clients, coordinating services, and providing interventions tailored to their unique circumstances. Social workers act as advocates and coordinators, ensuring clients receive comprehensive support.

Community Organizing: Social workers engage in community organizing to empower residents, strengthen social bonds, and address systemic issues affecting communities. This involves mobilizing community members, facilitating discussions, and initiating collaborative efforts to bring about positive change.

Crisis Intervention: This duty requires social workers to respond swiftly and empathetically to crises, such as natural disasters, emergencies, or individual crises. Social workers provide immediate support, connect individuals to resources, and assist in the recovery process, offering both emotional and practical assistance.

Education and Prevention: Involves designing and implementing educational programs to raise awareness about social issues and prevent future challenges. Social workers educate individuals and communities on topics such as mental health, domestic violence, and substance abuse, aiming for long-term positive outcomes.

Research and Evaluation: Social workers engage in research and evaluation activities to inform their practice. This includes conducting studies, analyzing data, and evaluating the effectiveness of interventions. By grounding their practice in evidence, social workers ensure that their methods are informed by the latest research findings.

Cultural Sensitivity: Recognizing and respecting cultural diversity is crucial in social work. Practitioners must adapt their approaches to align with the cultural backgrounds of clients. This involves understanding cultural nuances, addressing language barriers, and fostering inclusivity to ensure interventions are effective and culturally sensitive.

Reflective Practice: Reflective practice involves regularly evaluating and analyzing one's actions, decisions, and experiences. Social workers engage in self-reflection to enhance their awareness of personal biases, learn from successes and challenges, and continuously improve their practice. This process ensures ongoing growth and adaptability in the ever-evolving field of social work.

The diverse duties of social workers encompass a broad range of roles and responsibilities, from individual interventions to systemic advocacy. By understanding and navigating this spectrum, practitioners can effectively address the complex and dynamic needs of the individuals and communities they serve.

4.3 Roles and Responsibilities in the Field

In the field of social work, understanding and defining roles and responsibilities is paramount for practitioners, delineating the scope within which they operate. This section delves into the multifaceted dimensions of social work roles, emphasizing the diverse responsibilities that practitioners shoulder as they engage with individuals, families, and communities. By clarifying these roles, social workers can navigate the complexities of their profession, ensuring a comprehensive and impactful approach to their interventions.

Macro, Mezzo, and Micro Roles: Social workers operate on a spectrum of roles encompassing macro (systemic and policy-level), mezzo (community and group-level), and micro (individual and family-level) interventions. Balancing these roles requires a nuanced understanding of how they intersect and influence each other. Practitioners must navigate between advocating for systemic change, facilitating group interventions, and engaging in one-on-one therapeutic relationships to address the varied needs of their clients and communities.

Advocacy and Activism: A core responsibility of social workers is advocacy and activism, serving as catalysts for systemic change. This involves actively supporting and championing the rights of marginalized individuals and communities. Social workers engage in advocating for social justice, influencing policies, and addressing systemic inequalities to create a more equitable and just society.

Case Management and Intervention: Social work responsibilities often involve case management and intervention strategies to address the specific needs of individuals and families. This includes assessing clients, developing care plans, coordinating services, and providing therapeutic support. Practitioners navigate a diverse array of duties to enhance the well-being of those they serve, tailoring interventions to meet unique circumstances.

Community Organizing: In addressing broader community issues, social workers take on responsibilities related to community organizing. This involves mobilizing residents, fostering social cohesion, and addressing systemic challenges. Social workers facilitate discussions, initiate collaborative efforts, and empower communities to create positive and lasting change.

Crisis Intervention: Field assignments often require social workers to respond swiftly and empathetically to crises, whether they are individual emergencies or community-wide disasters. This responsibility involves providing immediate support, connecting individuals to resources, and assisting in the recovery process to alleviate immediate needs and support long-term resilience.

Education and Prevention: Social work responsibilities extend to education and prevention initiatives. Practitioners design and implement educational programs to raise awareness about social issues, empowering individuals and communities with the knowledge and skills needed to address challenges proactively and prevent future issues from arising.

Research and Evaluation: Social workers engage in responsibilities related to research and evaluation to inform evidence-based practice. This includes conducting studies, analyzing data, and evaluating the effectiveness of interventions. By grounding their practice in evidence, social workers ensure that their methods are informed by the latest research findings, fostering a culture of continuous improvement.

Cultural Sensitivity: Recognizing and respecting cultural diversity is a fundamental responsibility in social work. Practitioners must adapt their approaches to resonate with the cultural contexts of the individuals and communities they serve. This responsibility involves understanding cultural nuances, addressing language barriers, and fostering inclusivity to ensure interventions are effective and culturally sensitive.

Reflective Practice: An integral responsibility for social workers is engaging in reflective practice. This involves regularly evaluating and analyzing one's actions, decisions, and experiences. By engaging in self-reflection, practitioners enhance their awareness of personal biases, learn from successes and challenges, and continuously refine their approaches to navigate the complexities of their responsibilities.

Defining roles and responsibilities in the field of social work is essential for practitioners to effectively address the diverse and complex needs of individuals, families, and communities. By embracing these responsibilities, social workers contribute to positive social change and enhance the overall well-being of those they serve.

4.4 Effective Fieldwork Documentation

In the realm of social work, effective fieldwork documentation stands as a cornerstone for practitioners, providing a systematic and comprehensive method to capture the impact of interventions and glean valuable insights. This section delves into the importance of meticulous documentation, outlining the key elements and strategies that enable social workers to record, analyze, and communicate their efforts in the field. Documentation in social work serves multifaceted purposes, including recording client information, tracking progress, ensuring accountability, and facilitating communication among professionals. Effective documentation is crucial for demonstrating the impact of interventions, supporting evidence-based practice, and providing a basis for informed decision-making.

Key Elements of Fieldwork Documentation: These elements encompass clear and concise client information, assessment, and goal-setting details, intervention strategies employed, progress and outcomes achieved, and any challenges or modifications to the original plan. The inclusion of these elements ensures that the documentation serves as a robust record of the practitioner's engagement with clients and the effectiveness of interventions.

Strategies for Effective Documentation: Practitioners need to employ specific strategies to enhance the effectiveness of their documentation. This includes maintaining accuracy, timeliness, and confidentiality in recording information. Additionally, utilizing standardized formats, incorporating measurable goals and outcomes, and incorporating client input contribute to the clarity and comprehensiveness of the documentation. Regular updates and revisions ensure that the documentation remains reflective of the dynamic nature of social work interactions.

Legal and Ethical Considerations in Documentation: This aspect delves into the legal and ethical responsibilities associated with fieldwork documentation. Social workers must adhere to confidentiality standards, privacy regulations, and legal requirements in documenting client information. Balancing transparency with the protection of client rights is crucial, and practitioners need to be mindful of ethical considerations to ensure the integrity and trustworthiness of their documentation.

Communication and Collaboration Through Documentation: Documentation serves as a vital means of communication and collaboration among professionals involved in a client's care. Social workers must convey relevant information to colleagues, supervisors, and other stakeholders, fostering a collaborative approach to client welfare. Effective documentation facilitates continuity of care and ensures that all involved parties are well-informed and aligned in their efforts.

Reflective Practices in Documentation: Encouraging reflective practices in documentation promotes continuous learning and improvement. Practitioners should engage in self-reflection on their documentation practices, considering what worked well, what challenges were encountered, and how they can enhance their approach in the future. This reflective process contributes to ongoing professional development and the refinement of intervention strategies.

Technology Integration in Fieldwork Documentation: With advancements in technology, social workers can leverage electronic documentation systems for greater efficiency and accessibility. This section explores the integration of technology, emphasizing the benefits of electronic records, data analytics for insights, and secure platforms that enhance the overall quality and usability of fieldwork documentation.

Training and Professional Development: Fieldwork documentation is a skill that requires ongoing training and professional development. This aspect discusses the importance of training programs, workshops, and continuing education opportunities for social workers to enhance their documentation skills. Staying abreast of best practices and emerging trends ensures that practitioners are well-equipped to meet the evolving demands of fieldwork documentation.

Effective fieldwork documentation is a fundamental aspect of social work practice, capturing the impact of interventions and providing valuable insights for continuous improvement. By understanding the purpose, key elements, strategies, legal considerations, and the role of technology in documentation, social workers can elevate the quality of their documentation practices and contribute to the overall effectiveness of their interventions in the field.

4.5 Ethical Dimensions of Field Practice

In the arena of social work, navigating ethical dimensions (as discussed in Chap. 1, Sect. 1.3) is paramount for practitioners, demanding a delicate balance between personal values and professional duties. This section explores the ethical considerations inherent in field practice, shedding light on the complexities social workers face as they strive to uphold ethical principles while delivering effective and compassionate services.

Foundations of Ethical Practice: At the core of ethical dimensions in field practice lies a commitment to the foundational principles that govern social work. This includes upholding principles such as respect for the dignity and worth of individuals, promoting social justice, maintaining integrity in professional relationships, and ensuring confidentiality. Understanding and internalizing these principles provide the ethical compass that guides practitioners in their daily interactions and decision-making.

Navigating Value Conflicts: Social workers often encounter situations where their values may conflict with those of their clients or the broader societal context. This includes the challenges of navigating value conflicts, emphasizing the importance of self-awareness, cultural competence, and the ability to separate personal beliefs from professional obligations. Strategies for open dialogue, reflective practice, and seeking supervision are explored to ensure that practitioners can navigate these ethical dilemmas effectively.

Client Autonomy and Informed Consent: Respecting client autonomy is a cornerstone of ethical practice. Social workers must actively involve clients in the decision-making process, ensuring that they have the necessary information to make informed choices about their lives. The concept of informed consent, where clients understand the purpose, risks, and benefits of interventions, is discussed as a critical component of upholding ethical standards in field practice.

Confidentiality and Privacy Considerations: Maintaining the confidentiality of client information is a fundamental ethical duty. Social workers must be vigilant in protecting the privacy of the individuals they serve, recognizing the importance of trust and the potential consequences of breaches in confidentiality. This section explores the nuances of confidentiality in the context of client safety, mandated reporting, and collaboration with other professionals.

Cultural Competence and Diversity: Ethical practice in fieldwork involves a deep commitment to cultural competence and diversity. Social workers must be attuned to the diverse backgrounds, experiences, and values of their clients. This requires ongoing education, self-reflection, and a dedication to providing services that are inclusive and respectful of cultural differences. The ethical imperative of promoting social justice in the face of systemic inequalities is also emphasized.

Dual Relationships and Professional Boundaries: Maintaining professional boundaries is essential for ethical social work practice. This includes avoiding dual relationships that could compromise objectivity and the well-being of clients. Social workers must navigate situations where their personal and professional roles intersect, recognizing the potential risks and taking steps to minimize any harm to clients.

Ethical Decision-Making Models: This section explores models of ethical decision-making that guide social workers in navigating complex ethical dilemmas. Models such as the NASW Code of Ethics, the ethical decision-making framework, and reflective practice are discussed as tools that practitioners can utilize to analyze situations, consider potential consequences, and arrive at ethically sound decisions.

Supervision and Consultation: Seeking supervision and consultation is a crucial aspect of ethical field practice. Social workers must have access to support systems where they can discuss ethical challenges, seek guidance, and receive feedback. This collaborative approach ensures that practitioners remain accountable, continuously learn, and uphold the highest ethical standards in their work.

Ethical Challenges in Emerging Areas: As social work evolves, practitioners face new ethical challenges in emerging areas such as technology, social media, and global contexts. This section explores the ethical considerations in utilizing technology in practice, maintaining ethical online interactions, and addressing global issues with cultural sensitivity and social justice advocacy.

Ethical dimensions in field practice demand a nuanced and thoughtful approach from social workers. By grounding their practice in ethical principles, navigating value conflicts with sensitivity, and utilizing ethical decision-making models, practitioners can uphold the integrity of the profession while delivering services that prioritize the well-being and autonomy of those they serve.

4.6 Supervision and Guidance

In the realm of social work, supervision and guidance play pivotal roles in maximizing learning opportunities for practitioners in the field (detailed in Chap. 12). This section delves into the significance of effective supervision, outlining strategies to optimize learning, foster professional growth, and ensure the delivery of high-quality services to individuals, families, and communities.

Foundations of Effective Supervision: Effective supervision serves as the bedrock for learning and growth in social work field practice. This includes creating a supportive and collaborative environment where practitioners feel encouraged to reflect on their experiences, seek guidance, and enhance their skills. Supervision is not merely a form of oversight; rather, it is a dynamic process that promotes continuous learning and development.

Learning Goals and Professional Development: Establishing clear learning goals is essential for maximizing learning opportunities in the field. Social workers and their supervisors collaboratively identify specific areas for growth and skill development. This involves setting achievable objectives that align with the practitioner's professional development plan, ensuring that the learning process is intentional and targeted.

Reflective Practice and Self-Assessment: Encouraging reflective practice is integral to effective supervision. Social workers engage in self-assessment and critical reflection on their practice, exploring the impact of their interventions, identifying strengths, and recognizing areas for improvement. Supervisors guide this reflective process, helping practitioners gain deeper insights into their practice and fostering a habit of continuous self-improvement.

Case Consultation and Problem-Solving: Supervision provides a platform for case consultation and collaborative problem-solving. Social workers bring cases to supervision, presenting challenges, ethical dilemmas, and complex situations. Through dialogue and exploration, supervisors guide practitioners in analyzing cases, considering various perspectives, and developing effective intervention strategies. This process enhances critical thinking and decision-making skills.

Formative and Summative Feedback: Supervisors offer both formative and summative feedback to social workers, providing ongoing guidance and constructive evaluations. Formative feedback focuses on immediate improvement and skill development, while summative feedback assesses overall performance. This dual-feedback approach ensures that practitioners receive continuous support and have a comprehensive understanding of their strengths and areas for growth.

Cultural Competence and Inclusivity: Supervision plays a crucial role in promoting cultural competence and inclusivity in social work practice. Supervisors guide practitioners in navigating cultural nuances, addressing biases, and adapting interventions to diverse populations. This cultural sensitivity enhances the effectiveness of social work services and ensures that practitioners can meet the unique needs of individuals from various cultural backgrounds.

Professional Ethics and Ethical Decision-Making: Supervision is a key forum for discussing ethical considerations and promoting ethical decision-making. Social workers engage in dialogues with supervisors about ethical dilemmas they encounter in the field. Supervisors guide practitioners in navigating these challenges, applying ethical frameworks, and making decisions that align with professional ethical standards.

Support for Self-Care and Emotional Well-being: Recognizing the emotional toll of social work practice, supervision provides support for practitioners' self-care and emotional well-being. Supervisors help social workers identify signs of burnout, establish healthy boundaries, and implement self-care strategies. This holistic approach to supervision ensures that practitioners can sustain their well-being and remain effective in their roles.

Professional Networking and Resource Access: Supervisors facilitate professional networking and provide access to valuable resources. This includes connecting social workers with other professionals, experts, and organizations in the field. Supervisors guide practitioners in building a professional support network, attending relevant training opportunities, and staying informed about emerging trends and best practices.

Evaluation and Professional Growth Plans: Supervision involves a comprehensive evaluation of a social worker's performance and the development of professional growth plans. This process includes setting performance expectations, assessing progress, and collaboratively planning for future growth and skill enhancement. Regular evaluations and growth plans ensure that practitioners are on a trajectory of continuous improvement and career development.

Supervision and guidance are indispensable components of maximizing learning opportunities in the field of social work. By fostering a supportive and reflective supervisory environment, practitioners can enhance their skills, navigate challenges, and contribute to the well-being of the individuals and communities they serve. Effective supervision is not only a means of oversight but a dynamic process that nurtures professional growth and excellence in social work practice.

4.7 Adaptability in Action

Adaptability in the field of social work is a cornerstone for success, requiring practitioners to navigate dynamic and unpredictable situations. This section explores strategies for effectively applying adaptability in action during field assignments, emphasizing the importance of flexibility, resilience, and creative problem-solving.

Embracing Flexibility in Approaches: Adaptability begins with embracing flexibility in approaches to social work interventions. Practitioners must recognize that each client and situation is unique, requiring a tailored approach. Being open to modifying strategies, techniques, and plans based on the evolving needs of clients contributes to successful outcomes in the field.

Dynamic Assessment and Reassessment: Continuous assessment and reassessment are vital components of adaptability. Social workers must dynamically evaluate the needs, strengths, and challenges of clients throughout field assignments. Regular reassessment ensures that interventions remain relevant and effective, allowing practitioners to adjust their approaches in response to changing circumstances.

Creative Problem-Solving: Adaptability involves creative problem-solving in the face of challenges. Social workers encounter diverse issues, and the ability to think innovatively and generate alternative solutions is crucial. This section explores strategies such as brainstorming, collaboration, and drawing on community resources to address challenges creatively.

Effective Communication in Changing Environments: Adaptability relies on effective communication, especially in rapidly changing environments. Social workers must communicate clearly with clients, colleagues, and other stakeholders, keeping them informed about changes in plans or interventions. Open and transparent communication builds trust and ensures that all parties involved are on the same page.

Cultivating Resilience in Adversity: Resilience is a key aspect of adaptability, enabling social workers to bounce back from challenges. This section delves into strategies for cultivating resilience, such as self-care practices, seeking support from supervisors and colleagues, and maintaining a positive mindset. Resilience is a valuable asset in navigating the emotional demands of field assignments.

Collaborative Teamwork: Adaptability is enhanced through collaborative teamwork. Social workers often collaborate with other professionals, agencies, and community resources. Effective teamwork involves shared decision-making, flexibility in roles, and a collective commitment to adapt to changing circumstances. This section explores strategies for fostering collaborative partnerships to maximize adaptability.

Utilizing Technology for Flexibility: Technology plays a significant role in enhancing adaptability. Social workers can leverage technology for remote communication, virtual interventions, and accessing resources on the go. This section explores how practitioners can integrate technology into their field assignments to increase flexibility and responsiveness.

Proactive Planning for Contingencies: While adaptability is about responding to the unexpected, proactive planning for contingencies is equally important. Social workers can anticipate potential challenges, develop contingency plans, and establish protocols for unforeseen situations. This proactive approach ensures a level of preparedness while maintaining the capacity to adapt as needed.

Continuous Learning and Professional Development: Adaptability is closely linked to continuous learning and professional development. Social workers must stay abreast of evolving best practices, emerging trends, and relevant research. This section explores strategies for ongoing learning, including attending workshops, seeking additional training, and staying connected to professional networks.

Reflective Practices for Continuous Improvement: Reflection is a powerful tool for adaptability, allowing social workers to learn from their experiences and adjust their approaches accordingly. Practitioners engage in reflective practices to assess the effectiveness of interventions, identify areas for improvement, and refine their strategies for future field assignments.

Adaptability in action is a dynamic and multifaceted skill crucial for success in social work field assignments. By embracing flexibility, employing creative problem-solving, fostering resilience, and utilizing technology, practitioners can navigate the complexities of the field while continuously learning and improving their approaches. The strategies outlined in this section provide a roadmap for social workers to effectively apply adaptability in diverse and ever-changing environments.

4.8 Client-Centered Approaches

Client-centered approaches in social work underscore the importance of tailoring interventions to meet the unique needs and preferences of individuals (for details, please read Rothery & Tutty, 2008; Rowe, 2017). This section explores the key principles and strategies associated with client-centered practice, emphasizing the collaborative nature of the therapeutic relationship and the empowerment of clients in the decision-making process.

Empathy and Active Listening: At the core of client-centered approaches lies the cultivation of empathy and active listening. Social workers strive to understand the client's perspective, experiences, and emotions. By actively listening without judgment and demonstrating empathy, practitioners create a foundation of trust and rapport that forms the basis for collaborative intervention.

Collaborative Goal Setting: Client-centered interventions involve collaborative goal setting. Social workers work together with clients to identify their goals, aspirations, and areas for improvement. This process ensures that interventions are aligned with the client's priorities and that the client is actively engaged in defining the desired outcomes.

Individualized Assessment and Planning: Client-centered approaches prioritize individualized assessment and planning. Social workers conduct thorough assessments to understand the client's strengths, challenges, and contextual factors. The resulting intervention plans are tailored to address the specific needs and circumstances of the individual, recognizing the uniqueness of each client.

Cultural Competence and Sensitivity: Cultural competence is integral to client-centered practice. Social workers acknowledge and respect the cultural diversity of clients, adapting their approaches to be culturally sensitive. This involves understanding cultural nuances, incorporating culturally relevant practices, and recognizing the impact of cultural factors on the client's experiences and worldview.

Client Empowerment and Autonomy: Empowering clients and promoting their autonomy are fundamental principles of client-centered approaches. Social workers support clients in making informed decisions about their lives, respecting their autonomy, and acknowledging their capacity for self-determination. This empowerment fosters a sense of control and ownership in the client's journey.

Strengths-Based Perspective: A strengths-based perspective is a key component of client-centered practice. Social workers focus on identifying and building upon the client's strengths, resources, and resilience. This positive approach enhances the client's self-esteem, encourages a sense of agency, and facilitates the development of coping mechanisms and solutions.

Flexible and Responsive Interventions: Client-centered interventions are flexible and responsive to the evolving needs of clients. Social workers adapt their strategies based on the client's progress, feedback, and changing circumstances. This responsiveness ensures that interventions remain relevant, effective, and aligned with the client's current situation.

Promotion of Self-Reflection: Encouraging self-reflection is another aspect of client-centered practice. Social workers guide clients in exploring their thoughts, feelings, and behaviors, fostering self-awareness. This reflective process enables clients to gain insights into their challenges, strengths, and goals, contributing to their personal growth and decision-making.

Clear Communication and Transparency: Client-centered communication is characterized by clarity and transparency. Social workers straightforwardly communicate information, ensuring that clients have a clear understanding of the intervention process, goals, and any relevant information. Transparent communication builds trust and facilitates a collaborative relationship.

Ongoing Evaluation and Feedback: Client-centered approaches involve ongoing evaluation and feedback. Social workers regularly assess the effectiveness of interventions in collaboration with clients. This feedback loop allows for adjustments, refinements, and the identification of additional needs or priorities, ensuring that the intervention remains responsive to the client's evolving circumstances.

Client-centered approaches in social work prioritize tailoring interventions to individual needs, fostering collaboration, and empowering clients in their journey toward positive change. By incorporating these principles and strategies, social workers create a supportive and effective therapeutic environment that respects the uniqueness of each client and enhances the likelihood of successful outcomes.

4.9 Innovation and Technology in Field Assignments

In the contemporary landscape of social work, the integration of innovation and technology into field assignments is essential for enhancing efficiency and optimizing outcomes. This section explores the transformative impact of innovation and technology in the field, highlighting strategies for leveraging these tools to streamline processes, improve communication, and ultimately elevate the effectiveness of social work interventions.

Digital Case Management Systems: One of the key innovations in field assignments is the adoption of digital case management systems. These systems enable social workers to efficiently organize and access client information, track progress, and manage interventions in a secure and streamlined manner. Digital platforms facilitate collaboration among team members, ensuring that everyone involved in a case has real-time access to relevant information.

Mobile Applications for Fieldwork: Mobile applications tailored for social work field assignments provide practitioners with on-the-go tools for data collection, assessments, and intervention planning. These applications enhance the flexibility and responsiveness of social workers, allowing them to input information directly into digital platforms during client interactions. This real-time data entry minimizes paperwork, reduces errors, and improves overall efficiency.

Telehealth and Virtual Interventions: The integration of telehealth and virtual interventions represents a groundbreaking innovation in social work practice, especially relevant in situations where in-person interactions are challenging, such as during a pandemic. Telehealth platforms enable social workers to connect with clients remotely. This approach not only enhances accessibility for clients but also optimizes the allocation of resources and time for practitioners.

Data Analytics for Informed Decision-Making: The utilization of data analytics tools empowers social workers to make informed decisions based on comprehensive insights. These tools analyze large datasets to identify patterns, trends, and areas for improvement in social work interventions. By leveraging data analytics, practitioners can enhance their ability to assess the impact of interventions, identify effective strategies, and continuously refine their approaches.

Secure Communication Platforms: In the realm of confidentiality and communication, secure platforms play a critical role. Social workers can utilize encrypted communication tools to share sensitive information, collaborate with colleagues, and engage with clients in a secure digital environment. These platforms enhance privacy protections and ensure compliance with ethical standards related to confidentiality.

Virtual Training and Professional Development: Innovative technologies facilitate virtual training and professional development opportunities for social workers engaged in field assignments. Webinars, online courses, and virtual workshops enable practitioners to enhance their skills, stay updated on best practices, and engage in continuous learning without geographical constraints. This approach supports ongoing professional development and ensures that social workers remain well-equipped for their fieldwork.

Artificial Intelligence for Decision Support: Artificial intelligence (AI) applications offer decision support tools that can assist social workers in their assessments and interventions. AI algorithms can analyze complex datasets, identify patterns, and provide insights that complement practitioners' expertise. This innovative approach enhances the efficiency of decision-making processes and contributes to more targeted and effective interventions.

Remote Supervision and Consultation: Innovative technologies enable remote supervision and consultation, allowing social workers to connect with supervisors, consultants, and colleagues without physical proximity. Virtual platforms facilitate timely and convenient interactions, ensuring that practitioners receive guidance, support, and feedback in real time. This approach is particularly valuable in situations where face-to-face meetings are impractical.

Collaborative Online Platforms: Collaborative online platforms promote teamwork and information sharing among social work professionals. These platforms facilitate seamless collaboration, enabling practitioners to work on shared documents, exchange ideas, and coordinate interventions. The ability to collaborate in real time enhances communication and coordination, contributing to the overall efficiency of field assignments.

The integration of innovation and technology into social work field assignments has the potential to revolutionize the way practitioners operate. By embracing digital tools, social workers can enhance efficiency, improve communication, and ultimately provide more effective and responsive services to individuals and communities. The ongoing exploration and adoption of innovative technologies position social work practice at the forefront of positive and transformative change.

4.10 Global Perspectives on Social Work Assignments

Global perspectives on social work assignments offer a rich tapestry of learning experiences, allowing practitioners to glean insights from diverse contexts and apply culturally sensitive approaches to their practice. This section explores the importance of understanding global perspectives in social work assignments and highlights key lessons learned from contexts in Bangladesh, Pakistan, China, and India.

Cultural Competence as a Cornerstone: Incorporating global perspectives underscores the significance of cultural competence as a cornerstone of effective social work practice. Practitioners engaged in international assignments must be attuned to the cultural nuances, norms, and values prevalent in the specific regions they serve. This cultural sensitivity enhances the relevance and impact of interventions, fostering a deeper understanding of clients' backgrounds and experiences.

Recognizing Diversity in Problem Definition: Global perspectives emphasize the importance of recognizing diversity in defining social issues and problems. The challenges faced by individuals and communities can vary significantly across different regions and cultures. Social workers engaging in international assignments must approach problem definition with an openness to diverse perspectives, acknowledging the unique factors that contribute to social issues in each context.

Community Engagement and Empowerment: Learning from diverse global contexts underscores the importance of community engagement and empowerment. Social work assignments in countries like Bangladesh, Pakistan, China, and India often involve working closely with communities to understand their needs, strengths, and aspirations. This collaborative approach empowers communities to actively participate in the identification and implementation of solutions that are culturally relevant and sustainable.

Navigating Socio-Political Dynamics: Global perspectives highlight the necessity of navigating socio-political dynamics that influence social work assignments. Practitioners must be aware of the historical, political, and economic factors shaping the social landscape in different countries. Understanding these dynamics is crucial for effective advocacy, policy development, and addressing systemic barriers that impact the well-being of individuals and communities.

Innovative Solutions in Resource-Constrained Environments: Social work assignments in diverse global contexts often necessitate innovative solutions in resource-constrained environments. Learning from practices in Bangladesh, Pakistan, China, and India can inspire creative approaches to address challenges with limited resources. This includes leveraging community strengths, establishing partnerships, and adapting interventions to align with the available resources in each unique setting.

Localized Interventions with Global Relevance: While recognizing the uniqueness of each context, global perspectives in social work assignments emphasize the importance of interventions that have global relevance. Lessons learned from one region can inform and inspire practices in another, contributing to a broader understanding of effective social work strategies. Social workers can adapt successful interventions from diverse contexts to enhance their practice.

Building Cross-Cultural Competencies: Engaging with diverse global perspectives contributes to the development of cross-cultural competencies among social work practitioners. Exposure to different cultural norms, languages, and communication styles enhances practitioners' ability to work effectively in multicultural and international settings. This cross-cultural competence is invaluable for building meaningful relationships and promoting positive outcomes in social work assignments.

Learning from Indigenous Knowledge and Practices: Global perspectives in social work assignments encourage practitioners to learn from indigenous knowledge and practices prevalent in different regions. Indigenous wisdom often holds valuable insights into community resilience, coping mechanisms, and sustainable approaches to social issues. Integrating indigenous knowledge into social work practice fosters a more holistic and culturally grounded approach to interventions.

Promoting Social Justice on a Global Scale: Understanding global perspectives reinforces the commitment to promoting social justice on a global scale. Social work assignments provide opportunities to address inequities and advocate for the rights of marginalized populations in diverse contexts. Learning from the experiences of social workers in Bangladesh, Pakistan, China, and India contributes to a collective effort toward global social justice.

Reflective Practice for Cross-Cultural Competence: Engaging with global perspectives necessitates reflective practice for cross-cultural competence. Social workers involved in international assignments must continually reflect on their own cultural biases, assumptions, and communication styles. This reflective process enhances self-awareness and ensures that practitioners approach their work with humility, openness, and a willingness to learn from diverse global contexts.

Global perspectives on social work assignments offer a wealth of learning opportunities, enriching practitioners with insights from diverse cultures and contexts. By embracing cultural competence, recognizing diversity, engaging communities, and promoting global social justice, social workers can contribute to positive change on an international scale. The lessons learned from countries like Bangladesh, Pakistan, China, and India provide valuable benchmarks for developing effective and culturally responsive social work practices globally.

Review Questions

1. What are the key foundational principles of field assignments in social work practice?
2. How do roles and responsibilities in fieldwork contribute to client-centered approaches?
3. Why is effective fieldwork documentation crucial, and what ethical standards should be followed?
4. How can ethical challenges in field practice be navigated, considering ethical principles?
5. In what ways does supervision contribute to the professional development of social work practitioners?
6. Why is adaptability essential in responding to dynamic situations during field assignments?

Multiple Choice Questions

1. What is the primary purpose of effective fieldwork documentation?
   (a) To meet bureaucratic requirements
   (b) To ensure client-centered approaches
   (c) To avoid ethical considerations
   (d) To impress supervisors
2. How does adaptability contribute to successful field assignments?
   (a) By sticking to predetermined plans
   (b) By resisting changes in the field
   (c) By responding to dynamic situations
   (d) By avoiding client feedback
3. What role does supervision play in the fieldwork experience?
   (a) It hinders professional development
   (b) It provides constructive feedback

(c) It is unnecessary for experienced practitioners
(d) It adds bureaucratic layers

4. Why is understanding cultural sensitivity crucial in field practice?

(a) To enforce a single cultural perspective
(b) To undermine diversity
(c) To tailor interventions to client needs
(d) To avoid client communication

5. Which statement best describes the importance of ethical considerations in fieldwork?

(a) Ethical considerations are optional
(b) They are only relevant in crisis situations
(c) They guide professional conduct and decision-making
(d) Ethical principles hinder effective interventions

6. What is the main goal of client-centered approaches in field assignments?

(a) To tailor interventions to meet client needs
(b) To prioritize the social worker's preferences
(c) To streamline bureaucratic processes
(d) To enforce predetermined plans

References

Bogo, M. (2015). Field education for clinical social work practice: Best practices and contemporary challenges. *Clinical Social Work Journal, 43*, 317–324.

LaPorte, H. H., & Sweifach, J. (2011). MSW foundation students in the field: Reflections on the nature and quality of group work assignments and supervision. *Journal of Teaching in Social Work, 31*(3), 239–249.

Nuttman-Shwartz, O., & Berger, R. (2012). Field education in international social work: Where we are and where we should go. *International Social Work, 55*(2), 225–243.

Rothery, M., & Tutty, L. (2008). Client-centered theory. *Theoretical Perspectives for Direct Social Work Practice: A Generalist-Eclectic Approach, 2*, 299–320.

Rowe, W. S. (2017). *Client-centered theory and the person centered approach: Values-based, evidence-supported* (pp. 34–53). Social Work Treatment: Interlocking Theoretical Approaches.

Royse, D., Dhooper, S. S., & Rompf, E. L. (2016). *Field instruction: A guide for social work students*. Waveland Press.

Chapter 5
Culturally Responsive Diversity in Social Work Field Practice

Learning Objectives
After studying this chapter, you should be able to:

- Demonstrate cultural sensitivity in field practice by recognizing and respecting diverse perspectives and practices
- Implement anti-oppressive practices in fieldwork, promoting social justice and equality in interactions with clients
- Enhance cross-cultural communication skills to effectively engage with clients from different cultural backgrounds
- Evaluate personal biases and cultural assumptions to ensure unbiased and culturally competent interventions
- Collaborate with diverse stakeholders, recognizing the importance of engaging with various individuals and groups in the social work process
- Navigate ethical challenges in cross-cultural settings by applying ethical principles to culturally sensitive situations in field practice

5.1 Understanding Cultural Sensitivity in Field Practice

Understanding cultural sensitivity is a foundational aspect of social work field practice, ensuring practitioners can engage with diverse individuals and communities effectively (for details, please read Fernández-Borrero et al., 2016; Sousa & Almeida, 2018). Cultural sensitivity refers to the awareness, knowledge, and respect for the values, beliefs, practices, and traditions of different cultural groups. In the context of field practice, social work students must develop a deep understanding of the cultural nuances present in their interactions with clients. This involves recognizing that each individual brings a unique cultural background, and sensitivity requires an appreciation for the diversity that contributes to these differences.

M. R. Islam, *Fieldwork in Social Work*,
https://doi.org/10.1007/978-3-031-56683-7_5

Cultural sensitivity is not just about acknowledging differences; it is about cultivating a genuine respect for various cultural perspectives. It involves being attuned to the impact of cultural factors on individuals' experiences and recognizing that these factors shape their worldviews and responses to social issues. Social work students need to engage in continuous learning about various cultures and stay informed about cultural practices, rituals, and societal norms that may influence their clients. This knowledge forms the basis for building meaningful connections with individuals from diverse backgrounds.

In the field, cultural sensitivity manifests through open-mindedness, empathy, and a commitment to cultural competence. Social work students must actively seek to understand the lived experiences of their clients, considering cultural influences on their values, behaviors, and help-seeking preferences. Additionally, cultural sensitivity in field practice entails being aware of one's own cultural biases and avoiding stereotypes or assumptions that may hinder the development of a trusting client-practitioner relationship. Ultimately, a culturally sensitive approach contributes to the effectiveness and ethicality of social work interventions, fostering positive outcomes for diverse client populations.

5.2 Addressing Intersectionality and Diversity in Client Situations

Addressing intersectionality and diversity in client situations is a critical dimension of social work practice, requiring practitioners to recognize and respond to the overlapping and interconnected aspects of identity and oppression. Intersectionality acknowledges that individuals may face multiple forms of discrimination or disadvantage based on factors such as race, gender, class, sexuality, and ability, among others. In the field, social work students must be equipped to navigate the complex interplay of these intersecting identities to provide inclusive and tailored support to their clients.

For example, in the United States, a social work student working with a low-income transgender individual may need to address not only economic challenges but also discrimination and healthcare disparities related to both gender identity and socioeconomic status. Similarly, in India, a social work student may encounter caste-based discrimination intersecting with issues of poverty, emphasizing the importance of culturally sensitive interventions that consider both caste and economic factors.

Acknowledging and addressing intersectionality also means recognizing the impact of systemic inequalities on individuals with diverse identities. In South Africa, for instance, social work students may need to confront the historical legacy of apartheid and understand how it continues to influence the experiences of individuals from different racial backgrounds. In Australia, social work students may encounter issues related to the intersection of Indigenous identity and socioeconomic disadvantage among Aboriginal and Torres Strait Islander populations.

Social work students should be adept at recognizing the unique challenges and strengths that arise from the intersections of identity in client situations. This involves engaging in ongoing self-reflection and education to better understand the diverse contexts in which they work. By integrating an intersectional and diverse perspective into their field practice, social work students contribute to more equitable and inclusive outcomes for clients from various backgrounds.

5.3 Integrating Anti-oppressive Practices in Fieldwork

Integrating anti-oppressive practices in fieldwork is a fundamental aspect of social work that seeks to dismantle and challenge systemic forms of oppression and discrimination (for details, please read Radzikh, 2015; Bilotta, 2020; Thyberg, 2023). Social work students must actively engage in practices that promote equity, justice, and inclusivity, recognizing the historical and structural factors that contribute to oppression. This involves adopting an anti-oppressive lens, which entails critically examining power dynamics, biases, and systemic barriers that affect individuals and communities.

For instance, in the context of LGBTQ+ rights, a social work student may work to create inclusive and affirming spaces, challenging heteronormativity and advocating for policies that protect the rights of LGBTQ+ individuals. In a healthcare setting, a student might address the stigmatization of mental health issues by implementing anti-oppressive interventions that prioritize the mental well-being of clients.

Anti-oppressive practices also require social work students to collaborate with clients in ways that empower them and amplify their voices. In the global context, a student working in a postcolonial society might focus on decolonizing social work practices, valuing indigenous knowledge, and centering the experiences of marginalized communities.

Moreover, social work students need to engage in continuous self-reflection, education, and dialogue to understand their own biases and privileges. By challenging oppressive structures and advocating for systemic change, social work students contribute to fostering more just and inclusive environments. The integration of anti-oppressive practices in fieldwork aligns with the social work profession's commitment to social justice and human rights, empowering students to become advocates for positive social change.

5.4 Enhancing Cross-Cultural Communication Skills

Enhancing cross-cultural communication skills is a vital component of effective social work practice, especially when working in diverse and multicultural settings. Social work students need to develop the ability to navigate and communicate across various cultural contexts to ensure meaningful and respectful interactions with clients. This involves not only understanding cultural differences but also recognizing the impact of language, nonverbal cues, and communication styles on the therapeutic relationship.

Social work students can enhance cross-cultural communication by actively seeking cultural competence training, participating in language courses relevant to the populations they serve, and engaging in cultural immersion experiences. These experiences facilitate a deeper understanding of the cultural nuances that influence communication dynamics.

For example, a student working with immigrant communities in a Western country may focus on learning about the cultural norms related to family structures, gender roles, and healthcare beliefs. In another context, a student collaborating with indigenous communities may prioritize understanding traditional communication methods and protocols.

Moreover, social work students should be adept at adapting communication strategies to meet the unique needs of each client. This might involve using interpreters, incorporating culturally sensitive assessment tools, and employing alternative communication methods, such as visual aids or technology, to bridge language and cultural gaps.

By enhancing cross-cultural communication skills, social work students contribute to fostering a more inclusive and client-centered practice. This competency enables them to build trust, rapport, and understanding, ultimately leading to more effective interventions and positive outcomes for clients from diverse backgrounds.

5.5 Fostering Inclusive and Culturally Competent Interventions

Fostering inclusive and culturally competent interventions is a crucial aspect of social work practice, emphasizing the need to tailor interventions to the unique cultural contexts of clients. Social work students must recognize the diversity within populations and understand that a one-size-fits-all approach is inadequate for addressing the complex and varied needs of individuals and communities.

Inclusive interventions involve acknowledging and respecting clients' cultural backgrounds, values, and beliefs throughout the assessment, planning, and implementation stages. This requires social work students to engage in continuous self-reflection, challenge personal biases, and actively seek cultural competence in their professional development.

For instance, a student working with a diverse group of refugees may need to adapt trauma-informed interventions to consider the cultural nuances surrounding the experience of displacement and resettlement. In another scenario, a student working with LGBTQ+ youth should be aware of the unique challenges faced by this community and tailor support services accordingly.

Culturally competent interventions also involve collaboration with clients to ensure their active participation in the decision-making process. Social work students should prioritize empowering clients to express their preferences, values, and goals, fostering a sense of ownership over the intervention process.

Ultimately, fostering inclusive and culturally competent interventions contributes to the effectiveness of social work practice and promotes social justice. By recognizing and addressing the impact of cultural factors on clients' lives, social work students can enhance the relevance and success of their interventions, leading to more positive outcomes for the individuals and communities they serve.

5.6 Evaluating Personal Biases and Cultural Assumptions

Evaluating personal biases and cultural assumptions is an integral component of social work education and practice. Social work students must engage in ongoing self-reflection to identify and critically examine their own biases, stereotypes, and preconceived notions that may influence their interactions with clients from diverse backgrounds. This process is fundamental for promoting cultural humility and preventing the perpetuation of harmful stereotypes or discriminatory practices.

One example of this involves a student working in a healthcare setting who may hold unconscious biases about certain health practices based on cultural differences. Through self-reflection, the student can identify and challenge these biases, leading to more culturally sensitive and equitable healthcare interventions.

Additionally, social work students should be trained to recognize that cultural assumptions can contribute to misunderstandings and hinder effective communication. For instance, assuming that a client from a particular cultural group adheres to specific family structures or gender roles without confirming these aspects can lead to inaccurate assessments and inappropriate interventions.

By actively evaluating personal biases and cultural assumptions, social work students can enhance their cultural competence, build stronger rapport with clients, and provide more effective and ethical services. This reflective practice aligns with the profession's commitment to social justice and ensures that social workers contribute positively to the well-being of diverse individuals and communities.

5.7 Collaborating with Diverse Stakeholders

Understanding the global landscape is crucial for effective social work practice, where collaboration with stakeholders globally enhances the impact on diverse communities. For example, a student working on a community development project in Ghana might engage with local NGOs, government agencies, and community leaders to better understand and address unique challenges faced by the population.

Cultural competence in international collaboration is essential, exemplified by a student working with a refugee resettlement agency in Germany. Sensitivity to cultural nuances and effective communication with stakeholders from different backgrounds are critical components in ensuring the success of social work interventions.

Acknowledging intersectionality is vital for collaboration, as seen in South Africa, where a student working on gender-based violence initiatives collaborates with stakeholders considering the intersections of race, class, and gender to develop holistic and inclusive strategies.

Ethical considerations play a role in cross-cultural collaboration. Working in India, a student involved in mental health initiatives may collaborate with traditional healers, recognizing the importance of cultural competence and ethical engagement.

Community-based collaborations are crucial, especially in Latin American contexts. Students contributing to projects addressing poverty and education collaborate with local community leaders, schools, and grassroots organizations to understand and meet the specific needs of the population.

Ethical considerations play a role in cross-cultural collaboration. Working in India, a student involved in mental health initiatives may collaborate with traditional healers, recognizing the importance of cultural competence and ethical engagement.

Building bridges in conflict zones, like the Middle East, involves collaboration with international organizations, government agencies, and local communities to promote peace-building initiatives that respect diverse cultural perspectives. Social work students gain a comprehensive understanding of the significance of collaborating with diverse stakeholders, fostering inclusive practices, and addressing global challenges through culturally competent and ethical approaches.

5.8 Navigating Ethical Challenges in Cross-Cultural Settings

Navigating ethical challenges in cross-cultural settings requires a nuanced approach, and social work students must be equipped with the skills to address dilemmas that may arise. For instance, a student working on a public health project in a Southeast Asian country might encounter ethical challenges related to cultural differences in health practices. Balancing respect for cultural norms with the promotion of health interventions necessitates thoughtful consideration and cultural sensitivity.

In the context of humanitarian aid, a student engaged in refugee assistance in the Middle East may face ethical dilemmas regarding resource allocation and distribution. The ethical imperative to provide aid to those in need must be balanced with cultural considerations, ensuring that assistance respects local customs and values.

Collaborating with diverse stakeholders in Africa on community development initiatives may present ethical challenges related to power dynamics and decision-making processes. Social work students need to navigate these complexities while upholding ethical principles such as justice, autonomy, and beneficence.

In Latin American countries, where social work students participate in projects addressing indigenous rights, ethical considerations revolve around cultural respect and self-determination. Ensuring that interventions align with the cultural values and aspirations of indigenous communities is imperative for ethical practice.

In European contexts, a student working on LGBTQ+ rights might encounter ethical challenges related to varying cultural attitudes towards sexual orientation and gender identity. The need to advocate for inclusivity and equality while respecting cultural diversity demands a nuanced ethical approach.

The overarching theme in navigating ethical challenges in cross-cultural settings is the recognition that ethical principles are universal but must be applied with cultural sensitivity. Social work students learn to critically analyze and navigate complex ethical dilemmas while promoting culturally competent and respectful interventions in diverse global contexts.

Review Questions

1. How does cultural sensitivity contribute to effective fieldwork practice in social work?
2. Why is it important for social work practitioners to evaluate their personal biases and cultural assumptions?
3. What are the key elements of anti-oppressive practices, and how can they be integrated into fieldwork?
4. Explain the significance of enhancing cross-cultural communication skills in the context of social work.
5. In what ways can collaboration with diverse stakeholders positively impact the outcomes of social work interventions?

Multiple Choice Questions

1. What is the primary purpose of cultural sensitivity in social work field practice?

   (a) To enforce cultural norms
   (b) To identify cultural superiority

   (c) To enhance understanding and respect for diverse cultures
   (d) To isolate individuals based on cultural differences

2. Why is evaluating personal biases essential for social work practitioners?
   (a) To reinforce biases
   (b) To remain indifferent to cultural differences
   (c) To uphold prejudice
   (d) To provide equitable and unbiased services

3. What is a key aspect of anti-oppressive practices in fieldwork?
   (a) Reinforcing power imbalances
   (b) Ignoring systemic inequalities
   (c) Promoting fairness and challenging oppression
   (d) Advocating for discriminatory policies

4. How does cross-cultural communication contribute to effective social work interventions?
   (a) By promoting cultural homogeneity
   (b) By avoiding communication altogether
   (c) By fostering understanding and cooperation
   (d) By imposing one cultural perspective

5. What is the potential outcome of effective collaboration with diverse stakeholders in social work?
   (a) Positive impacts on intervention outcomes
   (b) Increased cultural segregation
   (c) Limited perspectives on client needs
   (d) Exclusion of marginalized communities

References

Bilotta, N. (2020). Anti-oppressive social work research: Prioritising refugee voices in Kakuma refugee camp. *Ethics and Social Welfare, 14*(4), 397–414.

Fernández-Borrero, M. A., Vázquez-Aguado, O., & Álvarez-Pérez, P. (2016). The influence of cultural sensitivity in social work practice with immigrants. *The British Journal of Social Work, 46*(2), 444–462.

Radzikh, O. (2015). *Social work students' perspectives on anti-oppressive practice* (Master's thesis).

Sousa, P., & Almeida, J. L. (2018). Culturally sensitive social work: Promoting cultural competence. In *Private troubles or public issues?* (pp. 232–250). Routledge.

Thyberg, C. T. (2023). Preparing social workers for anti-oppressive practice: Evaluating the role of critical social work education. *Journal of Social Work Education, 59*(2), 407–422.

Chapter 6
Developing Professional Skills in Social Work Field Practice

Learning Objectives
After studying this chapter, you will be able to:

- Master foundational skills in social work practice, emphasizing ethical principles and professional conduct
- Develop effective communication strategies for building meaningful relationships with clients and stakeholders
- Learn assessment and intervention planning techniques, exploring evidence-based approaches for comprehensive client support
- Acquire crisis intervention and conflict resolution skills to handle challenging situations with professionalism
- Cultivate cultural competence and diversity awareness for inclusive and effective social work interventions
- Advocate for social justice, understanding the role of advocacy in addressing systemic issues and promoting equitable access to resources

6.1 Foundations of Professional Skills

The foundation of professional skills in social work field practice is a critical aspect that shapes the competence and effectiveness of practitioners (for details, please read Kääriäinen & Muurinen, 2020; Brown & Gloyne, 2021). At the core of this foundation lies a comprehensive understanding of the multifaceted skills that contribute to successful social work interactions and interventions. This initiates by delving into the intricate definition of professional skills within the context of social work. It extends beyond mere technical expertise to encompass a spectrum of competencies, such as interpersonal communication, critical thinking, and ethical decision-making. These skills collectively form the building blocks for establishing

M. R. Islam, *Fieldwork in Social Work*,
https://doi.org/10.1007/978-3-031-56683-7_6

and maintaining meaningful connections with clients, colleagues, and the broader community.

A detailed overview of foundational skills follows, with a particular focus on communication skills. Social work is inherently relational, and effective communication is pivotal in establishing rapport, understanding client needs, and facilitating positive outcomes. The section explores the nuances of active listening, empathetic communication, and the ability to convey information clearly and respectfully. It also underscores the significance of problem-solving and critical thinking skills, emphasizing their role in assessing complex situations, identifying challenges, and devising creative and effective solutions. Critical thinking, in particular, emerges as a crucial tool for making informed decisions that align with ethical principles and professional standards.

Ethical considerations form an integral part of the foundation of professional skills. This expounds on the ethical principles that guide social work practice, illustrating how these principles intertwine with various professional skills. Navigating ethical dilemmas is explored, offering practitioners practical strategies for maintaining ethical integrity in the face of complex situations. This discussion establishes a framework for ethical decision-making, highlighting the interconnectedness of ethical considerations and professional skills in shaping responsible and morally sound practice.

Cultural competence and sensitivity emerge as pivotal aspects within the foundations of professional skills. Social work is inherently diverse, requiring practitioners to engage effectively with individuals from various cultural backgrounds. This elucidates the importance of understanding cultural competence, offering insights into how foundational skills contribute to working sensitively with diverse populations. It emphasizes the need for practitioners to be self-aware, open to diverse perspectives, and adaptable in their interventions to align with the cultural contexts of their clients.

Moreover, this introduces the concept of reflective practices as an essential component for continuous improvement in professional skills. It underscores the significance of practitioners engaging in ongoing self-reflection to assess personal biases, experiences, and the impact of interventions on clients. Reflective practices, intertwined with feedback from supervisors, colleagues, and clients, create a reciprocal process that enhances professional skills. This emphasis on continuous improvement aligns with the dynamic nature of social work practice and the evolving needs of clients and communities.

6.2 Communication and Relationship Building

Communication and relationship building stand as cornerstone elements in the intricate tapestry of social work field practice. This section delves into the nuanced dimensions of effective communication, emphasizing its pivotal role in establishing meaningful relationships with clients, collaborating with colleagues, and fostering positive change within communities.

Defining Communication in Social Work: Communication in social work extends far beyond the exchange of information. It encapsulates a complex interplay of verbal and nonverbal cues, empathy, active listening, and cultural sensitivity. This section lays the groundwork by defining the multifaceted nature of communication within the specific context of social work, emphasizing its central role in facilitating understanding and connection.

The Power of Active Listening: Active listening emerges as a paramount skill in social work communication. This explores how practitioners can cultivate active listening techniques to truly comprehend the nuances of clients' experiences, concerns, and aspirations. Through examples and practical guidance, social workers are equipped to harness the transformative power of active listening in building rapport and demonstrating genuine empathy.

Nonverbal Communication and Empathy: The nuances of nonverbal communication take center stage, acknowledging that gestures, body language, and facial expressions often convey messages as profound as spoken words. This unravels the art of interpreting and utilizing nonverbal cues effectively, emphasizing their role in conveying empathy and understanding. Practitioners learn to attune themselves to the subtle expressions that contribute to the richness of client interactions.

Tailoring Communication to Diverse Populations: Recognizing the diverse nature of the populations served in social work, this section underscores the importance of tailoring communication approaches. Cultural competence is woven into the discussion, emphasizing how an understanding of cultural norms and communication styles enhances the practitioner's ability to engage with individuals from various backgrounds. It explores strategies for overcoming language barriers and fostering inclusivity in communication.

Building Therapeutic Relationships: This extends beyond communication skills to explore the art of building therapeutic relationships. Practitioners are guided through the process of establishing trust, creating a safe and nonjudgmental space, and collaborating with clients to define their goals. Case examples illustrate the application of relationship-building techniques in diverse social work settings.

Addressing Challenges in Communication: Communication in social work is not without its challenges. This section candidly addresses common obstacles such as resistance, distrust, or communication breakdowns. Strategies for navigating these challenges are explored, empowering practitioners to adapt their communication approaches to diverse and sometimes difficult situations.

Collaborative Communication in Interdisciplinary Teams: Social work often involves collaboration with interdisciplinary teams. This section explores the dynamics of collaborative communication, emphasizing effective ways to communicate within teams comprised of professionals from different backgrounds. It delves into strategies for navigating diverse perspectives, fostering open dialogue, and aligning collective efforts toward client-centered outcomes.

Ethical Considerations in Communication: Ethical dimensions permeate communication in social work. This section delves into the ethical considerations inherent in client communication, confidentiality, and information sharing. It provides a framework for practitioners to navigate the delicate balance between transparency and confidentiality, ensuring that ethical principles guide communication practices.

Communication and relationship building serve as a comprehensive guide for social work practitioners seeking to enhance their communication skills and cultivate meaningful relationships with clients, colleagues, and communities. It navigates the intricate interplay of verbal and nonverbal communication, empathy, and cultural competence, positioning effective communication as an indispensable tool in the arsenal of social work professionals.

6.3 Assessment and Intervention Planning

Assessment and intervention planning are integral components of the social work process, guiding practitioners in understanding client needs, formulating effective strategies, and promoting positive change. This section delves into the complexities of these processes, providing a comprehensive exploration of assessment methods, intervention planning strategies, and the ethical considerations that underpin these crucial aspects of social work field practice.

The Role of Assessment in Social Work: Fundamentally, assessment is a dynamic and ongoing process within social work practice. It involves the continuous gathering, analysis, and interpretation of information concerning clients and their environments. The pivotal role of assessment lies in forming the foundation for informed decision-making and tailoring interventions to address the specific needs of individuals and communities.

Comprehensive Assessment Methods: Diving into the array of methods employed in comprehensive assessments, the exploration covers various tools. These include interviews, observations, standardized assessments, and ecological assessments. Insights into the strengths and limitations of each method empower practitioners to select the most appropriate approaches based on the unique needs and contexts of their clients.

Strengths-Based Assessment: Emphasizing a strengths-based perspective, this underscores the importance of recognizing and leveraging clients' strengths throughout the assessment process. Moving beyond a deficit-focused approach, practitioners gain insights into the inherent capabilities and resources individuals and communities possess. Case examples vividly illustrate the transformative impact of adopting a strengths-based lens in assessments.

Person-in-Environment Framework: Introduced as a guiding principle in assessment, the person-in-environment (PIE) framework emphasizes the interconnectedness of individuals with their environments. This framework informs a holistic understanding of clients, encouraging practitioners to consider the impact of social, cultural, and environmental factors on clients' well-being and challenges.

Developing Intervention Plans: Transitioning from assessment to intervention planning, this provides a comprehensive guide to formulating effective plans. The exploration encompasses the collaborative process of working with clients to set goals, outline measurable objectives, and select appropriate interventions.

Utilizing Client Strengths and Resources: Significantly emphasizing client strengths, practitioners are guided in identifying and mobilizing inherent capabilities. This approach empowers individuals and communities to actively participate in their own growth and change processes, creating a foundation for sustainable positive outcomes.

Ethical Considerations in Assessment and Intervention: Addressing the ethical dimensions inherent in assessment and intervention planning, this section navigates the principles governing social work practice. It explores issues of informed consent, confidentiality, cultural competence, and the responsibility of social workers to advocate for client well-being while respecting their autonomy.

Continuous Assessment and Adaptation: Emphasizing the dynamic nature of assessment and intervention planning, practitioners are encouraged to engage in continuous assessment. This advocates for regular revisiting and adaptation of plans based on clients' progress, changing circumstances, and evolving goals. Flexibility and responsiveness to dynamic client needs emerge as crucial elements for effective practice.

Navigating the intricacies of assessment methods highlights the importance of a strengths-based and person-in-environment approach. Emphasizing the collaborative and dynamic nature of intervention planning equips practitioners to engage in effective and ethical social work practices that promote positive outcomes for clients and communities.

6.4 Crisis Intervention and Conflict Resolution

Crisis intervention and conflict resolution are vital facets of social work field practice, requiring practitioners to navigate high-stress situations and facilitate resolution in complex interpersonal dynamics (Royse et al., 2016; Mansour, 2023). This section delves into the nuanced strategies and ethical considerations inherent in crisis intervention and conflict resolution, providing social work professionals with essential tools to address challenging scenarios and promote positive outcomes.

Understanding Crisis Intervention: It needs to define a crisis as a state of emotional or situational turmoil that exceeds an individual's coping mechanisms. The discussion explores the dynamics of crises and emphasizes the time-sensitive nature of effective intervention. Case studies illustrate the application of crisis intervention strategies in diverse social work settings.

Techniques for De-Escalation: A focal point of crisis intervention is the application of techniques for de-escalation. Practitioners are guided through methods to defuse heightened emotions, manage immediate risks, and create a supportive environment for clients in crisis.

Conflict Resolution Strategies: Transitioning to conflict resolution, this delineates various strategies for addressing interpersonal conflicts within the social work context. It explores collaborative approaches that prioritize open communication, mutual understanding, and negotiation. The importance of impartiality and cultural competence in resolving conflicts involving diverse populations is underscored.

Managing High-Stress Situations: Given the inherent stressors in crisis and conflict situations, this section delves into the techniques for managing high-stress environments. Social work practitioners learn stress management strategies for themselves and their clients, ensuring that interventions are conducted in a manner that minimizes additional distress and fosters a sense of safety and stability.

Promoting Client Safety: Client safety is a paramount consideration in crisis intervention. This explores protocols and strategies to ensure the physical and emotional well-being of clients during times of crisis. It addresses risk assessment, safety planning, and collaboration with other professionals or agencies to create a comprehensive approach to promoting client safety.

Ethical Considerations in Crisis Intervention and Conflict Resolution: Ethical dimensions permeate crisis intervention and conflict resolution. In this case, it needs to navigate the ethical principles and guidelines that govern these practices, emphasizing the importance of informed consent, confidentiality, and the prioritization of client well-being. Practitioners are guided in balancing ethical considerations while actively engaging in interventions.

Addressing Client Resistance: Acknowledging that client resistance is common in crisis and conflict scenarios, it needs to explore strategies for addressing resistance effectively. Social workers learn to navigate client pushback with sensitivity, understand the underlying reasons for resistance, and adapt interventions to align with clients' needs and concerns.

Cultural Sensitivity in Crisis and Conflict Resolution: Cultural competence is paramount in crisis and conflict resolution. This emphasizes the need for practitioners to approach interventions with cultural sensitivity, recognizing diverse perspectives, communication styles, and coping mechanisms.

Crisis intervention and conflict resolution equip social work practitioners with the knowledge and skills necessary to navigate challenging situations ethically and effectively. By addressing crisis dynamics, conflict resolution strategies, and the importance of cultural competence, this empowers social workers to engage in interventions that promote client safety, well-being, and positive outcomes in the face of crisis and conflict.

6.5 Cultural Competence and Diversity

Cultural competence and diversity lie at the heart of effective social work, requiring practitioners to navigate the intricate tapestry of human experiences and identities (Armour et al., 2004; Abrams & Moio, 2009). This section explores the multifaceted dimensions of cultural competence, emphasizing its significance in fostering meaningful connections with diverse populations and promoting equitable and inclusive social work practices.

Understanding Cultural Competence: Cultural competence is the ability to understand, respect, and effectively engage with individuals from diverse cultural backgrounds. Social work students should understand the dynamic and ongoing nature of cultural competence, emphasizing its role in enhancing the quality and relevance of social work interventions.

Cultivating Self-Awareness: At the core of cultural competence is self-awareness. Practitioners are guided through the process of examining their own cultural biases, values, and assumptions. This introspective journey is foundational to developing a humble and open-minded approach, allowing social workers to engage with clients from a place of cultural humility.

Recognizing Diversity in Social Work Practice: Diversity within the social work context is explored as a rich mosaic of experiences, identities, and perspectives. Social work students should underscore the importance of recognizing and celebrating this diversity. Practitioners are encouraged to approach clients as individuals with unique backgrounds, acknowledging the intersectionality of various identities, such as race, ethnicity, gender, sexual orientation, and socioeconomic status.

Tailoring Interventions to Cultural Contexts: Practical strategies for tailoring interventions to diverse cultural contexts are discussed. This includes adapting communication styles, incorporating culturally relevant assessment tools, and considering the impact of cultural factors on the interpretation of clients' needs.

Overcoming Language Barriers: Language is a fundamental aspect of culture, and this section explores strategies for overcoming language barriers in social work practice. From utilizing interpreters to embracing nonverbal communication cues, practitioners learn how to ensure effective communication with clients whose primary language may differ from their own.

Advocacy for Cultural Competence: Advocacy emerges as a key theme, emphasizing the role of social workers in advocating for cultural competence within the broader societal context. Social work students should be aware of the importance of challenging systemic barriers, promoting policies that support diversity, and actively engaging in advocacy efforts to address inequities experienced by marginalized communities.

Intersectionality in Social Work: Recognizing the interconnectedness of various social identities, this introduces the concept of intersectionality. Social workers are guided in understanding how intersecting identities influence clients' experiences and shape their needs. This awareness informs more nuanced and tailored approaches to intervention planning and advocacy.

Continuous Learning and Adaptation: This concludes by emphasizing the importance of continuous learning and adaptation in the pursuit of cultural competence. Social workers are encouraged to stay informed about evolving cultural dynamics, engage in ongoing education, and seek supervision and consultation to enhance their cultural competence throughout their careers.

Cultural competence and diversity provide a comprehensive guide for social work practitioners aiming to enhance their ability to engage effectively with diverse populations. By fostering self-awareness, recognizing the richness of diversity, tailoring interventions to cultural contexts, and advocating for inclusive practices, social workers can contribute to a more equitable and empowering field of social work that respects and celebrates the unique identities of each individual and community.

6.6 Advocacy and Social Justice

Advocacy and social justice form the ethical backbone of social work, compelling practitioners to actively engage in systemic change, address inequalities, and promote the well-being of marginalized populations. This section explores the integral role of advocacy and social justice in social work field practice, providing a comprehensive guide for practitioners committed to fostering positive societal transformations.

Defining Advocacy in Social Work: Advocacy is portrayed as a multifaceted and dynamic process that involves actively supporting and championing the rights, needs, and well-being of individuals and communities. It encompasses a range of actions, from individual client advocacy to broader social and policy advocacy initiatives.

The Intersection of Advocacy and Social Justice: Advocacy is intricately linked with the broader concept of social justice. Social work students will explore how social workers play a pivotal role in addressing systemic injustices, challenging oppressive structures, and working towards creating a more equitable and inclusive society.

Individual and Client Advocacy: Practical aspects of individual and client advocacy are illuminated, highlighting the importance of empowering clients to assert their rights, access resources, and navigate complex systems.

Community and Group Advocacy: Expanding the scope, this delves into community and group advocacy. Social workers are guided in mobilizing communities, facilitating grassroots movements, and advocating for social change at the community level. Case examples from field practices will help illustrate how community advocacy can address systemic issues and empower marginalized groups.

Policy Advocacy and Legislative Change: A crucial dimension of social work advocacy is the arena of policy and legislative change. Practitioners learn how to engage in policy analysis, lobby for legislative reforms, and contribute to the development of policies that promote social justice.

Addressing Systemic Barriers: Systemic barriers are explored as impediments to social justice, and social workers are equipped with strategies for addressing these barriers. Whether within organizations, institutions, or society at large, practitioners learn to identify and challenge systemic injustices, advocating for structural changes that foster equality and inclusion.

Collaborative Advocacy: Collaboration emerges as a powerful tool in advocacy efforts. In field practice, social work students have the opportunity to explore how social workers can collaborate with diverse stakeholders, including other professionals, organizations, and community members. This helps to understand the importance of building alliances to amplify advocacy efforts and achieve more significant social impact.

Ethical Considerations in Advocacy: Ethical considerations are woven into the need for social workers to engage in advocacy that upholds ethical principles. Here, students navigate the delicate balance between client confidentiality, informed consent, and the duty to advocate for social justice. Practitioners learn to navigate ethical challenges inherent in advocacy efforts.

Advocacy and social justice serve as a guiding compass for social work practitioners dedicated to effecting positive change. By embracing the interconnected nature of advocacy and social justice, social workers can contribute to a more just and equitable society, ensuring that their efforts extend beyond individual clients to address systemic issues and promote enduring social change.

6.7 Case Management and Documentation

Case management and documentation are critical components of social work practice, providing a structured approach to client care and ensuring accountability, continuity, and ethical standards (for details, please read Savaya, 2010; Jacobsson, 2016). This section delves into the intricacies of case management, exploring the processes of assessment, planning, intervention, and evaluation while emphasizing the significance of thorough and ethical documentation.

The Role of Case Management: Case management is defined as a collaborative and client-centered process that facilitates the coordination of services to meet the diverse needs of clients. Students will explore its importance in promoting holistic client well-being and fostering effective communication among various service providers.

Comprehensive Assessment and Goal Setting: A focal point of case management is a comprehensive assessment. Social workers are guided in conducting thorough assessments that consider not only the presenting issues but also the broader social, economic, and cultural contexts. Goal setting becomes a collaborative process, involving clients in defining their objectives and aspirations, and aligning interventions with their unique strengths and needs.

Developing and Implementing Intervention Plans: Social work students will learn to design strategies that align with client goals, incorporating evidence-based practices and drawing upon available resources. The collaborative nature of intervention planning is emphasized, emphasizing the importance of client engagement in decision-making.

Coordinating Services and Resources: Case management involves coordinating a myriad of services and resources. Practitioners learn effective strategies for navigating service systems, advocating for client needs, and leveraging community resources. Social work students will explore how social workers can build collaborative partnerships with other professionals and organizations to enhance the scope and impact of services.

Monitoring and Evaluation: The ongoing process of monitoring and evaluating intervention outcomes is essential in case management. Social work students will be equipped with tools to track progress, assess the effectiveness of interventions, and make necessary adjustments. Emphasis is placed on the importance of client feedback in the continuous improvement of service delivery.

Ethical Considerations in Case Management: Students must be aware of the ethical considerations inherent in case management, addressing issues such as confidentiality, informed consent, and the duty to advocate for client well-being. Practitioners learn to strike a balance between ensuring client privacy and sharing necessary information for effective collaboration among service providers.

Thorough Documentation Practices: Documentation is a cornerstone of case management, ensuring that client information is accurately recorded, accessible, and secure. This includes the use of standardized forms, maintaining client confidentiality, and adhering to legal and ethical standards. Practical tips are provided to streamline documentation processes.

Balancing Documentation and Client Engagement: While documentation is crucial, social workers are encouraged to strike a balance between fulfilling documentation requirements and maintaining authentic and meaningful engagement with clients for integrating documentation seamlessly into the workflow, allowing practitioners to focus on building trusting relationships and delivering client-centered care.

Case management and documentation provide social work practitioners with a comprehensive guide to navigating the complexities of client care. By emphasizing collaborative and client-centered approaches to case management and outlining ethical documentation practices, social workers can ensure that their interventions are effective, accountable, and grounded in principles that prioritize the well-being of those they serve.

6.8 Supervision and Professional Development

Supervision and ongoing professional development play crucial roles in shaping the landscape of social work practice, contributing significantly to the growth, competence, and ethical awareness of practitioners (for details, please read Kaba & Damaskos, 2015). This exploration delves into the multifaceted dimensions of supervision, underscoring its pivotal function in offering support, guidance, and avenues for reflective practice. Furthermore, it delves into the perpetual significance of continuous professional development, aiming to enrich the skills and knowledge base of social work professionals.

The Vital Role of Supervision in Social Work: Highlights the fundamental role of supervision in social work, depicting it as a structured and collaborative process. Its primary objective is to foster the professional growth and well-being of practitioners. Within the supervisory relationship, practitioners find a dedicated space for reflection, skill development, and the integration of theoretical knowledge into their practical endeavors. The dynamic nature of supervision is underscored, providing a supportive environment while maintaining a level of accountability.

Exploring Diverse Models of Supervision: Delves into various models of supervision, encompassing both traditional and contemporary approaches. Practitioners are encouraged to discern the unique needs of their clients, the organizational context, and their learning styles when selecting a supervision model. Explores the strengths and limitations of models such as the developmental model, the strengths-based model, and the integrative model, offering practitioners a nuanced understanding of the choices available.

The Significance of Reflective Practices in Supervision: Reflective practices take center stage as a crucial theme in supervision. Social workers are guided in utilizing reflective supervision as a potent tool for enhancing self-awareness, critical thinking, and continuous learning. This involves a meticulous examination of assumptions, biases, and reactions to refine the understanding of the impact of interventions on clients and to elevate professional skills. It emphasizes the transformative power of reflective practices in refining and enriching the practitioner's approach.

Striking a Balance between Support and Challenge: Effective supervision is portrayed as a delicate equilibrium between providing unwavering support and presenting constructive challenges. It explores how supervisors can establish an environment that encourages practitioners to explore their strengths while addressing areas for improvement. The overarching goal is to cultivate a safe space for practitioners to learn, grow, and adeptly navigate the intricacies of their roles. This balance is seen as a cornerstone for fostering resilient and competent professionals.

Crafting Personalized Professional Development Plans: Shifting the focus to professional development, this section equips practitioners with a framework to plan and pursue ongoing learning opportunities. Social workers are guided in assessing their strengths, identifying areas for growth, and crafting personalized professional development plans. It explores diverse avenues for professional development, encompassing workshops, conferences, academic pursuits, and networking. It emphasizes tailoring plans to individual needs for a well-rounded and impactful developmental journey.

Navigating Ethical Considerations in Supervision: Ethical considerations seamlessly weave throughout the discourse on supervision and professional development. This section addresses issues related to confidentiality, power dynamics inherent in the supervisory relationship, and the ethical responsibility of supervisors to foster a supportive and culturally competent environment. Practitioners gain insights into navigating ethical challenges within the supervisory context, emphasizing the importance of upholding ethical standards.

Mitigating Burnout and Vicarious Trauma: Acknowledging the demanding nature of social work, this section recognizes the potential for burnout and vicarious trauma. It positions supervision as a resource for addressing these challenges, providing practitioners with tools for self-care, stress management, and strategies to prevent burnout. It explores the role of ongoing professional development in building resilience and discusses practical approaches to mitigate burnout, emphasizing the importance of self-awareness and proactive strategies for well-being.

Embracing Lifelong Learning and Adaptation: Culminating by emphasizing the concept of lifelong learning in social work, it encourages social workers to perceive professional development as a continuous and evolving process. It unfolds how embracing a mindset of adaptability and curiosity contributes to ongoing competence and innovation in social work practice. This section highlights the value of remaining curious, open to new ideas, and adaptable to changes, fostering a culture of lifelong learning and professional growth.

Review Questions

1. What are the key components of foundational skills in social work practice?
2. How does effective communication contribute to building strong relationships in social work?
3. Discuss the significance of evidence-based approaches in assessment and intervention planning.
4. In what ways can crisis intervention and conflict resolution skills be applied in social work practice?
5. Why is cultural competence essential for providing inclusive and diverse social work interventions?

Multiple Choice Questions

1. What is the primary focus of foundational skills in social work?
   (a) Fundamental abilities
   (b) Specialized knowledge
   (c) Advanced technology use
   (d) Administrative tasks
2. How does effective communication contribute to social work practice?
   (a) It facilitates strong relationships
   (b) It is not relevant in social work
   (c) It hinders relationship-building
   (d) It only applies to paperwork
3. Why is cultural competence important in social work interventions?
   (a) It is optional
   (b) It perpetuates bias
   (c) It ensures inclusivity
   (d) It limits understanding

4. What is the purpose of crisis intervention in social work?
   (a) To create conflicts
   (b) To escalate situations
   (c) To ignore challenges
   (d) To resolve immediate issues
5. Why is supervision and professional development crucial for social workers?
   (a) It is unnecessary
   (b) It impedes growth
   (c) It fosters continuous improvement
   (d) It limits career options

References

Armour, M. P., Bain, B., & Rubio, R. (2004). Special section: Field education in social work. An evaluation study of diversity training for field instructors: A collaborative approach to enhancing cultural competence. *Journal of Social Work Education, 40*(1), 27–38.

Brown, S. C., & Gloyne, E. R. (2021). *The field training of social workers: A survey*. Routledge.

Jacobsson, K. (2016). Analysing documents through fieldwork. *Qualitative Research, 4*, 156–170.

Kääriäinen, A., & Muurinen, H. (2020). *Combining practice and theory in professional fieldwork: A guidebook to facilitate practice and theory groups*. University of Helsinki – Publications of the Faculty of Social Sciences.

Kaba, A., & Damaskos, P. (2015). Supervision and professional development. In *Handbook of oncology social work* (p. 715). Oxford University Press.

Mansour, R. (2023). Mapping crisis intervention course into social work academic curricula in Lebanon. *Open Journal of Trauma, 7*(1), 012–021.

Royse, D., Dhooper, S. S., & Rompf, E. L. (2016). *Field instruction: A guide for social work students*. Waveland Press.

Savaya, R. (2010). Enhancing student awareness of the importance of full and accurate documentation in social work practice. *Social Work Education, 29*(6), 660–669.

Chapter 7
Assessing and Planning for Agency-Level Field Practice in Social Work

Learning Objectives
After reading this chapter, you will be able to:

- Recognize the significance of agency assessment and analysis in social work.
- Distinguish between needs assessment and stakeholder analysis and comprehend their distinct roles.
- Apply needs assessment techniques to identify and prioritize critical client needs.
- Conduct a stakeholder analysis to recognize and engage relevant parties in the social work process.
- Develop strategic plans for social impact, incorporating goal setting, needs-driven action planning, and social work principles.
- Implement client-centered approaches in agency planning, emphasizing empathy and respect and tailoring interventions to client needs.
- Integrate cultural competence and diversity considerations into agency planning, fostering inclusivity and collaborative cross-cultural partnerships.

7.1 Agency Assessment and Analysis

In the dynamic landscape of social work, effective and impactful interventions often begin with a thorough understanding of the organizations that drive these initiatives. Agency assessment and analysis, as a crucial component of social work field practice, provide the necessary groundwork for practitioners to navigate the complexities of organizational dynamics (Netting et al., 2008). This process involves a comprehensive evaluation of an agency's structure, functioning, and mission alignment, aiming to optimize its capacity to meet the diverse needs of the communities it serves.

M. R. Islam, *Fieldwork in Social Work*,
https://doi.org/10.1007/978-3-031-56683-7_7

Understanding Agency Assessment: Agency assessment is a systematic and structured process of evaluating an organization's components, policies, and operations. It involves a meticulous analysis of various dimensions, including internal structures, external relationships, and the overall effectiveness of the agency's functioning. This critical evaluation serves as the foundation for informed decision-making, strategic planning, and ultimately, the delivery of high-quality social work services.

Navigating Organizational Analysis: Organizational analysis is a key facet of agency assessment, focusing on the examination of the agency's internal structures and dynamics. Social work students gain insights into the hierarchical arrangement, communication channels, and distribution of roles and responsibilities among staff members. Understanding the organizational framework is essential for recognizing potential bottlenecks, facilitating effective communication, and fostering a conducive work environment.

Mission Alignment and Coherence: An integral part of agency assessment is scrutinizing the alignment of the agency's activities with its stated mission. This involves assessing whether the organization's actions resonate with its intended purpose and values. Ensuring alignment and coherence between the agency's mission and its day-to-day operations is vital for maintaining focus and consistency in its pursuit of social work goals.

In-Depth Operational Functioning Analysis: Beyond the mission, a comprehensive analysis of operational functioning is paramount. This encompasses a close examination of the agency's daily operations, including workflow, resource utilization, and the efficiency of internal processes. Understanding how the agency operates on a practical level is crucial for identifying areas of improvement, streamlining processes, and optimizing the allocation of resources to enhance overall effectiveness.

Strategic Planning Foundation: The insights gained from agency assessment serve as the bedrock for strategic planning. By understanding the agency's strengths and weaknesses, social work practitioners can formulate strategic plans that capitalize on organizational strengths, address weaknesses, and align with broader social work principles. This forward-looking approach ensures that the agency is not only responsive to current needs but also well-prepared for future challenges and opportunities.

In essence, agency assessment and analysis in social work field practice are transformative processes. They empower practitioners to critically evaluate organizations, discern their unique dynamics, and lay the groundwork for interventions that are not only informed but also deeply rooted in the organizational context. As social work continues to evolve, the ability to conduct effective agency assessments becomes increasingly instrumental in shaping interventions that create lasting positive impacts on the individuals and communities served.

7.2 Needs Assessment and Stakeholder Analysis

In the realm of social work, addressing the needs of individuals and communities is at the core of effective practice (Beckett & Horner, 2015). The synergy between needs assessment and stakeholder analysis serves as a pivotal strategy, ensuring that interventions are not only responsive to the identified needs but also well-aligned with the expectations and perspectives of the diverse stakeholders involved.

7.2.1 Needs Assessment

Definition and Purpose: Needs assessment is a systematic and comprehensive process aimed at identifying, analyzing, and understanding the specific requirements and challenges faced by individuals or communities within a given context. The overarching purpose is to inform decision-making, program development, and resource allocation. Through this process, social work practitioners gain insights into the multifaceted aspects of the community's well-being, allowing for tailored and impactful interventions.

Methodology and Data Collection: Social work students are introduced to a spectrum of methodologies for needs assessment, each offering unique advantages based on the context and population. Surveys, interviews, focus groups, and community forums are among the tools employed to engage directly with individuals and collect both qualitative and quantitative data. This rich dataset provides a nuanced understanding of not only the surface-level needs but also the underlying social, economic, and cultural factors influencing the community's dynamics.

Holistic Approach: A critical aspect of needs assessment in social work is adopting a holistic approach. Beyond addressing immediate and visible needs, practitioners delve into understanding the systemic and structural factors contributing to challenges within the community. This broader perspective enables the development of interventions that not only provide short-term relief but also work towards sustainable and transformative change.

7.2.2 Stakeholder Analysis

Identification and Classification: Stakeholder analysis involves the identification and classification of individuals, groups, or organizations that have a vested interest in, or are affected by, the actions and outcomes of the social work agency. Stakeholders can encompass a wide spectrum, including clients, community members, staff, funders, governmental bodies, and collaborating organizations.

Understanding Perspectives and Influence: Social work students learn to scrutinize the perspectives, interests, and influence held by various stakeholders. Understanding the diverse needs and expectations of these entities is critical for developing interventions that are not only acceptable to the community but also aligned with the broader goals of funding entities and influential stakeholders. This understanding forms the basis for strategic decision-making and effective collaboration.

Facilitating Collaboration: Stakeholder analysis is not merely an information-gathering process; it is a strategic tool for fostering collaboration and partnership. By recognizing the roles and interests of different stakeholders, social work practitioners can facilitate inclusive decision-making processes. This collaborative approach not only ensures that interventions are well-received but also creates a network of advocates who are invested in the success and sustainability of the agency's initiatives.

Integration in Social Work Field Practice: In the field, social work practitioners seamlessly integrate needs assessment and stakeholder analysis into their practice. When working with a new community or initiating a program, they embark on a comprehensive needs assessment to understand the specific challenges, strengths, and aspirations of the individuals they aim to serve. Simultaneously, practitioners conduct stakeholder analyses to identify and engage with entities that can contribute to or influence the success of their interventions.

Key Challenges and Ethical Considerations: Needs assessment and stakeholder analysis come with challenges, including cultural sensitivity, ensuring representation of marginalized voices, and navigating power dynamics. Ethical considerations, such as confidentiality and informed consent, are paramount in both processes. Social work students learn to navigate these challenges ethically, ensuring that the rights and dignity of individuals and communities are upheld throughout the assessment and analysis phases.

7.3 Strategic Planning for Social Impact

Strategic planning is a dynamic and forward-thinking process that plays a pivotal role in shaping the impact and effectiveness of social work interventions. In the context of social work field practice, strategic planning involves the deliberate formulation of goals, actions, and initiatives to address identified needs and create lasting, positive change within communities. This multifaceted approach aligns social work practitioners with a purposeful and organized framework, ensuring that their efforts result in meaningful and sustainable social impact.

7.3.1 *Goal Setting and Clarity*

Defining Mission and Vision: Strategic planning begins with a clear articulation of the agency's mission and vision. Social work students learn to establish a purposeful mission statement that encapsulates the agency's overarching goals and aspirations. A well-defined vision sets the direction for the agency, guiding its efforts toward creating a positive and transformative impact on the individuals and communities it serves.

SMART Goals: Goal setting within strategic planning often follows the SMART criteria—Specific, Measurable, Achievable, Relevant, and Time-bound. Social work practitioners work towards formulating goals that are clear, quantifiable, realistic, aligned with the agency's mission, and time-sensitive. This ensures a focused and measurable approach to creating social impact.

7.3.2 *Needs-Driven Action Planning*

Linking Goals to Identified Needs: Strategic planning in social work is inherently needs-driven. Practitioners link their goals directly to the needs identified through comprehensive needs assessments. This alignment ensures that actions and interventions are targeted, responsive, and directly address the root causes of social issues within the community.

Resource Allocation and Optimization: Social work students learn the art of resource allocation within strategic planning, ensuring that available resources, whether human, financial, or technological, are optimally distributed to support the agency's goals. This involves careful consideration of the agency's capacity, potential collaborations, and the scalability of interventions.

7.3.3 *Integration of Social Work Principles*

Empowerment and Client-Centered Approaches: A hallmark of strategic planning in social work is the integration of social work principles, particularly those of empowerment and client-centered approaches. Social work practitioners prioritize interventions that empower individuals and communities, recognizing their strengths and capacities. Client-centered planning ensures that interventions are respectful, inclusive, and responsive to the unique needs and preferences of those served.

Cultural Competence and Diversity: Cultural competence and diversity considerations are woven into the fabric of strategic planning. Social work students learn to create interventions that respect and embrace the diverse backgrounds and perspectives within the community. This includes considerations for language, cultural practices, and the unique challenges faced by different demographic groups.

7.3.4 Monitoring and Evaluation

Continuous Assessment and Adaptation: Strategic planning is not a static process; it requires continuous assessment and adaptation. Social work practitioners implement monitoring and evaluation mechanisms to track the progress of interventions, measure outcomes against predefined indicators, and adapt strategies based on real-time feedback. This iterative approach ensures that interventions remain responsive and effective.

7.3.5 Collaboration and Networking

Building Alliances for Impact: Strategic planning encourages social work practitioners to actively seek collaborations and build alliances. By fostering partnerships with other organizations, governmental bodies, and community leaders, practitioners leverage collective expertise and resources. This collaborative approach enhances the overall impact and sustainability of social work interventions.

Advocacy and Systems Change: Strategic planning extends beyond direct service provision; it encompasses advocacy and systems change. Social work practitioners, through strategic planning, learn to identify systemic barriers and advocate for policy changes that address the root causes of social issues. This broader perspective ensures a comprehensive and lasting impact on the communities served.

7.4 Client-Centered Approaches in Agency Planning

Client-centered approaches in agency planning are foundational to providing effective and responsive social work services. This methodology places the individuals and communities being served at the forefront of decision-making, ensuring that interventions are respectful, inclusive, and aligned with the unique needs and preferences of clients (Grossmann et al., 2019). In social work field practice, incorporating client-centered approaches into agency planning enhances the relevance, accessibility, and impact of interventions.

7.4.1 Embracing Empathy and Respect

Understanding Client Perspectives: Client-centered approaches emphasize the importance of understanding the perspectives, values, and experiences of clients. Social work practitioners engage in active listening and empathy to gain insights into the lived realities of individuals and communities. This foundational understanding forms the basis for client-centered agency planning.

Respecting Autonomy and Self-Determination: The client-centered paradigm prioritizes the autonomy and self-determination of individuals. Social work students learn to respect the choices and decisions of clients, recognizing that empowerment comes from supporting clients in making choices that align with their goals and values. This respectful approach fosters a collaborative and trusting relationship between practitioners and clients.

7.4.2 Tailoring Interventions to Client Needs

Individualized and Culturally Responsive Planning: Agency planning incorporates the principle of tailoring interventions to the specific needs and preferences of clients. Social work practitioners recognize the diversity within the client population, including cultural backgrounds, socioeconomic statuses, and individual strengths. This approach ensures that interventions are culturally responsive and effective in meeting the unique needs of each client.

Collaborative Goal Setting: In client-centered agency planning, goal setting is a collaborative process between practitioners and clients. Social work students learn to involve clients in defining their goals, aspirations, and desired outcomes. This participatory approach empowers clients and ensures that interventions align with their individualized objectives.

7.4.3 Accessibility and Inclusivity

Removing Barriers to Access: Client-centered agency planning addresses barriers to access, ensuring that services are designed to be accessible to all individuals within the community. This involves considerations for physical accessibility, language preferences, and the removal of systemic barriers that may hinder certain groups from accessing services.

Inclusive Decision-Making: Inclusivity is a key element of client-centered approaches. Social work practitioners actively involve clients in decision-making processes related to their care. This inclusive approach not only respects the diversity of client perspectives but also contributes to the cultural competence and responsiveness of agency planning.

7.4.4 Flexibility and Responsiveness

Adapting to Changing Client Needs: Client-centered agency planning is characterized by flexibility and responsiveness. Social work practitioners recognize that client needs may evolve. By building flexibility into the planning process, practitioners can adapt interventions to meet the changing circumstances and priorities of clients.

Iterative Feedback Loops: Implementing feedback loops is integral to client-centered approaches. Social work practitioners establish mechanisms for ongoing communication and feedback, allowing clients to express their experiences, concerns, and suggestions. This iterative process ensures that interventions remain aligned with client needs and preferences.

7.4.5 Holistic and Strengths-Based Perspectives

Holistic Assessment and Planning: Client-centered agency planning takes a holistic view of clients, considering their physical, mental, and social well-being. Social work students learn to conduct comprehensive assessments that encompass various aspects of clients' lives, informing interventions that address the interconnected nature of individual challenges and strengths.

Strengths-Based Approaches: Building on the principles of empowerment, agency planning incorporates strengths-based approaches. Practitioners identify and leverage the inherent strengths and capacities of clients in the planning process. This positive and affirming perspective contributes to the resilience and self-efficacy of clients.

7.5 Cultural Competence and Diversity Integration

Cultural competence and diversity integration are fundamental pillars in social work agency planning. Recognizing and embracing the diversity within the client population is essential for developing interventions that are culturally responsive, inclusive, and effective. In social work field practice, cultural competence and diversity integration within agency planning contribute to a more nuanced, respectful, and impactful approach to addressing the needs of diverse individuals and communities.

7.5.1 Acknowledging Cultural Diversity

Cultural Awareness and Sensitivity: Cultural competence begins with an acknowledgment of the rich tapestry of cultures within the community. Social work practitioners develop cultural awareness and sensitivity, recognizing the diversity in beliefs, practices, languages, and customs. This foundational understanding forms the basis for creating interventions that respect and honor cultural differences.

Challenging Stereotypes and Biases: Cultural competence involves challenging stereotypes and biases that may influence perceptions and decision-making. Social work students learn to critically examine their cultural assumptions and biases, fostering a commitment to unbiased and equitable agency planning.

7.5.2 Inclusive Practices and Policies

Creating Inclusive Agency Policies: Diversity integration in agency planning extends to the development of inclusive policies. Social work practitioners actively participate in creating policies that account for the diverse needs and backgrounds of clients. This inclusivity ensures that agency services are accessible, respectful, and welcoming to individuals from all cultural backgrounds.

Promoting Linguistic Accessibility: Cultural competence encompasses linguistic accessibility. Agency planning considers language preferences and provides linguistic support to ensure effective communication with clients who may speak languages other than the dominant one. This commitment to linguistic accessibility enhances the inclusivity of services.

7.5.3 Tailoring Interventions to Cultural Contexts

Customizing Interventions: Cultural competence in agency planning involves customizing interventions to align with the cultural contexts of clients. Social work students learn to adapt practices to respect cultural norms and traditions, fostering interventions that are more likely to be accepted and effective within specific cultural communities.

Understanding Family Dynamics: Cultural competence extends to understanding family dynamics within different cultural contexts. Social work practitioners recognize the importance of family structures and dynamics in diverse communities. This understanding informs agency planning to consider family-based interventions that align with cultural values.

7.5.4 Collaborative Cross-Cultural Partnerships

Building Community Collaborations: Integration of diversity involves building collaborative partnerships with community organizations that represent diverse cultural groups. Social work practitioners actively engage with community leaders and organizations to ensure that agency planning reflects the perspectives and needs of various cultural communities.

Cross-Cultural Training for Staff: Cultural competence is not only external but internal to the organization. Social work agencies prioritize cross-cultural training for staff members. This training equips practitioners with the knowledge and skills needed to engage effectively with clients from diverse backgrounds, fostering a culturally competent and responsive work environment.

7.5.5 Continuous Learning and Adaptation

Ongoing Education and Awareness: Cultural competence is a dynamic process that requires ongoing education and awareness. Social work practitioners commit to continuous learning about different cultures, staying informed about cultural shifts, and adapting agency planning accordingly. This commitment ensures that interventions remain relevant and responsive over time.

Feedback and Reflection: Cultural competence is enhanced through feedback and reflection. Social work agencies establish mechanisms for obtaining feedback from clients and communities, reflecting on the cultural competence of interventions, and making necessary adjustments. This iterative process contributes to the agency's capacity for ongoing improvement.

7.6 Evaluation and Continuous Improvement

Evaluation and continuous improvement are integral components of effective agency planning in social work field practice (for details, please read Unrau et al., 2007; Shaw, 2018). These processes ensure that interventions are assessed for their impact, relevance, and alignment with goals, ultimately leading to enhancements that contribute to the ongoing development and success of social work agencies. In this context, evaluation serves as a dynamic tool for learning, adaptation, and the delivery of more effective and responsive services.

7.6.1 Establishing Clear Evaluation Criteria

Defining Measurable Objectives: Evaluation in agency planning begins with the establishment of clear and measurable objectives. Social work practitioners work collaboratively to define the outcomes they aim to achieve through their interventions. These objectives serve as the criteria against which the success of the agency's efforts will be assessed.

Selecting Appropriate Metrics: Social work agencies select appropriate metrics that align with their objectives. These metrics may include quantitative data, such as the number of individuals served or changes in specific indicators, as well as qualitative data that captures the nuanced impact of interventions on the well-being of clients and communities.

7.6.2 *Data Collection and Analysis*

Comprehensive Data Gathering: Evaluation involves comprehensive data gathering to assess the impact of interventions. Social work practitioners utilize a combination of quantitative and qualitative methods, including surveys, interviews, focus groups, and case studies. This multi-method approach provides a holistic understanding of the outcomes and experiences of those served.

Root Cause Analysis: In addition to measuring outcomes, social work agencies conduct root cause analysis to understand the factors influencing the success or challenges of interventions. This analysis helps practitioners identify systemic issues, gaps in services, or external factors that may impact the effectiveness of agency planning.

7.6.3 *Client and Community Feedback*

Incorporating Client Perspectives: Evaluation in agency planning prioritizes the incorporation of client perspectives. Social work practitioners actively seek feedback from clients regarding their experiences with interventions. This client-centric approach ensures that agency planning remains responsive to the evolving needs and preferences of those served.

Community Engagement in Evaluation: Social work agencies engage with the community throughout the evaluation process. Community members may participate in focus groups, community forums, or advisory committees to provide insights into the cultural, social, and economic factors that influence the impact of agency interventions.

7.6.4 *Continuous Learning and Adaptation*

Reflective Practices: Evaluation serves as a platform for reflective practices within social work agencies. Practitioners engage in critical reflection on the outcomes of their interventions, considering what worked well, what could be improved, and what unexpected challenges arose. This reflective process contributes to ongoing learning and professional development.

Adaptive Strategies: Continuous improvement is facilitated through the adaptation of strategies based on evaluation findings. Social work practitioners use the insights gained from evaluation to refine existing interventions, develop new approaches, or adjust service delivery models. This adaptive strategy ensures that agency planning remains responsive to the changing needs of the community.

7.6.5 Stakeholder Involvement

Engaging Stakeholders in Evaluation: Evaluation involves engaging various stakeholders, including staff, clients, community partners, and funders. Social work agencies recognize the importance of involving these stakeholders in the evaluation process, as their perspectives contribute to a comprehensive understanding of the impact and effectiveness of agency planning.

Transparency and Accountability: Social work agencies prioritize transparency and accountability in the evaluation process. Practitioners communicate evaluation findings to stakeholders, sharing successes, challenges, and areas for improvement. This transparency builds trust among stakeholders and reinforces the agency's commitment to continuous improvement.

Review Questions

1. Why is agency assessment and analysis crucial in social work field practice?
2. How does needs assessment contribute to effective social work planning at the agency level?
3. What are the key principles and goals of strategic planning for social impact in agency settings?
4. In what ways can client-centered approaches enhance the success of agency planning in social work?
5. Why are cultural competence and diversity integration important in the context of agency-level field practice?
6. What role does evaluation play in ensuring continuous improvement in agency planning in social work?
7. How can social workers effectively engage with stakeholders during the agency planning process?

Multiple Choice Questions

1. What is the primary purpose of agency assessment and analysis in social work?

   (a) Identifying personal learning goals
   (b) Evaluating continuous improvement

   (c) Recognizing cultural diversity
   (d) Establishing clear evaluation criteria

2. How does needs assessment contribute to effective social work planning?
   (a) By conducting stakeholder analysis
   (b) By prioritizing client needs
   (c) By implementing cultural competence
   (d) By fostering collaborative partnerships

3. What are the key components of strategic planning for social impact?
   (a) Client-centered approaches
   (b) Continuous learning and adaptation
   (c) Goal setting and clarity
   (d) Advocacy and social justice

4. In agency planning, why is it essential to embrace client-centered approaches?
   (a) To enhance cultural competence
   (b) To foster inclusivity and flexibility
   (c) To conduct stakeholder analysis
   (d) To establish clear evaluation criteria

5. How does cultural competence contribute to effective agency planning in social work?
   (a) By prioritizing client needs
   (b) By establishing clear evaluation criteria
   (c) By fostering inclusivity and collaborative partnerships
   (d) By conducting stakeholder analysis

6. What role does evaluation play in the continuous improvement of agency planning?
   (a) Establishing clear evaluation criteria
   (b) Recognizing cultural diversity
   (c) Conducting stakeholder analysis
   (d) Involving clients and communities in feedback processes

References

Beckett, C., & Horner, N. (2015). *Essential theory for social work practice*. Sage.

Grossmann, J., Shor, R., Schaefer, K., & Bennett Cattaneo, L. (2019). Development of a tool to assess client-centered practice on a domestic violence hotline. *Journal of Social Work, 19*(1), 102–120.

Netting, F. E., O'Connor, M. K., & Fauri, D. P. (2008). *Comparative approaches to program planning*. Hoboken, NJ: John Wiley & Sons.

Shaw, I. (2018). *Evaluating in practice*. Routledge.

Unrau, Y. A., Gabor, P. A., & Grinnell, R. M. (2007). *Evaluation in social work: The art and science of practice*. Oxford University Press.

Chapter 8
Implementation and Intervention in Field Practice at the Agency Level

Learning Objectives
After engaging with this chapter, learners will be able to:

- Demonstrate the skill of tailoring interventions to address the unique needs of individual clients, showcasing a client-centered approach in their practice
- Exhibit proficiency in collaborative goal setting and action planning, fostering effective partnerships with clients to achieve mutually agreed-upon objectives
- Apply evidence-based practices in social work interventions, utilizing research-supported methods to enhance the effectiveness of their approaches
- Address systemic factors in interventions, recognizing and addressing broader structural issues that may impact clients and communities
- Understand the key components of the Case Management Model, enabling them to implement this approach in their fieldwork practice for comprehensive client support

8.1 Tailoring Interventions to Client Needs

Tailoring interventions to meet the unique needs of clients is a fundamental aspect of effective social work practice (Trevithick, 2005; Coulshed & Orme, 2018). In the United States, for instance, a social worker engaging with a client experiencing homelessness may design interventions that prioritize access to shelter, food assistance, and job placement services (Bassuk et al., 2014). This client-centered approach acknowledges the immediate and pressing needs of the individual, ensuring that interventions address the root causes of their situation.

Moving to Norway, where social work often emphasizes holistic well-being, a social worker working with a client facing mental health challenges may tailor interventions to include a combination of counseling, outdoor activities, and

M. R. Islam, *Fieldwork in Social Work*,
https://doi.org/10.1007/978-3-031-56683-7_8

community engagement. This approach aligns with the cultural emphasis on nature and community support, demonstrating the importance of cultural competence in tailoring interventions.

In South Africa, where socioeconomic disparities are pronounced, a social worker may tailor interventions for a client affected by poverty by incorporating strategies that empower them economically. This could involve skills training, microfinance initiatives, or connecting the client with local entrepreneurial opportunities. This client-focused approach recognizes the systemic challenges prevalent in the region and aims to build sustainable solutions.

Shifting to Japan, where the cultural context places a high value on familial relationships, a social worker might tailor interventions for a client struggling with family dynamics by incorporating family therapy and communication-building exercises. This acknowledges the significance of family structures and interpersonal relationships in Japanese society, ensuring interventions are culturally sensitive and effective.

In Australia, a social worker addressing substance abuse issues may tailor interventions by incorporating harm reduction strategies, community support networks, and culturally appropriate rehabilitation programs. Recognizing the diverse indigenous cultures in Australia, the social worker ensures interventions are respectful and responsive to the unique needs of the client, reflecting a commitment to cultural competence.

These global examples underscore the importance of tailoring interventions to the specific needs and cultural contexts of clients, showcasing the versatility and adaptability required in social work practice across different countries and regions.

8.2 Collaborative Goal Setting and Action Planning

Collaborative goal setting and action planning form the cornerstone of effective social work practice, emphasizing the partnership between social workers and clients to achieve meaningful outcomes. In the United Kingdom, a social worker working with a client recovering from addiction may engage in collaborative goal setting, involving the client in decisions about treatment modalities, support networks, and relapse prevention strategies (Walton & Hall, 2016). This collaborative approach empowers the client, fostering a sense of agency and ownership in their recovery journey.

In Brazil, where social work often integrates community-based practices, a social worker may collaboratively set goals with a group of individuals facing economic challenges (de Araujo Lima Constantino et al., 2012). The action plan might involve organizing community workshops on financial literacy, creating small-scale entrepreneurial opportunities, and building a supportive network. This participatory approach aligns with the Brazilian cultural emphasis on collective well-being and community resilience.

Turning to India, where caste and class dynamics play a significant role, a social worker might collaborate with a marginalized community to set goals related to education, employment, and social inclusion (Nadkarni & Sinha, 2016). The action plan may involve advocating for policy changes, providing skill development programs, and creating awareness campaigns to address systemic inequalities. This collaborative process acknowledges the intersectionality of social issues and works towards comprehensive solutions.

In Canada, a social worker supporting a newcomer family may engage in collaborative goal-setting around acculturation and integration (Costigan et al., 2022). The action plan could include language classes, cultural orientation sessions, and connecting the family with community resources. This approach recognizes the importance of cultural sensitivity and individualized planning in facilitating a smooth transition for newcomers.

In South Korea, where mental health awareness is growing, a social worker may collaborate with a client experiencing anxiety to set goals related to mental well-being (Kim et al., 2015). The action plan may involve a combination of therapy, mindfulness practices, and community support groups. This collaborative approach recognizes the cultural nuances around mental health and strives to destigmatize seeking help.

These examples highlight the universality of collaborative goal setting and action planning in social work, demonstrating its adaptability to diverse cultural contexts while emphasizing the empowerment of individuals and communities in determining their trajectories.

8.3 Utilizing Evidence-Based Practices

Utilizing evidence-based practices (EBP) in social work involves integrating the best available research evidence with practitioner expertise and client values to inform decision-making and intervention strategies (Drisko & Grady, 2015). This approach ensures that social work interventions are not only grounded in empirical evidence but also responsive to the unique needs and preferences of clients. In the United States, for instance, a social worker addressing youth substance abuse might employ interventions supported by research demonstrating their efficacy, such as motivational interviewing or cognitive-behavioral therapy. By integrating evidence-based strategies, the social worker increases the likelihood of positive outcomes for the client.

In Sweden, where the social work profession emphasizes a strong research-practice connection, a social worker working with families facing domestic violence may rely on evidence-based interventions that have demonstrated effectiveness in similar cultural contexts (Alexanderson, 2004). This approach aligns with the Swedish commitment to maintaining a practice that is both scientifically informed and culturally sensitive.

In Kenya, a social worker addressing the mental health challenges of individuals in a community might draw on evidence-based practices that have been adapted to the local context. This adaptation could involve incorporating traditional healing practices alongside established therapeutic approaches and recognizing the importance of cultural relevance in achieving positive outcomes.

Australia, with its diverse population, may see social workers utilizing evidence-based practices in areas such as trauma-informed care for Indigenous communities (Bennett & Gates, 2022). This involves recognizing the historical and intergenerational trauma experienced by Indigenous populations and tailoring interventions accordingly. By incorporating evidence-based trauma interventions within a culturally competent framework, social workers in Australia strive for holistic and effective support.

In India, where social work often intersects with issues of poverty and education, a social worker may utilize evidence-based practices to enhance the effectiveness of interventions aimed at improving educational outcomes for marginalized children (Sharma et al., 2020). This may involve implementing evidence-based teaching strategies and community engagement programs to address educational disparities (Narzary et al., 2022).

The utilization of evidence-based practices in social work is a global imperative, transcending geographical boundaries. Social workers worldwide recognize the value of integrating research evidence into their practice to ensure the highest quality of care and intervention for diverse populations.

8.4 Addressing Systemic Factors in Interventions

Addressing systemic factors in social work interventions is crucial for creating sustainable and impactful change within communities. Social workers recognize that individual challenges are often intertwined with broader systemic issues, such as institutional discrimination, economic disparities, and social injustices. For example, in the United States, a social worker addressing poverty-related issues in a community may collaborate with local organizations to advocate for policy changes that address systemic barriers to economic stability. This might include supporting initiatives for affordable housing, equitable employment opportunities, and access to quality education.

In the complex sociocultural landscape of India, social workers grapple with the deep-rooted issue of caste-based discrimination, a systemic challenge that has persisted for centuries (Chander, 2019). This pervasive problem has led to the marginalization of specific communities, hindering their access to education, employment, and various social opportunities. Social workers operating in this context play a pivotal role in crafting interventions aimed at dismantling discriminatory practices, advocating for policy changes, and fostering social cohesion.

For example, a social worker might initiate collaborative efforts with local community leaders and organizations to raise awareness about the profound impacts of caste discrimination. Through strategically designed workshops, educational programs, and community dialogues, the social worker empowers individuals to challenge and question discriminatory norms prevalent within their communities. This proactive engagement seeks to catalyze a grassroots movement against entrenched biases.

Furthermore, the social worker may embark on advocacy endeavors, lobbying for policy changes at both local and national levels to secure equal rights and opportunities for all caste groups. By navigating the intricate web of social and political structures, social workers contribute significantly to dismantling systemic barriers that perpetuate discrimination. The holistic nature of their interventions extends beyond individual cases, aiming to transform societal attitudes and institutional frameworks.

In essence, this example from India exemplifies the multifaceted approach of social work interventions, where professionals actively engage with communities, challenge discriminatory norms, and advocate for structural changes. Through such efforts, social workers in India strive to create a more inclusive and just society, illustrating the transformative impact they can have on deeply ingrained systemic issues.

8.5 Case Management Model

Case management is a widely used and effective social work intervention that plays a pivotal role in the field of human services (for details, please read Gutheil & Chernesky, 1999; Gursansky & Harvey, 2020; Camilleri, 2020). The case management model has evolved and does not have a single origin or specific founder. Instead, it has developed in response to the changing needs of social services and the recognition of the importance of coordinating and integrating services for individuals and families. It is a client-centered and collaborative approach that aims to enhance the well-being of individuals and families by coordinating and facilitating access to a range of services. For social work students engaged in field practice, understanding and applying the case management model is essential as it equips them with valuable skills to navigate the complexities of real-world client scenarios.

8.5.1 Key Components of the Case Management Model

8.5.1.1 Assessment and Planning

Client Needs Assessment: The case management process begins with a comprehensive assessment of the client's needs, strengths, and challenges. Social work students learn to conduct thorough assessments to identify the most pertinent issues affecting the client (Fig. 8.1).

Fig. 8.1 Key components of the Case Management Model. (Source: Author)

Individualized Planning: Based on the assessment, students collaborate with clients to develop individualized plans that outline specific goals, objectives, and interventions. This phase emphasizes the importance of tailoring interventions to meet the unique needs of each client.

8.5.1.2 Linking and Coordinating Services

Resource Identification: Case managers assist clients in identifying and accessing relevant community resources, services, and supports. Social work students learn the skill of researching and connecting clients with appropriate resources to address their identified needs.

Collaboration with Service Providers: Effective case management involves building collaborative relationships with various service providers. Students engage in communication and coordination to ensure seamless delivery of services and address any barriers that may arise.

8.5.1.3 Monitoring and Advocacy

Progress Monitoring: Social work students involved in case management continually monitor the progress of clients toward their goals. Regular check-ins and assessments help adjust interventions as needed, promoting flexibility in the approach.

Advocacy: Students advocate on behalf of clients to ensure their rights are upheld, and they receive the necessary support. This involves navigating systems, addressing barriers, and promoting social justice for clients.

8.5.1.4 Empowerment and Skill Building

Client Empowerment: The case management model emphasizes empowering clients to actively participate in decision-making and goal-setting. Social work students learn to engage clients in the process, fostering a sense of autonomy and self-efficacy.

Skill Building: Case management involves supporting clients in acquiring the necessary skills to navigate challenges independently. Students work on developing interventions that promote skill-building and resilience.

8.5.1.5 Crisis Intervention

Prevention and Response: Social work students using the case management model are trained to identify potential crises and develop preventive strategies. In cases of crisis, they implement timely interventions to stabilize the situation and connect clients with appropriate crisis resources.

8.5.1.6 Challenges and Ethical Considerations

Social work students engaging in case management also explore the ethical considerations and potential challenges associated with this model. They learn about maintaining confidentiality, navigating dual relationships, and addressing issues related to client autonomy and informed consent.

The case management model, as a social work intervention, equips students with a holistic and client-centered approach to address the multifaceted needs of individuals and families. By integrating this model into their field practice, students enhance their problem-solving skills, cultural competence, and ability to advocate for clients within complex service systems. This valuable experience prepares them to be effective and ethical social work practitioners in diverse and dynamic settings.

8.6 Monitoring Progress and Adjusting Interventions

In the dynamic field of social work, the process of implementing interventions is not a static endeavor; it requires continuous monitoring, evaluation, and adaptive adjustments to ensure efficacy and responsiveness to evolving circumstances. This principle is exemplified in various countries, including Sweden, where social workers are actively engaged in monitoring progress and refining interventions to address the ever-changing needs of their diverse client populations.

For instance, in the context of Sweden's inclusive social welfare system, social workers often collaborate closely with government agencies, community organizations, and nonprofit entities to provide comprehensive support to individuals and families. Through the use of evidence-based practices and data-driven assessments, social workers monitor the impact of interventions on clients' well-being and adjust strategies accordingly.

In Sweden, a key aspect of monitoring progress involves regular consultations with clients to gather feedback and insights into the effectiveness of ongoing interventions. Social workers utilize client perspectives as valuable input to refine and tailor interventions, ensuring that they align with the unique circumstances and aspirations of those they serve. This collaborative approach not only enhances the relevance of interventions but also strengthens the client–worker relationship, fostering a sense of empowerment and mutual respect.

Additionally, social workers in Sweden leverage interdisciplinary collaboration, engaging with professionals from fields such as healthcare, education, and housing, to gain a comprehensive understanding of clients' multifaceted needs. Regular case reviews and team discussions allow for a collective evaluation of intervention outcomes, enabling social workers to make informed decisions about adjusting strategies, modifying goals, or introducing new resources.

In summary, the Swedish context illustrates how the ongoing monitoring of interventions is integral to the success of social work practices. By embracing a client-centered, collaborative, and data-informed approach, social workers in Sweden contribute to the continual improvement of services and the overall well-being of individuals and communities.

Review Questions

1. How does tailoring interventions to client needs contribute to the effectiveness of social work practice?
2. Why is collaborative goal setting essential in the client–worker relationship, and how does it enhance intervention outcomes?
3. What are the advantages of utilizing evidence-based practices in social work interventions, and how can practitioners stay updated on relevant research?
4. Explain the importance of addressing systemic factors in interventions and provide an example of how this consideration can positively impact clients.
5. Describe the key components of the Case Management Model and discuss how it can be applied to enhance client support in social work practice.

Multiple Choice Questions

1. What is the primary benefit of tailoring interventions to client needs?
   (a) Increased paperwork
   (b) Enhanced effectiveness
   (c) Longer intervention periods
   (d) Reduced client engagement
2. Collaborative goal setting in social work helps to:
   (a) Limit client involvement
   (b) Impose practitioner's goals
   (c) Enhance the client–worker relationship
   (d) Decrease intervention flexibility
3. Evidence-based practices in social work are based on:
   (a) Personal opinions
   (b) Latest research and empirical evidence
   (c) Traditional beliefs
   (d) Intuition and guesswork
4. Why is addressing systemic factors important in social work interventions?
   (a) It simplifies the intervention process
   (b) It ensures quick resolution of issues
   (c) It considers broader influences on clients
   (d) It avoids individualized approaches
5. The Case Management Model in social work involves:
   (a) Tailoring interventions to client needs
   (b) Ignoring client needs
   (c) Rigid and inflexible strategies
   (d) Limited documentation and assessment

References

Alexanderson, K. (2004). *Evidence in social work practice in England through Swedish eyes.* Dalarnas forskningsråd.

Bassuk, E. L., DeCandia, C. J., Tsertsvadze, A., & Richard, M. K. (2014). The effectiveness of housing interventions and housing and service interventions on ending family homelessness: a systematic review. *American Journal of Orthopsychiatry, 84*(5), 457.

Bennett, B., & Gates, T. G. (2022). Decolonization and trauma-informed truth-telling about indigenous Australia in a social work diversity course: A cultural safety approach. *Journal of Ethnic & Cultural Diversity in Social Work*, 1–14. https://doi.org/10.1080/15313204.2022.2154882

Camilleri, P. (2020). *The practice of case management: Effective strategies for positive outcomes*. Routledge.
Chander, R. K. (2019). *Combating social exclusion: Inter-sectionalities of caste, gender, class and regions*. Studera Press.
Costigan, C. L., Taknint, J. T., Mudryk, E., & Al Qudayri, B. (2022). Building community: Connecting refugee and Canadian families. *Cultural Diversity and Ethnic Minority Psychology, 28*(3), 338.
Coulshed, V., & Orme, J. (2018). *Social work practice*. Bloomsbury Publishing.
de Araujo Lima Constantino, P., Carlos, H. S. A., Ramalho, E. E., Rostant, L., Marinelli, C. E., Teles, D., et al. (2012). Empowering local people through community-based resource monitoring: A comparison of Brazil and Namibia. *Ecology and Society, 17*(4), 22.
Drisko, J. W., & Grady, M. D. (2015). Evidence-based practice in social work: A contemporary perspective. *Clinical Social Work Journal, 43*, 274–282.
Gursansky, D., & Harvey, J. (2020). *Case management: Policy, practice and professional business*. Routledge.
Gutheil, I. A., & Chernesky, R. H. (1999). Case management as a strategy of social work intervention with the mentally ill. In Turner, F. J. (Ed.). *Adult psychopathology: Social work perspective* (pp. 35–53). Simon and Schuster.
Kim, M. A., Hong, J. S., Ra, M., & Kim, K. (2015). Understanding social exclusion and psychosocial adjustment of North Korean adolescents and young adult refugees in South Korea through Photovoice. *Qualitative Social Work, 14*(6), 820–841.
Nadkarni, V. V., & Sinha, R. (2016). Transforming social work education in India: Integrating human rights. *Journal of Human Rights and Social Work, 1*(1), 9–18.
Narzary, V., Swargiary, B., Sharma, R., & Butterfield, A. K. (2022). Swastyayan, a commitment: Fieldwork through community engagement. In *The Routledge handbook of social work field education in the global south* (pp. 26–38). Routledge.
Sharma, S., Mehra, D., Akhtar, F., & Mehra, S. (2020). Evaluation of a community-based intervention for health and economic empowerment of marginalized women in India. *BMC Public Health, 20*(1), 1–16.
Trevithick, P. (2005). *Social work skills*. Open University Press.
Walton, M. T., & Hall, M. T. (2016). The effects of employment interventions on addiction treatment outcomes: A review of the literature. *Journal of Social Work Practice in the Addictions, 16*(4), 358–384.

Chapter 9
Data Collection for Field Reports in Social Work Practice

Learning Objectives
After studying this chapter, you will be able to:

1. Understand the fundamental purpose and significance of data collection in social work field practice
2. Master various qualitative data collection techniques, such as in-depth interviews, focus group discussions, key informant interviews (KIIs), participant observation, and content analysis
3. Familiarize yourself with essential quantitative data collection methods, including surveys, questionnaires, standardized tests, and statistical analysis in the context of social work research
4. Integrate mixed-methods approaches effectively, gaining an understanding of both the advantages and challenges associated with combining qualitative and quantitative data collection methods in social work field research
5. Navigate and apply ethical considerations in the process of data collection, including obtaining informed consent, ensuring confidentiality, and upholding participant autonomy and privacy
6. Utilize technology proficiently for efficient data collection in social work field practices, exploring tools such as electronic surveys and data management systems while adhering to ethical considerations related to technology-mediated data collection

9.1 Overview of Data Collection Techniques in Social Work Field Practice

In the realm of social work field practices, effective data collection is pivotal for understanding and addressing the complex needs of clients and communities (Gray et al., 2009). This section provides a comprehensive overview of the diverse

M. R. Islam, *Fieldwork in Social Work*,
https://doi.org/10.1007/978-3-031-56683-7_9

methodologies employed in gathering data during field practices for subsequent field reports. Data collection is a systematic process that involves the acquisition of relevant information to inform decision-making and intervention strategies. In social work, this process is nuanced, considering the intricacies of human behavior, social structures, and cultural contexts.

Purpose of Data Collection: The primary purpose of data collection in social work field practices is to obtain a comprehensive understanding of the challenges, strengths, and dynamics within the client population or community. This information serves as the foundation for evidence-based interventions, program development, and policy recommendations.

Types of Data: Social work field practices involve the collection of both qualitative and quantitative data. Qualitative data, such as narratives, interviews, and observations, provide rich insights into individuals' experiences and perspectives. Quantitative data, on the other hand, involve numerical information and statistical analyses, offering a more structured and measurable view of social phenomena.

Methods of Data Collection: Various qualitative and quantitative methods are employed in social work data collection, including interviews, surveys, focus groups, observations, and document analysis. Each method is chosen based on the research question, the nature of the data needed, and ethical considerations. Social workers employ their skills in active listening, empathy, and cultural competence to elicit meaningful information from clients and communities.

Cultural Sensitivity and Ethical Considerations: Given the diverse backgrounds of clients and communities, cultural sensitivity is paramount in data collection. Social workers must navigate ethical considerations, ensuring informed consent, confidentiality, and respect for the autonomy of participants. Adhering to professional codes of ethics is integral to maintaining trust and integrity in the data collection process.

Data Analysis and Interpretation: Once collected, data undergo thorough analysis, involving techniques such as thematic coding for qualitative data and statistical analyses for quantitative data. Social workers interpret the findings within the context of social work theories and frameworks, guiding subsequent interventions and recommendations.

This overview lays the groundwork for the subsequent sections, delving into specific qualitative and quantitative data collection techniques, the integration of mixed-methods approaches, ethical considerations, and the role of technology in optimizing the data collection process during social work field practices.

9.2 Data Collection Techniques for Field Report

Data collection techniques refer to the systematic methods employed to gather information or data for research, analysis, evaluation, or reporting purposes. These techniques involve the process of obtaining data from various sources, such as individuals, documents, observations, or digital records, to gain insights, make informed decisions, or address specific research questions. Data collection techniques are primarily categorized into two main types: qualitative and quantitative (Table 9.1). Qualitative data collection techniques focus on gathering non-numerical data that provides insights into underlying motivations, attitudes, behaviors, and perceptions. These techniques often involve open-ended questions, observations, interviews, and content analysis to explore complex phenomena in-depth. Qualitative data collection aims to capture the richness and depth of human experiences and social interactions, providing contextually rich data for analysis and interpretation. Quantitative data collection techniques involve gathering numerical data that can be quantified and statistically analyzed. These techniques typically utilize structured surveys, questionnaires, standardized tests, or assessments to collect data from a large sample size. Quantitative data collection aims to measure specific variables, establish relationships, and identify patterns through statistical analysis, providing objective and measurable insights into phenomena or trends.

Social work students engaged in field practice at the agency level often need to collect data for reporting purposes using both qualitative and quantitative methods. By employing a combination of qualitative and quantitative data collection techniques, students can gain a comprehensive understanding of clients' needs, evaluate the effectiveness of interventions, and contribute to evidence-based practice within

Table 9.1 Data collection technique for field report

Data collection technique	Description
Qualitative data collection	
In-depth interviews	Conducted to delve into lived experiences, perspectives, and narratives, offering nuanced understanding.
Focus group discussions	Assemble diverse participants for facilitated discussions around specific topics, elucidating shared perspectives.
Key informant interviews	Gather insights from individuals with specialized knowledge or experience relevant to the research context.
Participant observation	Immersive method involving observation and participation in daily activities to understand lived experiences and social dynamics.
Content analysis	Systematic examination of textual, visual, or audio content to identify patterns, themes, and underlying meanings.
Quantitative data collection	
Surveys and questionnaires	Administered to gather specific responses that can be quantified and analyzed, providing a scalable approach for collecting data.
Standardized tests	Systematically administered and scored assessments designed to measure specific attributes, providing quantitative insights into individuals' functioning.
Statistical analysis	Utilized to identify patterns, relationships, and trends within quantitative data sets, enabling evidence-based practice and informed decision-making.

Source: Author

the field of social work. Qualitative methods enable students to explore the lived experiences and perspectives of clients, while quantitative methods offer measurable data for analysis and evaluation, enhancing the rigor and validity of their fieldwork and reporting efforts.

9.3 Qualitative Data Collection Techniques for Field Report

9.3.1 In-Depth Interviews

In-depth interviews stand as a cornerstone in the arsenal of data collection methods within social work practice (Azam, 2022). Social work practitioners often employ this method to delve into the lived experiences, perspectives, and narratives of clients, offering a nuanced understanding of their unique situations. The depth and richness of information derived from in-depth interviews contribute to the formulation of tailored interventions, grounded in the contextual realities of those being served. Additionally, the empathetic and interactive nature of these interviews fosters a therapeutic alliance between practitioners and clients, facilitating trust and openness essential for uncovering hidden complexities. As an invaluable tool in the social work toolkit, in-depth interviews serve to amplify the voices of individuals and communities, enriching the profession's capacity for holistic and person-centered interventions.

9.3.1.1 A Sample Guideline of an In-Depth Case Interview

Title: In-Depth Case Interview Guideline for Qualitative Data Collection from Registered Patients in [Hospital Name]
Research Objective: To gain a comprehensive understanding of the healthcare experiences and perspectives of registered patients at [Hospital Name].
Preparation:

1. **Ethical Considerations:** Ensure that you have received all necessary ethical approvals and that patients have given informed consent.
2. **Familiarity:** Familiarize yourself with the hospital's policies, procedures, and relevant medical terminology.
3. **Interviewer Training:** Interviewers should be well-trained in qualitative research methods, empathetic communication, and maintaining patient confidentiality.

Interview Setup:

1. **Location:** Choose a comfortable and private location within the hospital for the interview.

(continued)

2. **Recording:** Seek permission to audio-record the interview for accurate data capture.
3. **Duration:** Plan for interviews to last approximately 45 minutes to 1 hour.
4. **Materials:** Have consent forms, interview questions, and recording equipment ready.

Interview Structure:

1. **Introduction (5 minutes):**
   - Greet the patient warmly.
   - Explain the purpose of the interview and your role as the interviewer.
   - Reiterate confidentiality and informed consent.
   - Invite the patient to ask questions.
2. **Patient Background (10 minutes):**
   - Gather basic demographic information (age, gender, occupation, etc.).
   - Ask about their previous healthcare experiences and any relevant medical history.
   - Build rapport by showing empathy and active listening.
3. **Hospital Experience (15 minutes):**
   - Explore the patient's specific experiences at [Hospital Name]:
     - Why did they seek care at this hospital?
     - What was their initial impression?
     - How were they greeted and registered?
   - Ask about their interactions with healthcare providers, including doctors, nurses, and support staff.
   - Inquire about the quality of care they received, any concerns, and how those concerns were addressed.
4. **Communication and Information (10 minutes):**
   - Probe into how information was communicated to them about their condition, treatment options, and prognosis.
   - Assess their satisfaction with the clarity and comprehensibility of the information provided.
   - Explore any challenges they faced in understanding medical jargon.
5. **Patient-Centered Care (10 minutes):**
   - Ask about their perception of patient-centered care.
   - Discuss their involvement in healthcare decision-making.
   - Inquire about their overall satisfaction with the care received.

(continued)

6. **Closing (5 minutes):**
   - Summarize key points discussed during the interview.
   - Ask if the patient has any additional comments or concerns.
   - Thank the patient for their participation and provide contact information for follow-up questions.

Post-Interview:

1. Transcribe and analyze the interview data.
2. Ensure data security and anonymity.
3. Share findings with relevant stakeholders as appropriate.

Remember to be flexible during the interview, allowing patients to share their experiences in their own words. Adapt your questions and approach based on the patient's responses to encourage open and honest dialogue.

9.3.2 Focus Group Discussions (FGDs)

Focus group discussions (FGDs) emerge as a dynamic and participatory data collection method integral to social work practice. This subsection navigates the terrain of FGDs, shedding light on their purpose and application in gathering qualitative insights (Khan & Abedin, 2022). Unlike one-on-one interviews, FGDs assemble a diverse group of participants to engage in facilitated discussions around a specific topic. This method proves particularly effective in elucidating shared perspectives, collective experiences, and group dynamics within communities. In social work, FGDs offer a platform for clients to interact, express differing viewpoints, and collectively contribute to the co-creation of knowledge. Practitioners leverage this method to explore common themes, identify patterns, and uncover the underlying factors influencing social issues. By fostering a collaborative atmosphere, FGDs empower participants, ensuring their voices are not only heard but also incorporated into the development of contextually relevant interventions.

9.3.2.1 A Sample Guideline of a Focus Group Discussion (FGDs)

Title: Focus Group Discussion Guideline with a Hospital Nurses
Objective: To facilitate a focused group discussion with nurses from [Hospital Name] to gather insights on [Specify the research or discussion topic].
Preparation:

1. **Define the Purpose:** Clearly outline the objectives and goals of the FGD. Determine the specific topic or issues you want to explore with the nurses.

(continued)

2. **Participant Selection:** Identify and invite a diverse group of nurses from different departments or units, with varying levels of experience.
3. **Location and Logistics:** Secure a comfortable and private meeting room within the hospital. Ensure that the room is equipped with audio recording equipment and any necessary materials.
4. **Moderator Training:** Train the FGD moderator(s) in qualitative research methods, active listening, and facilitation skills.

Focus Group Discussion Structure:

1. **Introduction (10 minutes):**
   - Welcome participants and introduce yourself and any co-moderators.
   - Explain the purpose of the FGD and its relevance to hospital practices.
   - Emphasize the importance of open and respectful dialogue.
   - Ensure informed consent and confidentiality.
2. **Icebreaker (5 minutes):**
   - Use a brief icebreaker activity or question to help participants get comfortable and open up.
3. **Topic Exploration (40 minutes):**
   - Present the main topics or questions you want to discuss.
   - Encourage participants to share their experiences, opinions, and perspectives.
   - Use open-ended questions to spark discussions. Sample questions may include:
     - "Can you describe your experiences with [the topic]?"
     - "What challenges have you encountered in your role related to [the topic]?"
     - "What suggestions or solutions do you have?"
4. **Group Interaction (15 minutes):**
   - Promote interaction and exchange of ideas among participants.
   - Encourage participants to respond to each other's comments and build on the discussion.
   - Keep the conversation focused on the designated topics.
5. **Summarization and Clarification (10 minutes):**
   - Summarize key points and themes discussed during the FGD.
   - Ask for clarification or further input on important issues.
   - Ensure that all participants have had an opportunity to share their views.

(continued)

6. **Closing (5 minutes):**
   - Thank the participants for their valuable contributions.
   - Remind them of the confidentiality of the discussion.
   - Provide contact information for follow-up questions or feedback.

Post-FGD:

1. **Transcription:** Transcribe the FGD audio recording, if available, for analysis.
2. **Data Analysis:** Analyze the collected data using qualitative analysis methods such as thematic analysis.
3. **Reporting:** Prepare a report summarizing the FGD findings, key themes, and relevant insights.
4. **Feedback:** Consider sharing the findings with the participating nurses and relevant hospital staff to inform decision-making.
5. **Storage:** Safely store all FGD data and transcripts for future reference or auditing purposes.

Continuous Improvement:

1. **Feedback and Evaluation:** Collect feedback from participants about their experience in the FGD and use it to improve future discussions.
2. **Iterative Process:** Adapt the FGD process and topics as needed based on emerging research needs or new insights.

Customize this guideline to suit your specific research or discussion topic and ensure that it aligns with the goals of your FGD with hospital nurses.

9.3.3 Key Informant Interviews (KIIs)

Key Informant Interviews (KIIs) are a valuable qualitative data collection method employed in social work fieldwork to gather in-depth insights from individuals with specialized knowledge or experience relevant to the research context (Akhter, 2022). Key informants, often experts in their respective fields, provide unique perspectives and nuanced information that contribute to a comprehensive understanding of the social issues under investigation. The success of KIIs hinges on the careful selection of informants based on their expertise, credibility, and relevance to the research objectives. During these interviews, social work practitioners employ open-ended questions to encourage detailed responses, allowing key informants to share their expertise, experiences, and observations. KIIs serve as a powerful tool in enriching the qualitative data collected during fieldwork, providing a deeper understanding of complex social phenomena, and informing the development of effective interventions and strategies within the social work practice.

9.3.3.1 A Sample Checklist of Key Informant Interviews (KIIs)

Title: Key Informant Interview Checklist with the Head of the Orthopedic Department
Objective: To conduct a structured interview with the Head of the Orthopedic Department at [Hospital Name] to gather insights on departmental management, patient care, and future directions.

Preparation:

1. **Define the Purpose:** Clearly outline the objectives and goals of the KII. Determine the specific topics or issues you want to explore with the department head.
2. **Participant Selection:** Identify and schedule the interview with the Head of the Orthopedic Department, ensuring their availability and willingness to participate.
3. **Interviewer Training:** Train the interviewer(s) in qualitative research methods, active listening, and interview techniques.
4. **Location and Logistics:** Secure a private and comfortable meeting room within the hospital. Ensure that the room is equipped with audio recording equipment and any necessary materials.

Key Informant Interview Structure:

1. **Introduction (5 minutes):**
    - Welcome the department head and introduce yourself.
    - Explain the purpose of the KII and its relevance to hospital practices.
    - Ensure informed consent and confidentiality.
    - Confirm the duration of the interview.
2. **Background and Role (10 minutes):**
    - Ask the department head to provide background information about their professional history, role in the department, and responsibilities.
    - Inquire about their vision for the Orthopedic Department.
3. **Departmental Operations (15 minutes):**
    - Explore the daily operations of the Orthopedic Department:

    - Patient flow and admission procedures.
    - Staffing and team dynamics.
    - Workflow and patient care pathways.
    - Key challenges and successes.
4. **Patient Care (15 minutes):**
    - Discuss patient care practices within the department:

(continued)

- Quality of care and patient outcomes.
- Patient safety initiatives.
- Patient satisfaction and feedback mechanisms.
- Notable cases or innovations in patient care.

5. **Challenges and Solutions (15 minutes):**
   - Inquire about the major challenges faced by the Orthopedic Department.
   - Ask for potential solutions or strategies employed to address these challenges.
6. **Future Directions (10 minutes):**
   - Explore the department head's vision for the future of orthopedic care at the hospital.
   - Discuss plans for improvements, expansion, or innovation.
7. **Closing (5 minutes):**
   - Thank the department head for their time and insights.
   - Remind them of the confidentiality of the interview.
   - Provide contact information for follow-up questions or feedback.

Post-KII:

1. **Transcription:** Transcribe the KII audio recording, if available, for analysis.
2. **Data Analysis:** Analyze the collected data using qualitative analysis methods such as thematic analysis.
3. **Reporting:** Prepare a report summarizing the KII findings, key themes, and relevant insights.
4. **Feedback:** Share the findings with relevant hospital staff or stakeholders to inform decision-making and departmental improvements.
5. **Storage:** Safely store all KII data and transcripts for future reference or auditing purposes.

Continuous Improvement:

1. **Feedback and Evaluation:** Collect feedback from the department head about their experience in the KII and use it to improve future interviews or research processes.
2. **Iterative Process:** Adapt the interview process and topics as needed based on emerging research needs or new insights.

Customize this checklist to fit your specific research goals and ensure it aligns with the objectives of your key informant interview with the Head of the Orthopedic Department.

9.3.4 Participant Observation

Participant Observation emerges as a nuanced and immersive data collection method within the realm of social work practice. This subsection delves into the significance and application of participant observation as a qualitative research approach. In social work, practitioners engage in participant observation by embedding themselves within the communities, organizations, or settings under study. This method involves not only observing but actively participating in the daily activities and interactions of the subjects. By becoming an integral part of the environment, social workers gain firsthand insights into the lived experiences, social dynamics, and contextual nuances that may not be fully captured through other means (Islam, 2022). Participant observation offers a unique vantage point for understanding the complexities of social issues, cultural norms, and power structures within diverse settings. It fosters a holistic understanding that goes beyond surface-level observations, enabling practitioners to tailor interventions that are contextually informed and responsive to the needs of the populations they serve.

9.3.4.1 A Sample Guideline of an Observation Checklist

Title: Observation Checklist Guideline for Qualitative Data Collection from Registered Patients in [Hospital Name]
Objective: To collect non-verbal and environmental data during interactions between healthcare providers and registered patients at [Hospital Name].
Preparation:

1. **Define the Purpose:** Clearly outline the objectives and goals of the observation. Determine what specific aspects you want to capture through non-verbal behaviors and environmental factors.
2. **Select Observers:** Identify and train the observers responsible for conducting the observations. Ensure that they understand the purpose, criteria, and procedures.
3. **Select the Setting and Time:** Determine the specific locations (e.g., waiting areas and examination rooms) and times for the observations. Ensure that it aligns with the context you want to study.

Checklist Development:

1. **Identification of Key Variables:** Determine the specific non-verbal behaviors, interactions, and environmental factors you want to observe. These should align with your research objectives.
2. **Item Design:** Create clear and concise items/questions for the checklist. Each item should be observable and measurable.

(continued)

3. **Pilot Testing:** Test the checklist in a similar hospital setting to identify any issues with clarity, completeness, or usability. Revise as necessary.

Observation Process:

1. **Introduction (if applicable):** If required, introduce yourself to the individuals being observed, explaining the purpose of the observation and ensuring their consent (if necessary).
2. **Observation Period:** Begin the observation at the predetermined time and location. Follow the checklist items systematically.
3. **Recording Observations:**
   - Use a structured format to record observations, such as a table with columns for items, date, time, location, and observer's name.
   - For each item on the checklist, record observations accurately and objectively.
   - Note any relevant contextual information that might influence the observation.
4. **Non-Verbal Behaviors:** Observe and record non-verbal cues, such as facial expressions, body language, and gestures, exhibited by both patients and healthcare providers.
5. **Interactions:** Record details of interactions between patients and healthcare providers, including communication styles, tone of voice, and responsiveness.
6. **Environmental Factors:** Take note of environmental factors that may affect the patient experience, such as cleanliness, noise levels, comfort, and accessibility.

Completion:

1. **Review:** Double-check the completed checklist for completeness, accuracy, and clarity. Ensure that all items have been addressed.
2. **Data Entry:** Transfer the recorded observations into a digital database or spreadsheet for analysis, if applicable.

Post-Observation:

1. **Data Analysis:** Analyze the collected data based on your research objectives. Use appropriate qualitative analysis methods, such as thematic coding.
2. **Reporting:** Prepare a report or summary of the observations, including key findings, trends, and any recommendations or conclusions related to the patient experience.
3. **Feedback:** If relevant, provide feedback or share the observation results with relevant hospital staff or stakeholders.
4. **Storage:** Store the completed checklists and raw data securely for future reference or auditing purposes.

(continued)

Continuous Improvement:

1. **Feedback and Evaluation:** Collect feedback from observers about the checklist's effectiveness and usability, and make improvements as needed.
2. **Iterative Process:** Continuously refine the checklist based on changing research needs or new insights.

Customize this guideline to suit your specific research needs and ensure that it aligns with the qualitative data collection requirements for studying the patient experience in a hospital setting.

9.3.5 Content Analysis

Content analysis stands out as a systematic and objective method of extracting meaningful insights from various forms of communication within the field of social work. This subsection illuminates the importance and application of content analysis as a data collection technique. In social work, content analysis involves the systematic examination of textual, visual, or audio content to identify patterns, themes, and underlying meanings. This method allows practitioners to analyze and interpret the messages conveyed in documents, media, or any other communication channels. By categorizing and coding the content, social workers can uncover prevalent narratives, identify recurring themes, and discern the implicit messages embedded in the material. Content analysis proves particularly valuable in assessing the portrayal of certain issues, public perceptions, or organizational communication within the social work context. It offers a structured and replicable approach to making sense of vast amounts of qualitative data, contributing to evidence-based practice and informed decision-making in the field.

9.3.5.1 A Sample Checklist of a Content Analysis

Fieldwork Data Collection Checklist for Novice Social Workers in a Hospital
Objective: To systematically collect essential data and information for preparing a comprehensive fieldwork report in a hospital setting.

I. Preparation:

A. **Clarify Fieldwork Objectives**—Clearly define the objectives and goals of your fieldwork to guide your data collection efforts.
B. **Hospital Familiarization**—Acquaint yourself with the hospital's layout, departments, and the role of a social worker within the healthcare team.

(continued)

C. **Ethical Considerations**—Ensure strict compliance with ethical standards and seek the necessary permissions for data collection.

II. Secondary Sources:

A. **Hospital Records Department**—Responsible Person: Hospital Records Manager or Coordinator—Data Available: Patient demographics, medical history, admission and discharge records, and billing information.
B. **Hospital Policy and Procedure Manuals**—Responsible Person: Hospital Administration or Compliance Officer—Data Available: Information on hospital policies, procedures, and guidelines related to patient care, ethics, and social work services.
C. **Patient Feedback and Satisfaction Surveys**—Responsible Person: Quality Improvement Department or Patient Experience Coordinator—Data Available: Feedback from patients regarding their hospital experience, including social work services.
D. **Clinical Social Workers**—Responsible Person: Clinical Social Work Team or Department Head—Data Available: Insights from experienced social workers regarding their experiences, best practices, and challenges in providing support to patients.
E. **Hospital Reports and Publications**—Responsible Person: Hospital Public Relations or Communications Department—Data Available: Access to hospital annual reports, newsletters, or research publications relevant to patient care and social work services.

III. Responsible Persons:

A. **Hospital Social Work Department**—Responsible Person: Head of Social Work Department or Clinical Supervisor—Data Available: Guidance on departmental procedures, caseload information, and access to experienced social workers for mentorship.
B. **Hospital Ethics Committee**—Responsible Person: Ethics Committee Chair or Coordinator—Data Available: Information on ethical considerations, policies, and decisions related to patient care and social work involvement.
C. **Hospital Administrators**—Responsible Person: Hospital CEO, Chief Medical Officer (CMO), or Chief Nursing Officer (CNO)—Data Available: Insights into hospital management, strategic goals, and priorities related to patient care.
D. **Patient Relations Office**—Responsible Person: Patient Relations Coordinator or Officer—Data Available: Information on patient complaints, grievances, and resolutions, which can provide insights into areas of improvement.
E. **Quality Improvement Department**—Responsible Person: Quality Improvement Director or Manager—Data Available: Data related to hospital quality measures, patient outcomes, and initiatives for improvement.

F. **Hospital Research Department**—Responsible Person: Research Director or Coordinator—Data Available: Access to research studies, clinical trials, or data relevant to patient care and social work interventions.
G. **Hospital IT Department**—Responsible Person: IT Manager or Data Analyst—Data Available: Assistance with data retrieval, management, and analysis of electronic health records (EHRs) and other digital resources.

IV. Data Collection Process:

A. **Structured Interviews**—Conduct structured interviews with patients to gather information on their needs, concerns, and experiences.
B. **Documentation**—Accurately and confidentially document patient interactions, assessments, and interventions.
C. **Review Hospital Policies**—Review and document relevant hospital policies and guidelines related to social work and patient care.
D. **Data Analysis**—Analyze collected data to identify trends, challenges, and areas for improvement.

V. Reporting:

A. **Report Preparation**—Prepare a comprehensive fieldwork report including an introduction, methodology, findings, recommendations, and conclusions.
B. **Review and Validation**—Review your report with your supervisor or responsible persons for validation and feedback before final submission.

VI. Continuous Learning:

A. **Training Opportunities**—Identify and participate in relevant training programs or workshops to enhance your knowledge and skills.
B. **Self-Reflection**—Engage in self-reflection to assess your fieldwork experiences and continuously strive for personal and professional growth.

Customize this checklist to match the specific requirements and objectives of your fieldwork as a novice social worker in the hospital setting.

9.4 Quantitative Data Collection Techniques for Field Report

9.4.1 Surveys and Questionnaires

Surveys and questionnaires have emerged as pivotal tools in the realm of quantitative data collection within social work practices. This subsection explores the significance and application of surveys and questionnaires, shedding light on their role in systematically gathering numerical data for analysis. Surveys typically involve the administration of structured questionnaires to a targeted sample, aiming to elicit specific responses that can be quantified and analyzed. This method proves beneficial in collecting data on attitudes, opinions, behaviors, or demographic characteristics. Questionnaires, on the other hand, offer a written or verbal set of questions designed to gather standardized information from respondents. Both surveys and questionnaires provide a scalable approach, allowing social work practitioners to collect data from a large number of participants efficiently. The quantitative nature of the data garnered through these techniques facilitates statistical analysis, making it a valuable asset in empirical research, program evaluation, and evidence-based decision-making within the social work domain.

Human Rights Organization Data Collection Survey

Introduction: Thank you for participating in our survey. Your feedback is crucial in helping us understand and enhance our efforts in promoting and protecting human rights. Please provide honest and thoughtful responses. Your answers will remain confidential.

Demographic Information:

1. Gender:
   - Male
   - Female
   - Non-binary
   - Prefer not to say
   - Other (please specify)
2. Age:
   - Under 18
   - 18–24
   - 25–34
   - 35–44
   - 45–54
   - 55–64
   - 65 or older
3. Educational Background:
   - High School
   - Bachelor's Degree
   - Master's Degree
   - Doctoral Degree
   - Other (please specify)
4. Occupation:
   - Student
   - Professional
   - Activist
   - Other (please specify)

(continued)

5. Geographical Location:
   - Urban
   - Suburban
   - Rural
6. How did you become aware of our organization?

Perceptions and Awareness:

7. How would you rate your awareness of human rights issues before engaging with our organization?
   - Very Low
   - Low
   - Moderate
   - High
   - Very High
8. Which specific human rights issues are you most passionate about? (Open-ended)

Engagement and Participation:

9. Have you attended any events or activities organized by our organization?
   - Yes
   - No
10. If yes, please describe your experience. If not, what would encourage you to participate in future events? (Open-ended)
11. Are you a member or volunteer of our organization?
    - Yes
    - No
12. If yes, how satisfied are you with your involvement in the organization?

Communication Channels:

13. How do you prefer to receive updates and information from our organization?
    - Email
    - Social Media
    - Website
    - Newsletter
    - Events/Workshops
    - Other (please specify)
14. How often do you check or engage with our organization's social media channels?

(continued)

15. Would you be interested in attending webinars or online events hosted by our organization?
    - Yes
    - No
    - Maybe

Effectiveness and Impact:

16. How would you rate the effectiveness of our organization in addressing human rights issues?
    - Not Effective
    - Somewhat Effective
    - Effective
    - Very Effective
17. In your opinion, what impact has our organization had on the community or specific human rights issues? (Open-ended)

Suggestions for Improvement:

18. What suggestions do you have for improving our organization's initiatives, outreach efforts, or communication strategies? (Open-ended)

Advocacy and Action:

19. Have you participated in any advocacy campaigns or actions led by our organization?
    - Yes
    - No
20. If yes, please describe your experience. If not, what would encourage you to participate in advocacy initiatives?

Overall Satisfaction:

21. On a scale of 1–10, how satisfied are you with our organization's work?
    - 1 (Not satisfied at all)
    - 10 (Extremely satisfied)
22. How likely are you to recommend our organization to others?
    - Not Likely
    - Somewhat Likely
    - Likely
    - Very Likely
23. Do you have any additional comments or feedback you would like to share with us? (Open-ended)

Thank you for taking the time to complete our survey. Your input is invaluable in helping us better serve the community and advance human rights.

9.4.2 Standardized Tests and Assessments

Standardized tests and assessments serve as integral components of quantitative data collection methodologies in social work. This subsection delves into the importance and application of standardized tests and assessments, elucidating their role in obtaining measurable and comparable data. Standardized tests are systematically administered and scored based on a consistent set of rules, ensuring uniformity in the assessment process. These assessments are designed to measure specific attributes, such as cognitive abilities, emotional well-being, or behavioral traits, providing quantitative insights into the individual's functioning. Social work practitioners often utilize standardized tests and assessments to evaluate clients, identify strengths and challenges, and inform intervention strategies. The standardized nature of these instruments facilitates reliable and objective data collection, enabling practitioners to make informed decisions in various practice settings, from clinical interventions to program evaluations.

9.4.3 Statistical Analysis in Social Work Research

Statistical analysis plays a pivotal role in social work research, contributing to the robustness and validity of quantitative data. In this subsection, we explore the significance of statistical analysis in the context of social work, emphasizing its role in deriving meaningful insights from data sets. Statistical methods are employed to identify patterns, relationships, and trends within the collected quantitative data, providing a foundation for evidence-based practice. Social work researchers use statistical analyses to draw inferences, test hypotheses, and make informed decisions about the effectiveness of interventions or the prevalence of social issues. Techniques such as regression analysis, t-tests, and ANOVA enable researchers to examine the impact of variables, establish correlations, and assess the significance of findings. This subsection sheds light on the integration of statistical analysis into the research process, highlighting its importance in elevating the quality and reliability of social work research endeavors.

9.5 Integrating Mixed-Methods Approaches in Social Work Field Research

9.5.1 Integrating Qualitative and Quantitative Data

Integrating qualitative and quantitative data in social work research is a strategic and holistic approach that combines the strengths of both methodologies to provide a more comprehensive understanding of complex social issues. This method involves collecting and analyzing qualitative data, such as in-depth interviews or focus group discussions, alongside quantitative data obtained through surveys or experiments. By employing a mixed-methods design, researchers can triangulate findings, ensuring a more robust and nuanced exploration of their research questions. This approach allows for a richer interpretation of social phenomena, offering depth and breadth to the analysis. Researchers benefit from the flexibility to capture the intricacies of human experiences through qualitative insights while also obtaining measurable data for statistical analysis. The integration of qualitative and quantitative data stands as a powerful tool, enhancing the depth and validity of social work research endeavors.

9.5.2 Benefits and Challenges of Mixed-Methods Research

Engaging in mixed-methods research in social work presents both benefits and challenges, reflecting the dynamic nature of combining qualitative and quantitative approaches. One key advantage is the ability to triangulate data, validating research findings through multiple lenses and enhancing the overall reliability and validity of the study. Researchers can gain a more comprehensive understanding of complex social phenomena, tapping into both the depth of qualitative insights and the breadth of quantitative measures. This approach also allows for a more nuanced exploration of the interplay between variables, fostering a deeper understanding of the research context. However, challenges arise in terms of the complexity of design and analysis, requiring researchers to navigate methodological intricacies and effectively integrate diverse data sources. Striking a balance between the two methods, managing logistics, and ensuring ethical considerations are met are essential aspects that researchers must address to harness the full potential of mixed-methods research in the field of social work.

9.6 Ethical Considerations in Data Collection for Field Reports

9.6.1 Informed Consent and Confidentiality

In the realm of social work research, ensuring ethical standards is paramount, and this is particularly evident in the key principles of informed consent and confidentiality. Obtaining informed consent from research participants involves transparently communicating the purpose, procedures, and potential risks and benefits of the study, allowing individuals to make voluntary and informed decisions about their participation (Pollock, 2012). Respecting confidentiality is equally crucial, emphasizing the protection of participants' privacy by safeguarding their identities and sensitive information. These ethical considerations serve as a foundation for establishing trust between researchers and participants, contributing to the overall integrity and credibility of social work research endeavors. Practitioners and researchers must navigate the delicate balance between obtaining valuable data and upholding the ethical principles that underpin the profession, ensuring that the well-being and dignity of individuals remain central throughout the research process.

9.6.2 Ensuring Participant Autonomy and Privacy

In the ethical landscape of social work research, upholding participant autonomy and privacy is a fundamental commitment. This principle recognizes the right of individuals to make independent decisions regarding their involvement in research endeavors. Respecting participant autonomy involves providing clear and comprehensive information about the study, ensuring that individuals can make informed choices based on their values and preferences. Simultaneously, safeguarding participant privacy extends beyond mere confidentiality, emphasizing the protection of personal information from unauthorized access. Social work researchers are tasked with establishing robust procedures that prioritize participant autonomy and privacy, fostering a research environment built on trust and ethical responsibility. By integrating these principles, the research process aligns with the foundational values of social work, promoting the welfare and dignity of all involved individuals.

9.7 Utilizing Technology for Effective Data Collection in Social Work Field Practices

9.7.1 Electronic Surveys and Data Management

The utilization of technology in social work data collection signifies a transformative shift in research methodologies (Margaryan et al., 2011). Electronic surveys and data management systems offer unprecedented efficiency and accessibility, streamlining the data collection process. Electronic surveys enable researchers to reach a broader and more diverse audience, fostering inclusivity in research endeavors. Additionally, advanced data management systems facilitate the secure storage and organization of vast data sets, enhancing the overall research infrastructure. Embracing technology in data collection not only expedites the research process but also opens avenues for innovative and dynamic approaches, aligning social work research with the evolving landscape of the digital age. This section explores the benefits and considerations associated with the integration of electronic surveys and data management technologies, providing insights into their practical application within the social work context.

9.7.2 Ethical Considerations in Technology-Mediated Data Collection

In Technology-Mediated Data Collection, several ethical principles guide social work practitioners to ensure responsible and respectful research practices. Key considerations include obtaining informed consent from participants, emphasizing transparency about the data collection process, and communicating the purpose and potential risks associated with technology use. Upholding participant autonomy and privacy is paramount, necessitating measures to protect confidential information and ensure data security. Social work researchers must also remain vigilant about the potential for technological biases and disparities, addressing these issues to maintain fairness and justice in the research process. Overall, ethical considerations in technology-mediated data collection underscore the importance of aligning research practices with the values and principles of social work, fostering trust and integrity in the profession.

Review Questions

1. What is the primary purpose of data collection in social work field practice?
2. Name two qualitative data collection techniques discussed in this chapter and briefly explain their applications.
3. Briefly outline the ethical considerations related to participant autonomy and privacy in data collection.
4. Why is it beneficial to integrate mixed-methods approaches in social work field research?
5. Discuss the role of technology in data collection for social work field practices, highlighting its advantages and potential ethical considerations.

Multiple Choice Questions

1. What is the main advantage of utilizing mixed-methods approaches in social work field research?

   (a) Simplicity in data analysis
   (b) Increased depth and breadth of understanding
   (c) Limited perspectives on the research question
   (d) Narrow scope of data collection

2. Which of the following is an example of a qualitative data collection technique?

   (a) Surveys
   (b) Statistical analysis

   (c) Content analysis
   (d) Standardized tests

3. What is a key ethical consideration in technology-mediated data collection?
   (a) Limited access to data
   (b) Participant anonymity
   (c) Informed consent
   (d) Avoidance of data encryption

4. In quantitative data collection, what method involves asking participants to respond to a series of predetermined questions?
   (a) Participant observation
   (b) Focus group discussions
   (c) Surveys and questionnaires
   (d) Key informant interviews

5. Why is ensuring participant autonomy important in social work field research?
   (a) It protects the participants' rights and choices.
   (b) It simplifies the research process.
   (c) It reduces the need for informed consent.
   (d) It limits the diversity of collected data.

References

Akhter, S. (2022). Key informants' interviews. In M. R. Islam, N. A. Khan, & R. Baikady (Eds.), *Principles of social research methodology. Springer. Principles of social research methodology* (pp. 389–403). Springer Nature Singapore.

Azam, M. G. (2022). In-depth case interview. In M. R. Islam, N. A. Khan, & R. Baikady (Eds.), *Principles of social research methodology. Springer. Principles of social research methodology* (pp. 347–364). Springer Nature Singapore.

Gray, M., Plath, D., & Webb, S. (2009). *Evidence-based social work: A critical stance*. Routledge.

Islam, M. R. (2022). Participatory research. In M. R. Islam, N. A. Khan, & R. Baikady (Eds.), *Principles of social research methodology. Springer. Principles of social research methodology* (pp. 291–311). Springer Nature Singapore.

Khan, N. A., & Abedin, S. (2022). Focus group discussion. In M. R. Islam, N. A. Khan, & R. Baikady (Eds.), *Principles of social research methodology. Springer. Principles of social research methodology* (pp. 377–387). Springer Nature Singapore.

Margaryan, A., Littlejohn, A., & Vojt, G. (2011). Are digital natives a myth or reality? University students' use of digital technologies. *Computers & Education, 56*(2), 429–440.

Pollock, K. (2012). Procedure versus process: Ethical paradigms and the conduct of qualitative research. *BMC Medical Ethics, 13*, 1–12.

Chapter 10
Navigating Field Settings and Agency Dynamics

Learning Objectives
After studying this chapter, you will be able to:

- Understand the diversity of agency environments, specializations, and cultures in social work to navigate and adapt effectively to different contexts
- Comprehend the complex interplay of roles and structures within social work agencies to navigate organizational dynamics and contribute effectively to the agency's mission
- Apply SWOT analysis as a strategic tool to assess and understand the strengths, weaknesses, opportunities, and threats in various fieldwork situations
- Utilize SWOT analysis principles in social work practice, enhancing decision-making skills and contributing to more effective interventions within agencies
- Gain practical insights into SWOT analysis by exploring real-world examples in diverse fieldwork settings, enriching your understanding of its application in social work practice

10.1 Exploration of Various Agency Environments, Specializations, and Cultures

As we delve into the realm of social work practice, our exploration encompasses various dimensions, including agency environments, specializations, and cultural dynamics. Understanding the diverse settings where social work operates, from public to private agencies, rural to urban contexts, and population-specific organizations, equips us with contextual awareness crucial for effective interventions. Specializations such as clinical, medical, school, and community development social work offer nuanced pathways within the field, each addressing unique client needs. Moreover, recognizing the cultural fabric of agencies informs our practice,

M. R. Islam, *Fieldwork in Social Work*,
https://doi.org/10.1007/978-3-031-56683-7_10

emphasizing the importance of cultural competence and rapport-building. This holistic approach to exploration lays the foundation for the comprehensive summary table (Table 10.1) that follows, encapsulating the key points for our understanding and application in social work practice.

10.1.1 Unveiling Diverse Agency Environments

In the exploration of diverse agency environments within the realm of social work, a nuanced understanding of the distinct settings where fieldwork takes place becomes paramount. Agencies represent the operational hubs where social work practitioners engage with clients, systems, and societal issues.

Public and Private Agency Distinctions: Public agencies, such as government departments and community service organizations, operate with a focus on serving the broader community. Private agencies, on the other hand, may include non-profit organizations, healthcare institutions, or advocacy groups, each contributing to social welfare in distinctive ways. Understanding the operational disparities between these settings equips social work students with insights into the diverse landscapes they might encounter during their field placements.

Organizational Structures: Exploring diverse agency environments involves an examination of organizational structures. Hierarchies, communication channels,

Table 10.1 Summary table of various agency environments, specializations, and cultures

Section	Main points
Exploration of agency environments	Understanding public and private agency distinctions, exploring organizational structures, community-based vs. institutional settings, population-specific agencies, rural vs. urban dynamics, technological integration, political and cultural influences, interagency collaboration, environmental considerations
Delving into specializations	Clinical social work, medical social work, school social work, child and family social work, gerontological social work, community development, criminal justice social work, international social work
Understanding agency cultures	Defining organizational culture, impact on social work practice, cultural competence, diversity and inclusion policies, communication styles and decision-making processes, adapting to cultural dynamics
Navigating role dynamics	Roles within agencies, supervisory relationships, interdisciplinary collaboration, structures and hierarchies, team dynamics, client–professional relationships, adapting to change
Adapting to challenges and opportunities	Agency-specific challenges, opportunities for innovation, cultural competence in agency contexts, building resilience, collaborative problem-solving, professional development opportunities
Building rapport in agency cultures	Cultural sensitivity and awareness, active listening and observation, adapting communication styles, establishing trust and credibility, collaborative relationship building, flexibility and adaptability

Source: Author

and decision-making processes significantly impact the daily functions of social work practitioners within these settings.

Community-Based vs. Institutional Settings: The nature of agency environments extends to the communities they serve. Community-based organizations often operate directly within the neighborhoods they impact, fostering a grassroots approach. In contrast, institutional settings, such as hospitals or schools, address social issues on a broader scale. This exploration sheds light on the implications of working in various settings, emphasizing the importance of contextual awareness in effective social work practice.

Population-Specific Agencies: Diverse agency environments also cater to specific populations, such as children, the elderly, or individuals with disabilities. Whether it's a childcare facility, a nursing home, or an organization supporting people with disabilities, understanding the intricacies of these environments is crucial for effective social work.

Rural vs. Urban Dynamics: The geographical location of agencies, whether in rural or urban settings, contributes to distinct operational dynamics. Urban environments may involve a higher volume of cases and diverse challenges, while rural settings might have a more close-knit community with specific needs. This exploration helps social work students comprehend the variations in practice based on the geographical context of the agency.

Technological Integration: Modern agencies increasingly integrate technology into their operations, impacting service delivery and communication. Students will explore how technology, such as electronic record-keeping or virtual counseling, influences the practice of social work. Understanding the role of technology in different agency environments prepares students for the evolving landscape of social work practice.

Political and Cultural Influences: Agencies are not immune to the influences of politics and culture. Students will know how political ideologies and cultural nuances can shape the mission, policies, and practices of social work agencies. Recognizing these influences is essential for social work practitioners to navigate the complexities of diverse agency environments effectively.

Interagency Collaboration: Many social work scenarios involve collaboration between different agencies and organizations. This includes the dynamics of interagency collaboration, emphasizing the importance of teamwork, communication, and shared goals in addressing complex social issues. Social work students gain insights into how collaborative efforts contribute to holistic and impactful interventions.

Environmental Considerations: In certain contexts, agencies may be involved in environmental or ecological issues. Students will look at how social work extends beyond individual and community levels to engage with broader environmental challenges. Understanding the agency's role in environmental advocacy and sustainability contributes to a comprehensive understanding of social work practice.

By encompassing these additional points, the exploration of diverse agency environments provides a thorough and nuanced perspective for social work students, preparing them for the intricacies they may encounter in their field placements.

10.1.2 Delving into Specializations: A Spectrum of Social Work Practice

In the exploration of social work agency dynamics, it is essential to delve into the various specializations that define the spectrum of social work practice.

Clinical Social Work: One prominent specialization is clinical social work, which involves direct therapeutic interventions with individuals or groups. Students will explore the intricacies of clinical practice, including assessment, diagnosis, and the application of therapeutic modalities. Social work students gain insights into working with clients dealing with mental health issues, addiction, or trauma.

Medical Social Work: In healthcare settings, medical social work plays a crucial role. This specialization involves addressing the psychosocial aspects of illness and working with patients and families facing medical challenges. Here students will explore collaboration with healthcare professionals, navigating ethical dilemmas in medical settings, and providing support during critical health situations.

School Social Work: School social work is another specialization focused on supporting students' academic success and overall well-being. This explores the role of social workers in educational settings, including addressing behavioral issues, facilitating communication between school and home, and advocating for students' needs. Social work students gain insights into the unique challenges and rewards of working within the educational system.

Child and Family Social Work: Dedicated to supporting children and families, this specialization involves interventions related to child welfare, family dynamics, and parenting. The exploration delves into the complexities of working with families in crisis, navigating child protection services, and implementing interventions to enhance family functioning.

Gerontological Social Work: The aging population necessitates expertise in gerontological social work. This specialization involves addressing the unique needs of older adults, including healthcare, housing, and social inclusion. Social work students gain insights into promoting the well-being of the elderly, navigating end-of-life issues, and advocating for age-friendly policies.

Community Development: Focusing on the broader community, community development social work aims to enhance the overall well-being of communities. This includes community engagement, empowerment, and social change. Social work students gain insights into mobilizing community resources, fostering social cohesion, and addressing systemic challenges.

Criminal Justice Social Work: Within the criminal justice system, social workers play a crucial role in rehabilitation and reintegration. This specialization involves working with individuals involved in the legal system, addressing issues of incarceration, parole, and community reintegration. The exploration sheds light on the challenges and ethical considerations in the criminal justice context.

International Social Work: Global issues require social workers with expertise in international social work. This explores the role of social workers in addressing global challenges such as migration, humanitarian crises, and human rights. Social work students gain insights into cultural competence, cross-border collaboration, and advocating for social justice on a global scale.

By delving into these specializations, social work students gain a comprehensive understanding of the diverse pathways available within the field. This exploration prepares them for the richness and complexity of social work practice across various specializations.

10.1.3 Understanding the Cultural Fabric of Agencies

In the exploration of social work agency dynamics, understanding the cultural fabric of agencies emerges as a critical aspect.

Organizational Culture Defined: Organizational culture encompasses the shared values, beliefs, practices, and norms within an agency. It shapes how individuals within the organization interact, make decisions, and approach their work. This delves into the various components that contribute to the formation of organizational culture, including leadership styles, communication patterns, and the agency's history and mission.

Impact on Social Work Practice: The organizational culture of an agency significantly influences social work practice. This exploration sheds light on how cultural elements within an agency can either support or pose challenges to social work interventions. For example, a culture that prioritizes collaboration and open communication may enhance interdisciplinary teamwork, while a culture resistant to change may hinder innovative approaches.

Cultural Competence in Social Work: Cultural competence is a key consideration in social work practice, and this subsection explores how organizational culture plays a role in fostering or impeding cultural competence. It delves into strategies for developing a culturally responsive organizational culture, including ongoing training, diversity initiatives, and the promotion of inclusivity.

Diversity and Inclusion Policies: Agencies with a commitment to diversity and inclusion contribute to a more enriching work environment. This includes the development and implementation of diversity and inclusion policies within agencies, and examining how these policies impact the recruitment of staff, the provision of services, and the overall agency culture.

Communication Styles and Decision-Making Processes: The way communication flows within an agency and the methods employed in decision-making are integral components of organizational culture. This explores how different communication styles and decision-making processes can either facilitate or hinder effective social work practice. It addresses the importance of transparent communication and inclusive decision-making in fostering a positive cultural environment.

Adapting to Cultural Dynamics: Social work practitioners must be adept at navigating and adapting to the cultural dynamics of the agencies in which they work. This exploration provides insights into how practitioners can navigate cultural nuances, build rapport with colleagues from diverse backgrounds, and contribute to the positive cultural fabric of their workplace.

By comprehensively understanding the cultural fabric of agencies, social work students and practitioners can navigate the complexities of organizational dynamics, contribute meaningfully to their workplace, and enhance the overall effectiveness of social work interventions. This subsection equips them with the knowledge and skills needed to thrive within diverse organizational cultures and contribute to positive cultural shifts within agencies.

10.1.4 Navigating Complex Dynamics: The Interplay of Roles and Structures

In the realm of social work, agency dynamics are characterized by intricate interplays of roles and structures that significantly influence the effectiveness of social work practice.

Roles Within Agencies: The first layer of exploration involves the diverse roles present within social work agencies. From frontline practitioners to supervisors, administrators, and support staff, each role contributes uniquely to the overall functioning of the agency. This includes the expectations, responsibilities, and collaborative aspects of these roles, emphasizing the importance of cohesive teamwork in achieving organizational goals.

Supervisory Relationships: Supervision is a crucial component of social work practice, and this part of the exploration focuses on the dynamics between supervisors and social work practitioners. It delves into effective supervisory practices, the role of feedback, and the establishment of a supportive supervisory relationship that fosters professional growth and development.

Interdisciplinary Collaboration: Social work rarely operates in isolation, and interdisciplinary collaboration is integral to addressing complex social issues. This examines the dynamics of collaboration with professionals from other disciplines within agencies, emphasizing the importance of effective communication, shared goals, and a mutual understanding of each discipline's contributions.

Structures and Hierarchies: The organizational structure and hierarchies within agencies shape the dynamics of authority, decision-making, and communication. This exploration delves into how hierarchical structures can impact the flow of information, the delegation of responsibilities, and the overall functioning of social work practice within agencies.

Team Dynamics: Teamwork is a cornerstone of effective social work, and this subsection explores the dynamics of teamwork within agencies. It addresses the importance of clear communication, mutual respect, and a collaborative approach to problem-solving. Understanding team dynamics equips social work practitioners to navigate challenges and contribute meaningfully to collective efforts.

Client–Professional Relationships: At the heart of social work practice are the relationships formed with clients. This exploration delves into the dynamics of client–professional relationships within agency settings, emphasizing the principles of empathy, cultural competence, and client-centered approaches that enhance the quality of social work interventions.

Adapting to Change: The social work landscape is dynamic, and agencies must adapt to changes in policies, practices, and societal needs. This exploration addresses the challenges and opportunities associated with adapting to change within agency structures, emphasizing the resilience and flexibility required of social work practitioners.

By comprehensively navigating the complex dynamics of roles and structures within agencies, social work students and practitioners gain insights into the intricacies of organizational life. This subsection equips them with the knowledge and skills needed to engage effectively with diverse roles, collaborate within interdisciplinary teams, and contribute meaningfully to the dynamic and ever-evolving field of social work.

10.1.5 Adapting to Agency-Specific Challenges and Opportunities

Navigating the landscape of social work agencies involves a nuanced understanding of the challenges and opportunities specific to each organizational context. This subsection delves into the dynamic interplay between challenges and opportunities, providing social work students and practitioners with insights into adapting effectively within diverse agency settings.

Agency-Specific Challenges: Every agency presents unique challenges influenced by factors such as size, mission, and population served. This identifies and analyzes the common challenges faced within social work agencies, ranging from resource constraints and bureaucratic hurdles to client-specific difficulties. Understanding these challenges is essential for developing strategies that enhance resilience and problem-solving skills.

Opportunities for Innovation: Amid challenges lie opportunities for innovation and improvement. This subsection emphasizes the identification and exploration of opportunities within agency settings. From implementing new interventions to leveraging community resources, social work practitioners can proactively contribute to positive changes. Recognizing and capitalizing on opportunities fosters a proactive and forward-thinking approach to social work practice.

Cultural Competence in Agency Contexts: The cultural fabric of agencies plays a pivotal role in shaping the experiences of both practitioners and clients. This exploration focuses on the importance of cultural competence within agency settings, addressing the diverse cultural backgrounds of clients, colleagues, and the broader community. Social work practitioners are encouraged to develop cultural humility and adaptability to ensure responsive and inclusive service delivery.

Building Resilience in the Face of Challenges: Resilience is a key attribute in the field of social work, and this part of the exploration provides strategies for building and maintaining resilience in the face of agency-specific challenges. Whether overcoming systemic barriers or addressing client needs in complex situations, resilience equips practitioners to navigate adversity and sustain their commitment to social work values.

Collaborative Problem-Solving: Agency-specific challenges often require collaborative problem-solving approaches. This explores the dynamics of collaborative problem-solving within agency contexts, highlighting the importance of teamwork, effective communication, and shared responsibility. Social work practitioners are encouraged to actively engage with colleagues, clients, and community partners to address challenges collectively.

Professional Development Opportunities: Agencies can serve as fertile ground for ongoing professional development. This exploration underscores the importance of identifying and leveraging opportunities for skill enhancement, training, and mentorship within agency settings. Social work students and practitioners are encouraged to actively pursue avenues for continuous learning, contributing to their professional growth.

By comprehensively addressing the agency-specific challenges and opportunities within the field of social work, this subsection equips practitioners with the knowledge and skills needed to navigate diverse organizational contexts. It encourages a proactive and adaptive mindset, fostering resilience, cultural competence, and collaborative approaches that enhance the overall effectiveness of social work practice within agencies.

10.1.6 Strategies for Building Rapport Within Unique Agency Cultures

Building rapport within unique agency cultures is a critical aspect of effective social work practice. This explores strategies and techniques for establishing meaningful connections, trust, and collaborative relationships within the specific cultural dynamics of diverse agencies.

Cultural Sensitivity and Awareness: Navigating unique agency cultures requires a foundation of cultural sensitivity and awareness. Social work practitioners are encouraged to develop a keen understanding of the values, norms, and communication styles prevalent in a particular agency. This emphasizes the importance of respecting and appreciating diverse cultural nuances within the organizational context.

Active Listening and Observation: Building rapport hinges on active listening and keen observation. Practitioners are guided on the art of active listening, which involves fully engaging with clients, colleagues, and stakeholders to comprehend their perspectives and needs. Additionally, the power of observation is highlighted, allowing practitioners to discern non-verbal cues and contextual factors that contribute to a deeper understanding of agency cultures.

Adapting Communication Styles: Effective communication is pivotal in rapport-building, and this subsection delves into the importance of adapting communication styles to align with unique agency cultures. Social work practitioners are encouraged to be flexible in their approach, tailoring communication methods to resonate with the specific context and preferences of the agency environment.

Establishing Trust and Credibility: Trust is the cornerstone of rapport, and practitioners are provided with strategies for establishing and maintaining trust within diverse agency cultures. Building credibility involves consistency, transparency, and ethical conduct, contributing to a positive reputation and fostering stronger relationships with clients, colleagues, and other stakeholders.

Collaborative Relationship Building: This practitioner is guided in developing collaborative relationships with colleagues, supervisors, and other professionals involved in the agency's operations. Strategies for effective teamwork and interprofessional collaboration are explored to enhance overall rapport within the organizational context.

Flexibility and Adaptability: The dynamic nature of agency cultures necessitates flexibility and adaptability. Social work practitioners are encouraged to embrace change, learn from diverse experiences, and adapt their approaches to suit evolving organizational dynamics. This subsection provides insights into cultivating a mindset of flexibility to navigate challenges and foster positive connections within unique agency cultures.

By addressing the intricacies of building rapport within unique agency cultures, this subsection equips social work practitioners with actionable strategies to enhance their effectiveness in diverse organizational contexts. It emphasizes the importance of cultural sensitivity, active listening, adaptability, and collaborative relationship building as essential components of successful rapport-building within the dynamic landscape of social work agencies.

10.2 Adapting to and Understanding Unique Agency Dynamics and Structures

Organizational Hierarchy and Decision-Making Processes: In examining organizational hierarchy and decision-making processes, social work practitioners must delve into the intricate layers of an agency's structural framework. The organizational hierarchy delineates the distribution of authority and responsibilities, encompassing various levels from frontline staff to managerial roles and executive positions. Understanding the intricacies of organizational hierarchy is crucial for practitioners to navigate their roles effectively within the agency. It provides clarity on reporting structures, facilitating streamlined communication and collaboration. Moreover, comprehending decision-making processes is integral to contributing meaningfully to the agency's direction. This exploration encompasses the criteria influencing decisions, the involvement of different staff levels, and mechanisms for conflict resolution. By gaining insights into organizational hierarchy and decision-making processes, social work practitioners enhance their capacity to engage proactively within the agency. This knowledge equips them to participate in decision-making forums, ensuring that their contributions align with ethical standards and the overarching mission of the organization. It fosters a collaborative and transparent working environment, where practitioners can navigate the complexities of agency structures with efficacy and uphold the values integral to social work practice.

Communication Channels and Protocols: In the realm of adapting to and understanding unique agency dynamics and structures, the examination of communication channels and protocols emerges as a pivotal aspect of effective social work practice. Communication channels encompass a spectrum of methods, from formal avenues such as meetings, reports, and official memos to informal channels such as team discussions and interdepartmental interactions. Understanding these channels is essential for social work practitioners to ensure that vital information reaches the relevant stakeholders in a timely and accurate manner. By gaining proficiency in communication channels and protocols, social work practitioners enhance their ability to convey information effectively and to engage in collaborative efforts. This knowledge fosters a transparent and cohesive working environment, enabling practitioners to align their communication strategies with the agency's goals and values. It underscores the significance of clear and respectful communication as an essential component of successful social work within the dynamic context of diverse agency structures.

Roles and Responsibilities: Within the context of adapting to and understanding unique agency dynamics and structures, the exploration of roles and responsibilities becomes integral to effective social work practice. Roles and responsibilities within an agency are often multifaceted, ranging from direct client interactions to administrative tasks and collaborative efforts with colleagues. It emphasizes the significance of role clarity, ensuring that each team member comprehends their specific duties and how they align with the agency's mission and objectives. Furthermore, the exploration extends to the collaborative nature of roles, emphasizing the interconnectedness of tasks within an agency. Understanding the interdependence of roles facilitates effective teamwork, promoting a cohesive approach to addressing the diverse needs of clients and communities. By gaining insights into roles and responsibilities, social work practitioners enhance their capacity to contribute meaningfully to the agency's overarching goals, fostering a collaborative and purpose-driven organizational culture.

Team Dynamics and Collaboration: In the realm of adapting to and understanding unique agency dynamics and structures, the exploration of team dynamics and collaboration emerges as a pivotal aspect of effective social work practice. Team dynamics encompass the interactions, relationships, and communication patterns among team members. Understanding these dynamics is crucial for creating a positive and supportive work environment that enhances the overall well-being of both staff and clients. This subsection unravels the factors that contribute to effective team collaboration, including clear communication channels, shared goals, and mutual respect among team members. Collaboration extends beyond individual teams to interdepartmental and interdisciplinary cooperation within an agency. Social work practitioners often collaborate with professionals from diverse fields to provide holistic and comprehensive services. This exploration sheds light on the benefits and challenges of interdisciplinary collaboration, offering insights into how social work professionals can navigate and contribute to collective efforts aimed at achieving positive outcomes for clients. Ultimately, the subsection on team dynamics and collaboration underscores the importance of fostering a collaborative ethos within agencies, where teamwork is not only valued but actively cultivated to optimize the impact of social work interventions.

Organizational Culture and Values**:** In the intricate landscape of adapting to and understanding unique agency dynamics and structures, the subsection on organizational culture and values assumes a central role. Organizational culture refers to the shared beliefs, values, and practices that shape the working environment within an agency. Understanding the prevailing organizational culture is paramount for social work students and professionals alike, as it provides insights into the agency's mission, priorities, and expectations. Values, another integral component, form the ethical backbone of an agency. The alignment of personal values with organizational values is crucial for maintaining professional integrity. Ultimately, the exploration of organizational culture and values underscores the significance of cultural congruence for effective social work practice. It emphasizes the need for practitioners to be cognizant of and adaptable to the cultural nuances within an agency, fostering an environment where ethical values are not only articulated but also upheld in daily professional endeavors.

Client Interaction Models: In the realm of adapting to and understanding unique agency dynamics and structures, the subsection focusing on client interaction models is pivotal. Client interaction models elucidate the frameworks and approaches employed by social work practitioners when engaging with clients within the agency setting. This exploration delves into various client interaction models, such as the strengths-based perspective, person-in-environment framework, and empowerment model. Each model offers distinctive lenses through which social work practitioners assess, understand, and intervene in the lives of their clients. The subsection outlines the theoretical foundations of these models and elucidates how they are practically applied within the agency context. Furthermore, it emphasizes the dynamic nature of client interactions, acknowledging the diverse needs, backgrounds, and circumstances of clients served by the agency. Social work students and practitioners gain insights into tailoring their approaches, interventions, and communication styles based on the specificities of each client interaction model.

Adapting to Change and Innovation**:** Within the broader exploration of adapting to and understanding unique agency dynamics and structures, the subsection on adapting to change and innovation takes center stage. In the dynamic landscape of social work agencies, the ability to navigate and embrace change is crucial for practitioners and students alike. It explores strategies employed by agencies to foster innovation, adapt to emerging trends, and incorporate technological advancements into their service delivery models. Social work students gain insights into the importance of flexibility, continuous learning, and a proactive approach to change within the agency context. Moreover, the subsection emphasizes the role of leadership, organizational culture, and the willingness of practitioners to embrace new methodologies. It showcases examples of agencies that have successfully navigated change and leveraged innovation to enhance the effectiveness of their services. In essence, the exploration of adapting to change and innovation within this sub-section provides a holistic understanding of the evolving nature of social work agencies. It equips social work students with the knowledge and skills needed to thrive in dynamic environments and contribute to the ongoing improvement and innovation within the field.

Conflict Resolution Mechanisms: Within the realm of adapting to and understanding unique agency dynamics and structures, the subsection on conflict resolution mechanisms is a critical component. Conflict is inherent in any organizational setting, and social work agencies are no exception. Social work students gain insights into the importance of open communication, active listening, and constructive dialogue in addressing conflicts within the agency. Furthermore, real-world examples and case studies illustrate instances where conflict resolution mechanisms have been successfully implemented within social work agencies. This provides students with practical knowledge and skills to navigate conflicts professionally and collaboratively. By understanding conflict resolution mechanisms, social work students are better prepared to contribute to positive organizational cultures, build strong collaborative relationships, and ensure the continuity of effective service delivery within the agency context.

10.3 Integrating SWOT Analysis for Effective Fieldwork Situations

Understanding the Foundations of SWOT Analysis: In the exploration of SWOT analysis as a foundational tool in social work practice, it is imperative to dissect its components, elucidating each element's role in strategic planning (Westhues et al., 2001; Raines, 2006; Harrikari et al., 2021). SWOT, an acronym for Strengths, Weaknesses, Opportunities, and Threats, serves as a structured framework for assessing the internal and external factors influencing fieldwork situations. Understanding the foundations of SWOT analysis involves a deep dive into discerning an agency's internal strengths and weaknesses, encompassing aspects such as organizational culture, resources, and operational efficiency. Simultaneously, the analysis extends to the external landscape, identifying opportunities for growth and potential threats that may impede successful fieldwork. This subsection aims to provide social work students with a comprehensive grasp of the theoretical underpinnings of SWOT analysis, enabling them to approach fieldwork situations with a strategic mindset and enhancing their ability to navigate complexities and make informed decisions in the dynamic context of social work practice.

Real-World Applications of SWOT Analysis in Social Work: In the practical application of SWOT analysis within the realm of social work, this subsection illuminates real-world scenarios where the framework proves invaluable. By examining case studies and examples, social work students gain insights into how SWOT analysis can be effectively employed to assess and address challenges encountered in fieldwork situations. Whether evaluating an agency's internal strengths to optimize service delivery or identifying external threats that may impact client well-being, the application of SWOT analysis comes to life through tangible illustrations. By delving into these real-world applications, this subsection equips students with the skills to translate theoretical knowledge into practical strategies, fostering a holistic understanding of SWOT analysis as a dynamic and adaptable tool in the social work toolkit.

Collaborative SWOT Analysis: Involving Stakeholders: Collaborative SWOT analysis stands as a pivotal aspect of effective fieldwork situations, emphasizing the engagement of various stakeholders in the process. This subsection explores the importance of involving not only social work practitioners and students but also clients, community members, and other relevant stakeholders in the SWOT analysis. By fostering collaboration, a more comprehensive and nuanced understanding of the fieldwork context emerges. The collective insights of diverse perspectives contribute to a holistic SWOT analysis, enriching the identification of strengths, weaknesses, opportunities, and threats within the social work practice setting. This collaborative approach not only enhances the quality of the analysis but also promotes inclusivity and empowers those directly impacted by social work interventions.

Leveraging Strengths in Fieldwork Practice: Leveraging strengths in fieldwork practice is a strategic dimension within the SWOT analysis framework, emphasizing the identification and optimization of inherent strengths. This subsection delves into the practical application of recognizing and capitalizing on the positive attributes and capacities within the social work practice setting. By harnessing and amplifying these strengths, practitioners and students can enhance the overall effectiveness of their interventions. Examples of leveraging strengths may include building on established community partnerships, utilizing advanced technological resources, or tapping into the diverse skills of the social work team. Understanding how to leverage strengths is crucial for cultivating a proactive and empowered approach to fieldwork, fostering positive outcomes for both practitioners and the communities they serve.

Addressing Weaknesses and Mitigating Challenges: Addressing weaknesses and mitigating challenges is an integral aspect of applying SWOT analysis in social work fieldwork. Social work practitioners and students learn to conduct a thorough assessment of weaknesses, which may include resource limitations, communication gaps, or skill gaps within the team. Through targeted interventions and collaborative efforts, the aim is to mitigate these challenges effectively, ensuring a more resilient and adaptive approach to fieldwork practice. This proactive stance contributes to the overall quality of social services and strengthens the foundation of social work practice within diverse settings.

Capitalizing on Opportunities in Fieldwork: Capitalizing on opportunities in fieldwork is a strategic endeavor explored in this subsection. Here, social work students and practitioners are guided in recognizing and leveraging opportunities that arise within the dynamic context of their practice settings. Opportunities could encompass new partnerships, community resources, or emerging trends that align with the mission of social work. By incorporating a proactive approach, individuals involved in fieldwork learn to assess, prioritize, and harness these opportunities for the betterment of their clients and the community. This process aligns with the broader goal of enhancing the impact and effectiveness of social work interventions by capitalizing on favorable circumstances and fostering positive developments within the field.

Mitigating Threats to Fieldwork Success: Mitigating threats to fieldwork success is a crucial aspect addressed in this subsection. Here, social work students and practitioners learn how to identify and navigate potential threats that may impede the achievement of their objectives during fieldwork. Threats could arise from external factors, internal challenges, or systemic issues within the agency or community. This part of this emphasizes the importance of proactive risk management, offering strategies and tools to assess, address, and minimize potential threats. By developing this skill set, individuals engaged in fieldwork enhance their ability to navigate uncertainties, ensuring a more resilient and successful implementation of social work practices in various settings.

Developing Action Plans from SWOT Analysis: Developing action plans from SWOT analysis is a critical component explored in this subsection. Once the strengths, weaknesses, opportunities, and threats have been identified and assessed, the focus shifts to translating these insights into actionable plans. Social work students and practitioners learn the art of crafting strategic interventions and initiatives based on the SWOT analysis findings. This involves aligning organizational or individual strengths with available opportunities, addressing weaknesses to mitigate threats, and formulating plans that capitalize on identified strengths.

10.4 Application of SWOT Analysis in Fieldwork Practice

Integrating SWOT Analysis into Fieldwork Planning: The seamless integration of SWOT analysis into fieldwork planning marks a pivotal phase in enhancing the strategic approach of social work practitioners. As professionals navigate the dynamic landscape of fieldwork assignments, incorporating SWOT analysis becomes a foundational step. This process involves a systematic examination of internal strengths and weaknesses, as well as external opportunities and threats pertinent to the specific fieldwork context. By identifying these factors, practitioners can proactively design tailored intervention plans, anticipate potential challenges, and align their strategies with the overarching goals of social work practice. The integration of SWOT analysis into fieldwork planning not only fosters a proactive mindset but also lays the groundwork for informed decision-making, ensuring a comprehensive and strategic approach to addressing the multifaceted challenges within the fieldwork setting.

Tailoring SWOT Analysis to Specific Fieldwork Assignments: In the realm of social work field practice, the adaptation of SWOT analysis to specific assignments emerges as a dynamic and context-sensitive strategy. Recognizing that each assignment presents a unique set of challenges and opportunities, social work practitioners learn to conduct a focused SWOT analysis that aligns with the objectives of the assignment. This tailored approach involves a meticulous examination of internal strengths and weaknesses directly relevant to the assignment's goals, as well as an exploration of external factors that may impact its successful execution. By customizing the application of SWOT analysis to specific fieldwork assignments, practitioners can enhance their ability to formulate targeted intervention plans that respond effectively to the distinctive dynamics of each case. This adaptive use of SWOT analysis becomes a valuable tool for navigating the diversity of challenges encountered in the fieldwork setting.

Utilizing SWOT Analysis for Case Management and Client Interventions: Within the landscape of social work, effective case management and client interventions demand a strategic approach, and the integration of SWOT analysis serves as a powerful instrument in this regard. Social work practitioners, equipped with a thorough understanding of their clients' situations, leverage SWOT analysis to assess internal strengths and weaknesses, considering the clients' resources, capacities, and potential barriers. Simultaneously, they scrutinize external opportunities and threats that may influence the success of interventions. The tailored insights derived from SWOT analysis enable practitioners to formulate client-specific intervention plans, ensuring a holistic and personalized approach. By integrating SWOT analysis into case management, social work professionals enhance their ability to address the complex and unique needs of each client, fostering a client-centered and strengths-based practice. This strategic utilization of SWOT analysis becomes an integral component in the arsenal of tools employed for comprehensive and effective social work interventions.

SWOT Analysis in Decision-Making Processes During Fieldwork: Navigating the dynamic fieldwork landscape requires adept decision-making processes, and SWOT analysis emerges as a valuable companion in this endeavor. This subsection delves into the nuanced application of SWOT analysis in guiding decision-making during various stages of fieldwork. Social work practitioners, armed with a thorough SWOT assessment, gain clarity on the potential impact of decisions on clients, agencies, and broader systems. SWOT analysis aids in identifying decision options aligned with organizational strengths, mitigating weaknesses, capitalizing on opportunities, and addressing potential threats. Whether making choices in client interventions, agency policies, or collaborative efforts, practitioners employ SWOT analysis as a systematic and strategic tool. By incorporating this analysis into decision-making processes, social work professionals enhance their ability to make informed, contextually relevant, and ethical decisions, contributing to the overall success and impact of their fieldwork endeavors.

Adapting SWOT Analysis for Macro-Level Social Work Initiatives: Adapting SWOT analysis for macro-level social work initiatives involves extending the application of this strategic tool to address broader societal challenges and systemic issues. In this context, the focus shifts from individual case management to influencing large-scale policies, programs, and community interventions. Practitioners utilize SWOT analysis to assess the strengths, weaknesses, opportunities, and threats inherent in macro-level social work initiatives, such as advocacy campaigns, policy reforms, and community development projects. This adaptation allows social workers to leverage their understanding of the broader socio-political landscape, incorporating systemic perspectives into the strategic planning process. By tailoring SWOT analysis to macro-level contexts, practitioners can contribute to transformative changes in social structures, fostering sustainable impact and positive outcomes on a larger societal scale.

Evaluating the Impact of SWOT Analysis on Fieldwork Outcomes: Evaluating the impact of SWOT analysis on fieldwork outcomes involves a comprehensive assessment of how strategic planning, informed by SWOT insights, translates into tangible and positive changes in social work practice. This rigorous examination delves into the practical effectiveness of implementing action plans derived from SWOT analysis, assessing their real-world influence on client interventions, case management, and broader social work initiatives. Through this evaluative process, practitioners gain a nuanced understanding of the concrete results and transformative shifts achieved at both micro- and macro-levels. The analysis serves as a crucial feedback mechanism, enabling practitioners to fine-tune their application of SWOT analysis and ensuring its ongoing relevance and its role in contributing meaningfully to positive fieldwork outcomes.

Challenges and Considerations in Applying SWOT Analysis in Fieldwork: Applying SWOT analysis in fieldwork is not without its challenges and considerations, necessitating a thoughtful approach for its effective implementation. One key challenge involves the potential oversimplification of complex issues, as SWOT analysis tends to distill multifaceted situations into four categories: strengths, weaknesses, opportunities, and threats. Practitioners need to be mindful of the nuanced and interconnected nature of social work dynamics to avoid overlooking intricacies. Additionally, the subjective nature of identifying and interpreting factors within each category can introduce bias, requiring a reflective and collaborative effort to ensure a comprehensive analysis. Another consideration involves the dynamic nature of social work environments, where factors can evolve rapidly. As such, practitioners must regularly revisit and reassess the SWOT analysis to account for changes in the field. Despite these challenges, acknowledging and addressing them enhances the utility of SWOT analysis as a dynamic and adaptive tool in the realm of social work fieldwork.

Collaborative SWOT Analysis: Involving Field Instructors and Peers: Collaborative SWOT analysis in the context of fieldwork proves to be a valuable strategy, emphasizing the importance of involving field instructors and peers in the analytical process. This collaborative approach fosters a comprehensive understanding of the fieldwork environment, drawing on diverse perspectives and experiences. Field instructors, with their wealth of practical knowledge, contribute valuable insights into the strengths, weaknesses, opportunities, and threats present in the field. Peers, on the other hand, bring a fresh and varied viewpoint, enriching the analysis with different interpretations and considerations. The collaborative nature of this approach not only enhances the depth and accuracy of the SWOT analysis but also promotes a shared learning experience. Moreover, involving both field instructors and peers creates a supportive environment for social work students, encouraging mutual growth and the development of effective strategies for addressing challenges and leveraging opportunities in the field.

10.5 SWOT Analysis Examples

10.5.1 Example 1: Field Practice in a Hospital Setting in Canada

In the context of field practice within a Canadian hospital setting, applying the SWOT analysis brings to light the specific nuances and considerations relevant to the Canadian healthcare landscape.

Strengths: In a Canadian hospital, strengths may encompass a robust universal healthcare system, fostering inclusivity and accessibility to medical services for all citizens. Social work practitioners benefit from a healthcare infrastructure that values collaborative interdisciplinary approaches, providing an environment where patients can access comprehensive care. The integration of social work within this system allows practitioners to address the social determinants of health effectively.

Weaknesses: Weaknesses in this setting might include potential gaps in mental health services, resource constraints, and variations in social work roles across different provinces. Social work practitioners in Canadian hospitals may face challenges in addressing mental health issues due to resource limitations, and the variability in provincial policies could lead to inconsistencies in the delivery of social work services.

Opportunities: Opportunities within the Canadian hospital setting may involve active participation in community-based health promotion programs, collaboration with Indigenous health initiatives, and engagement in research to enhance the effectiveness of social work interventions. The Canadian healthcare context encourages social work practitioners to contribute to community well-being beyond the hospital walls, aligning with national health priorities.

Threats: Threats could include potential budget cuts, evolving healthcare policies, and the strain on mental health resources. Social work practitioners must be aware of these threats and advocate for adequate funding, actively participate in policy discussions, and develop strategies to cope with increased demands on mental health services.

This tailored SWOT analysis for a hospital setting in Canada emphasizes the importance of contextual considerations, enabling social work practitioners to navigate the intricacies of the Canadian healthcare system effectively.

10.5.2 Example 2: Field Practice in a Community Development-Based Organization in Mexico

In the context of field practice within a community development-based organization in Mexico, applying the SWOT analysis reveals specific dynamics and opportunities inherent to the Mexican socio-cultural landscape.

Strengths: Within a Mexican community development organization, strengths may include vibrant community engagement, cultural richness, and strong community bonds. Social work practitioners benefit from a deeply ingrained sense of community, allowing for effective collaboration and cultural sensitivity in addressing local issues.

Weaknesses: Weaknesses might involve economic disparities, limited resources, and potential cultural misunderstandings. Social work practitioners could face challenges in addressing economic inequalities within the community and may need to navigate resource constraints that impact the scope of their interventions.

Opportunities: Opportunities within this setting could involve leveraging local cultural practices for community empowerment, facilitating skill-building initiatives, and collaborating with local authorities for sustainable development. Social work practitioners in Mexico have the chance to align their interventions with community values and traditions, fostering a more resonant impact.

Threats: Threats may include external economic pressures, shifts in cultural norms, and potential resistance to external interventions. Social work practitioners should be mindful of external factors that may influence community dynamics and work collaboratively to ensure that interventions align with local perspectives and needs.

This SWOT analysis tailored to a community development-based organization in Mexico underscores the importance of understanding the unique socio-cultural context, enabling social work practitioners to craft interventions that are culturally competent and responsive to the community's specific needs.

10.5.3 Example 3: Field Practice in a Group Work-Based Gender Empowerment Organization in India

In the realm of gender empowerment organizations in India, conducting a SWOT analysis unveils distinctive features that shape the field practice landscape.

Strengths: Strengths within a group work-based gender empowerment organization in India may encompass a rich tapestry of cultural diversity, strong community ties, and a historical context of grassroots movements for gender equality. Social work practitioners benefit from the wealth of cultural insights and community-driven initiatives, fostering impactful gender empowerment interventions.

Weaknesses: Weaknesses could involve deeply ingrained gender norms, economic disparities, and limited accessibility to education and resources for women. Social work practitioners might grapple with challenging societal attitudes toward gender roles and the need to address barriers hindering women's access to education and economic opportunities.

Opportunities: Opportunities in this setting may revolve around advocacy for legal reforms, educational initiatives for women, and the cultivation of grassroots movements. Social work practitioners have the chance to collaborate with local communities, policymakers, and grassroots activists to affect positive change and challenge systemic barriers to gender equality.

Threats: Threats may include conservative societal attitudes, resistance to gender equality initiatives, and potential backlash against empowerment efforts. Social work practitioners need to navigate these challenges sensitively, acknowledging and addressing the societal resistance that may impede progress in gender empowerment.

This SWOT analysis tailored to a group work-based gender empowerment organization in India underscores the need for social work practitioners to navigate complex cultural and societal dynamics, emphasizing the importance of collaborative efforts to achieve meaningful gender empowerment outcomes.

Review Questions

1. How does exploring diverse agency environments contribute to the effectiveness of social work practice?
2. What role does understanding unique agency dynamics and structures play in successful fieldwork experiences?
3. How can SWOT analysis be applied as a strategic tool in social work fieldwork situations?
4. Why is the integration of SWOT analysis crucial for adapting to and addressing challenges within agencies?
5. Provide an example from the SWOT analysis in fieldwork settings and explain how it influenced decision-making and interventions.

Multiple Choice Questions

1. What is the primary purpose of exploring various agency environments in social work field practice?

   (a) To find employment opportunities
   (b) To build rapport with colleagues

(c) To enhance the effectiveness of social work practice
(d) To gather information for personal interest

2. Why is understanding unique agency dynamics important for social work practitioners?

(a) It helps in avoiding workplace conflicts.
(b) It contributes to the success of fieldwork experiences.
(c) It is a requirement for professional certification.
(d) It ensures personal career advancement.

3. In what way does SWOT analysis contribute to effective fieldwork situations in social work?

(a) By assessing internal and external factors influencing practice
(b) By identifying personal strengths and weaknesses only
(c) By analyzing agency policies and procedures
(d) By creating promotional materials for the agency

4. What is the main benefit of applying SWOT analysis in fieldwork practice?

(a) It ensures financial success for social work agencies.
(b) It helps practitioners avoid challenges and difficulties.
(c) It provides a systematic approach to decision-making.
(d) It is primarily used for academic research purposes.

References

Harrikari, T., Romakkaniemi, M., Tiitinen, L., & Ovaskainen, S. (2021). Pandemic and social work: Exploring Finnish social workers' experiences through a SWOT analysis. *The British Journal of Social Work, 51*(5), 1644–1662.

Raines, J. C. (2006). SWOT! A strategic plan for school social work in the twenty-first century. *School Social Work Journal, 31*(3), 132–150.

Westhues, A., Lafrance, J., & Schmidt, G. (2001). A SWOT analysis of social work education. *Social Work Education, 20*(1), 35–56.

Chapter 11
Working Within Systems: Applications of Assessment Planning Interventions

Learning Objectives
After reading this chapter, you will be able to:

- Demonstrate effective engagement skills with clients and their families
- Apply group work strategies for effective engagement with diverse groups
- Implement community engagement techniques for collaborative work with local communities
- Analyze policies to understand their impact on individuals and communities
- Navigate political systems and structures to advocate for social change
- Create a comprehensive case record, including client information, home visits, and problem assessments
- Develop intervention plans that encompass a range of supports and services for clients

11.1 Engaging with Clients and Their Families

Initiating meaningful connections with clients and their families is a cornerstone of effective social work practice. This section underscores the essential skills and strategies crucial for social work students during the engagement phase of field practice. The process involves building rapport, active listening, and establishing trust, which are foundational elements that pave the way for collaborative relationships.

Understanding Cultural Sensitivity: In the multicultural landscape of the United Kingdom, a social work student engaging with a family of immigrants learns to navigate diverse cultural norms. Sensitivity to the impact of social policies, such as immigration laws, becomes imperative. Similarly, in China, where Confucian values influence family dynamics, respecting hierarchical structures is essential for effective engagement.

M. R. Islam, *Fieldwork in Social Work*,
https://doi.org/10.1007/978-3-031-56683-7_11

Ecological Systems Perspective: The ecological systems emphasize the interconnectedness of individual, family, community, and societal factors. In China, with its collectivist values, students recognize the integral role of family and community in an individual's life. Contrastingly, in the UK, the examination of how social policies influence families, particularly in cases of immigration, adds depth to the understanding of engagement.

Ethical Considerations and Informed Consent: Ethical considerations take center stage, emphasizing the maintenance of confidentiality, informed consent, and the principles of autonomy and beneficence. Case studies illuminate ethical dilemmas, allowing students to navigate complexities. For instance, understanding and addressing mental health stigma in the context of Chinese culture or ensuring the rights of immigrant families in the United Kingdom are key considerations.

Initial Assessments and Cultural Competence: This covers techniques for initial assessments, urging a culturally competent approach. In China, this might involve navigating cultural nuances related to mental health stigma. Conversely, in the United Kingdom, understanding the diverse needs of immigrant families is essential for a comprehensive assessment.

Reflective Practice and Cultural Humility: Reflective exercises encourage self-awareness and cultural humility. Students critically examine biases and assumptions, fostering a deeper understanding of the impact of their identity on the client engagement process. Through reflection, social work students enhance their ability to engage authentically and respectfully with clients from diverse backgrounds.

Collaborative Approaches in Family Engagement: Effective engagement extends to collaborative approaches with families. In China, where family honor is highly regarded, involving the extended family in decision-making processes can be pivotal. In the United Kingdom, acknowledging and respecting diverse family structures, including LGBTQ+ families, underscores the importance of inclusive practices.

Trauma-Informed Engagement: The trauma-informed engagement recognizes the prevalence of trauma in diverse client populations. In both China and the United Kingdom, understanding historical and cultural contexts is crucial for providing trauma-informed care. Students explore approaches to create safe spaces and mitigate potential retraumatization during the engagement process.

Case Examples: Real-world case examples from China and the United Kingdom bring theoretical concepts to life. In China, a case involving intergenerational conflicts due to societal changes showcases the importance of adapting traditional practices to modern contexts. In the United Kingdom, a case involving an immigrant family navigating the complexities of the healthcare system illustrates the intersectionality of cultural and systemic factors in engagement.

By seamlessly integrating theoretical frameworks with practical examples, this equips social work students with the skills and knowledge needed to initiate culturally competent engagements. Whether navigating the intricate social landscape of China or addressing the multicultural dynamics of the United Kingdom, students gain a holistic understanding of client engagement in diverse contexts.

11.2 Engaging with Groups

Engaging with groups within Systems: Applications of Assessment, Planning, and Interventions delve into the crucial aspect of engaging with groups within the field of social work. Recognizing the power of collective dynamics, this section focuses on the various dimensions, methods, and ethical considerations involved in working with groups.

Understanding Group Dynamics: Social work often involves addressing issues and fostering change at the group level. Understanding group dynamics is foundational to effective practice. Social work students explore the complexities of how individuals interact within a group, the emergence of roles, power dynamics, communication patterns, and the influence of group norms. By grasping these dynamics, practitioners can navigate the challenges and opportunities inherent in group work.

Types of Groups in Social Work: This section introduces students to the diverse range of groups encountered in social work practice. From support groups and therapy groups to educational groups and task-oriented groups, social work students learn to differentiate the purposes and structures of various group formats. Understanding the unique goals and dynamics of each group type is essential for tailoring interventions to meet specific needs.

Group Assessment and Planning: Social work students are guided through the process of assessing groups and identifying strengths, challenges, and goals. Group assessments involve understanding the composition of the group, its purpose, and the contextual factors influencing its dynamics. Planning interventions for groups requires a nuanced approach, considering the collective needs and aspirations of group members.

Intervention Strategies for Groups: This section explores a spectrum of intervention strategies designed to address the identified goals of a group. Social work students learn about facilitating group discussions, employing psychoeducational techniques, promoting skill-building exercises, and utilizing expressive therapies. The emphasis is on creating a safe and inclusive environment that encourages active participation and collaboration among group members.

Leadership and Facilitation Skills: Effective group work demands strong leadership and facilitation skills. Social work students develop an understanding of different leadership styles, the role of the facilitator in guiding group processes, and the importance of balancing structure and flexibility. Learning to manage conflicts, encourage participation, and foster a sense of cohesion is a vital skill for successful group engagement.

Ethical Considerations in Group Work: Ethics play a central role in group work, and this section highlights the ethical considerations unique to working with groups. Topics include confidentiality within the group setting, managing dual relationships, addressing power differentials, and ensuring the well-being of all group members. Social work students engage in discussions and case studies that illuminate the ethical complexities of group interventions.

Challenges and Opportunities in Group Work: Social work students explore the challenges inherent in group work, such as resistance, conflicts, and issues related to diversity. Simultaneously, they recognize the opportunities for mutual support, shared learning, and the potential for transformative group experiences. Strategies for overcoming the challenges and maximizing the benefits of group work are discussed.

Evaluation and Continuous Improvement: The section concludes with a focus on evaluating the effectiveness of group interventions and the importance of continuous improvement. Social work students learn to assess the impact of their interventions, solicit feedback from group members, and make adjustments to enhance the overall experience and outcomes.

11.3 Engaging with Community

In the realm of social work, engaging with the community is a fundamental and dynamic aspect that goes beyond individual and group interventions. This explores the intricacies of community engagement, emphasizing the significance of understanding, collaborating with, and empowering communities to address social issues and promote positive change.

Understanding Community Dynamics: Social work students delve into the complexities of community dynamics, recognizing that communities are diverse, interconnected, and shaped by historical, cultural, and structural factors. Understanding the unique strengths, challenges, and aspirations of a community is essential for effective social work practice. This helps to explore the importance of cultural competence, contextual understanding, and the recognition of community assets.

Community Assessment and Mapping: Engaging with communities requires a comprehensive assessment of their needs, resources, and systems. Social work students learn to conduct community assessments, employing methods such as asset mapping, stakeholder analysis, and understanding community demographics. The goal is to gain insights into the social, economic, and environmental factors that impact community well-being.

Collaborative Planning and Capacity Building: Collaboration is a key theme in community engagement. Social work students explore strategies for building collaborative partnerships within communities, involving residents, organizations, and other stakeholders. The focus is on identifying and enhancing the existing capacities within the community to address challenges and capitalize on opportunities for positive change.

Community-Based Interventions: Social work students should know a variety of community-based interventions designed to address identified needs. From community organizing and development to advocacy and policy change, students learn how to mobilize resources and empower community members to actively participate in the decision-making processes that affect their lives.

Advocacy and Social Justice in Community Work: Engaging with the community inherently involves advocating for social justice. Social work students explore the role of advocacy in addressing systemic issues, promoting equity, and challenging oppressive structures. This emphasizes the importance of social work practitioners serving as advocates for marginalized and disenfranchised communities.

Ethical Considerations in Community Engagement: Ethics play a crucial role in community engagement, and social work students examine the ethical considerations unique to working at the community level. Topics include ensuring community participation, maintaining cultural sensitivity, and navigating power dynamics within community partnerships. Ethical decision-making within the broader context of social justice is a key focus.

Challenges and Opportunities in Community Engagement: Social work students critically analyze the challenges and opportunities associated with community engagement. Challenges may include addressing diverse perspectives, managing conflicts, and overcoming barriers to participation. Opportunities lie in fostering community empowerment, building social capital, and creating sustainable solutions to community issues.

Evaluation of Community Initiatives: Social work students learn to assess the impact of community interventions, measure community outcomes, and use feedback to adapt and improve strategies over time. The goal is to create sustainable, community-driven solutions that foster long-term positive change.

Engaging with the community is a cornerstone of social work practice. This equips social work students with the knowledge, skills, and ethical considerations needed to effectively engage with and contribute to the well-being of communities. Through a comprehensive understanding of community dynamics, collaborative planning, and advocacy, social work practitioners can play a vital role in promoting social justice and enhancing the resilience of diverse communities.

11.4 Engaging with Policy Assessment

Social work's impact extends beyond individual and community levels to influencing broader societal structures through policy engagement (Morley et al., 2019). This explores the role of social work in policy assessment. This section emphasizes the importance of understanding, analyzing, and influencing policies to address systemic issues and promote social justice.

Understanding Policy Dynamics: Social work students delve into the complexities of policy dynamics, recognizing that policies shape the social, economic, and political landscape. Understanding how policies are formulated, implemented, and evaluated is crucial for social work practitioners aiming to address the root causes of social issues.

Policy Assessment Methods: Engaging with policy assessment involves a systematic examination of existing policies and proposals. Social work students learn methods for policy analysis, including examining the historical context, assessing the intended and unintended consequences, and evaluating the equity and justice implications. Examples of policy assessment tools and frameworks are explored.

Global Examples of Policy Impact: Drawing on global examples, social work students analyze instances where policies have had significant social impact. This may include examining policies related to healthcare, education, poverty alleviation, and human rights. Case studies from different countries showcase how policies can shape social conditions and influence the well-being of diverse populations.

Advocacy for Policy Change: Policy engagement goes hand in hand with advocacy. Social work students explore strategies for advocating policy change, whether at the local, national, or international levels. This emphasizes the importance of social workers serving as advocates for policies that promote social justice, equity, and the well-being of marginalized populations.

Ethical Considerations in Policy Engagement: Ethical considerations are paramount in policy engagement. Social work students examine ethical dilemmas related to policy advocacy, ensuring that policies uphold human rights, social justice, and inclusivity. The ethical responsibility of social workers to advocate for policies that address systemic inequalities is a central focus.

Challenges in Policy Engagement: Social work students critically analyze the challenges inherent in policy engagement. These challenges may include navigating political landscapes, addressing conflicting interests, and overcoming barriers to policy change. Real-world examples illuminate how social workers can navigate these challenges while maintaining ethical integrity.

Global Perspectives on Policy: Social work students explore how policies vary across countries and cultures, impacting populations differently. Comparative analyses highlight the importance of cultural competence and sensitivity in understanding the global implications of policy decisions.

Policy Evaluation and Reform: Social work students learn to assess the effectiveness of policies, measure their impact on diverse populations, and advocate for reforms that align with social work values and principles.

By understanding policy dynamics, advocating for change, and navigating ethical considerations, social work students are equipped to contribute to the development of just and equitable policies that address the root causes of social issues at systemic levels.

11.5 Engaging with Political System and Structure

This section recognizes that political contexts significantly influence social issues and emphasizes the importance of social work practitioners understanding, navigating, and actively participating in political processes to effect positive change.

Understanding Political Systems: Social work students begin by developing a foundational understanding of political systems (Delgado, 1999). This includes exploring different political structures, such as democracies, authoritarian regimes, and hybrid systems. Understanding the distribution of power, decision-making processes, and the role of various actors within political systems is crucial for effective engagement.

Political Advocacy and Social Justice: Political engagement in social work is inherently tied to advocacy for social justice. Social work students explore strategies for advocating within political systems to address systemic inequalities, promote human rights, and advance the well-being of marginalized populations.

Lobbying and Coalition Building: Practical skills in political engagement are a focus of this section. Social work students learn about lobbying techniques, coalition building, and how to effectively communicate with policymakers. They will deal with case studies and examples illustrating instances where social workers have successfully influenced political decisions to benefit the communities they serve.

Intersectionality in Political Engagement: The intersectionality of social issues is explored in the context of political engagement. Social work students analyze how factors such as race, gender, socioeconomic status, and other identities intersect with political structures to create unique challenges and opportunities. Understanding these intersections informs more nuanced and effective political advocacy.

Ethical Considerations in Political Engagement: Ethics play a central role in political engagement. Social work students critically examine the ethical dimensions of participating in political processes, considering issues such as transparency, accountability, and the potential for unintended consequences. Balancing advocacy with ethical principles is crucial for maintaining the integrity of social work practice.

Challenges and Opportunities in Political Engagement: Political engagement is not without challenges, and this section critically analyzes the obstacles social work practitioners may face. Challenges may include navigating partisan divides, addressing power imbalances, and overcoming barriers to entry into political processes. Opportunities lie in leveraging political platforms to amplify the voices of marginalized communities.

Global Perspectives on Political Engagement: Social work students explore how political systems vary internationally and examine instances where political engagement has led to positive social change on a global scale. Comparative analyses offer insights into the diverse strategies employed by social workers in different political contexts.

Evaluation of Political Advocacy: Social work students learn to assess the impact of their political engagement, measure outcomes, and adapt strategies based on the evolving political landscape. This evaluative approach ensures that political advocacy remains an effective tool for advancing social justice.

By understanding political contexts, advocating for social justice, and navigating the complexities of political processes, social work practitioners can contribute to shaping political decisions that promote equity, justice, and the well-being of diverse populations.

11.6 Structure of Case Record: An Example

A structured case record is a foundational tool in social work practice, facilitating comprehensive assessment, intervention, and collaboration within larger systems (Table 11.1).

Here's a detailed breakdown of the components and their significance within a case record structure:

11.6.1 Client and Family Information

This section provides essential identification details for the client and their family members. It includes contact information, birth dates, and emergency contact details. Clear identification ensures accurate communication and tracking.

Family Structure*:* Here, the composition of the client's family is outlined, including family members' relationships and demographic information. This helps practitioners understand the client's support network and context.

Client and Family Study: The "Client and Family Study" section of the case record is a critical component that provides a comprehensive understanding of the client and their family's dynamics, circumstances, and challenges. This thorough assessment informs the development of tailored interventions and strategies that address the client's unique needs within the larger context of their family and community. Here's an expanded explanation of each aspect within the "Client and Family Study" section:

Table 11.1 Summary of the structure of a case process record

Section	Components	Significance
Client and family information	Identification details, family structure	Accurate communication and understanding of support network
Client and family study	Economic, social, psychological, cultural, political assessment	Tailored interventions and comprehensive understanding
Home visit	Visit date, observations, family interactions	Holistic understanding of client's living environment
Problem assessment	Presenting issues, underlying causes	Focused and client-centered interventions
Interventions	Supports and services, timeline	Action-oriented and client-centered approach
Follow-up	Follow-up dates, progress update	Continuous assessment and client engagement
Evaluation	Progress review, outcomes	Informed decision-making and quality improvement

Source: Author

Economic Assessment

Purpose: This assessment focuses on understanding the client's financial situation and its impact on their overall well-being.

Components: Gather information about the client's sources of income, employment status, expenses, debts, and any financial support from family members or social services.

Significance: An economic assessment helps identify financial stressors that may contribute to the client's challenges, guiding the development of interventions related to economic stability and resource access.

Social Assessment

Purpose: The social assessment aims to explore the client's social connections, support systems, and community engagement.

Components: Assess the quality and extent of the client's social network, relationships, and interactions with friends, family, neighbors, and community groups.

Significance: Understanding the client's social context helps identify potential sources of support and collaboration. It also sheds light on any social isolation or challenges in building meaningful connections.

Psychological Assessment

Purpose: This assessment delves into the client's mental and emotional well-being, identifying factors that may impact their mental health.

Components: Assess the client's emotional state, coping mechanisms, any history of mental health concerns, and the presence of stressors or triggers.

Significance: A psychological assessment informs interventions aimed at enhancing the client's emotional resilience and promoting mental health. It also helps identify the need for specialized mental health services.

Cultural Assessment

Purpose: This assessment examines the client's cultural background, beliefs, and values, recognizing the influence of culture on their experiences and needs.

Components: Explore the client's cultural identity, religious affiliations, traditional practices, and any cultural challenges they may face.

Significance: A cultural assessment ensures that interventions are culturally sensitive and respectful. It helps avoid cultural misunderstandings and promotes a client-centered approach.

Political Assessment

Purpose: The political assessment involves understanding the client's engagement with political and advocacy activities.

Components: Explore whether the client is involved in community organizations, advocacy groups, or any activities related to social or political change.

Significance: A political assessment provides insights into the client's active participation in community and social change efforts. It informs interventions that align with their values and aspirations.

Application of the Client and Family Study

The information gathered through the client and family study informs the creation of holistic intervention plans that address multiple dimensions of the client's life. Practitioners can tailor interventions to target specific challenges identified in each assessment area, promoting a comprehensive approach to client care. The client and family study also guides practitioners in recognizing potential interactions between different aspects of the client's life, allowing for more effective interventions.

11.6.2 Home Visit

The "Home Visit" section of the case record involves documenting observations and interactions during a visit to the client's living environment. Conducting home visits is a valuable practice in social work as it provides firsthand insights into the conditions in which the client lives, offering a deeper understanding of their context and challenges. Here's a comprehensive look at the components and significance of the "Home Visit" section.

Purpose of Home Visit

The primary purpose of a home visit is to gain a more holistic understanding of the client's living conditions, family dynamics, and the environment in which they navigate their challenges.

Home visits allow social work practitioners to observe aspects that may not be apparent in office settings, such as cleanliness, safety, family interactions, and potential stressors.

Components of Home Visit Documentation

Visit Date and Time: Document the date and time of the home visit to provide context for the observations.

Observations: Record detailed observations of the living environment, including the physical condition of the home, cleanliness, organization, safety measures, and any visible signs of stress or challenges.

Family Interactions: Document interactions between family members present during the visit. Observe the dynamics, communication styles, and level of support and cohesion within the family.

Client Interaction: Note the client's demeanor, mood, and reactions during the visit. Assess their comfort level and any concerns they may express.

Physical Environment: Describe the physical surroundings, such as the layout of the home, available amenities, and any factors that may influence the client's well-being.

Personal Artifacts: Take note of personal items, decorations, or mementos that provide insights into the client's interests, values, and personal history.

Significance of Home Visits

Contextual Understanding: Home visits provide a more comprehensive understanding of the client's context, which is crucial for tailoring interventions that address their unique challenges.

Safety Assessment: Observations during a home visit can identify safety hazards or concerns that may impact the client's well-being.

Family Dynamics: Direct observations of family interactions shed light on the family's dynamics, communication patterns, and potential sources of support or stress.

Cultural Insights: The physical environment may reflect the client's cultural background and values, offering insights into their identity and preferences.

Holistic Assessment: Home visits complement other assessments and enrich the overall assessment of the client's needs and strengths.

Application of Home Visits

Home visits are particularly valuable when clients face challenges that are intertwined with their living conditions, family dynamics, or safety concerns. Practitioners can identify environmental factors that may contribute to the client's challenges and strategize interventions that address these factors. Home visits support the creation of interventions that are contextually relevant and client-centered, promoting a more accurate and effective approach to care.

11.6.3 Problem Assessment

The "Problem Assessment" section of the case record focuses on identifying and understanding the client's presenting challenges or issues. This assessment serves as the foundation for developing targeted interventions that address the root causes of these challenges. Here's a comprehensive breakdown of the components and significance of the "Problem Assessment" section.

Purpose of Problem Assessment

The primary purpose of the problem assessment is to clearly define and analyze the challenges/problems that the client is facing. This assessment sets the stage for the development of interventions that are specific and relevant to the client's needs.

Components of Problem Assessment

Presenting Issues: Clearly articulate the challenges that the client is currently experiencing. This could include emotional, psychological, social, economic, or environmental difficulties.

Underlying Causes: Explore the factors that contribute to or exacerbate the identified challenges. These underlying causes provide insights into the root of the issues and guide intervention strategies.

Strengths and Resources: Highlight the client's strengths, assets, and resources that can be leveraged to address the challenges. This is an essential aspect of a strengths-based approach to intervention.

Significance of Problem Assessment

Focused Intervention: A well-defined problem assessment guides practitioners in tailoring interventions that directly address the identified challenges, optimizing the chances of positive outcomes.

Understanding Complexity: Analyzing the underlying causes helps practitioners understand the complexity of the client's situation, which in turn informs the choice of intervention strategies.

Strengths-Based Approach: Recognizing the client's strengths empowers them and contributes to their active participation in the intervention process.

Ethical Decision-Making: Problem assessment helps practitioners prioritize interventions that align with the client's well-being and ethical considerations.

Application of Problem Assessment

Problem assessments are central to initial client meetings and assessments. They lay the groundwork for a deeper exploration of the client's needs. Problem assessments are essential when clients present with multifaceted challenges that require a targeted and comprehensive approach. Practitioners use problem assessments to identify the areas in which the client requires support, ensuring that interventions are focused and relevant.

11.6.4 Interventions: Supports and Services

The "Interventions" section of the case record outlines the specific strategies, supports, and services that social work practitioners employ to address the challenges identified in the problem assessment. This section serves as a roadmap for guiding client-centered interventions that promote positive change and improved well-being. Here's an in-depth look at the components and significance of the "Interventions" section.

Purpose of Interventions

The primary purpose of interventions is to provide practical and targeted solutions to the challenges identified in the problem assessment. Interventions are action-oriented steps that practitioners take to support the client's progress.

Components of Interventions

Supports and Services: List the supports, resources, and services that will be provided to the client. These could include counseling, educational workshops, referrals to community programs, financial assistance, and more.

Timeline: Specify the timeline for each intervention or service. This helps track progress and ensures that interventions are implemented within appropriate timeframes.

Responsibility: Identify the parties responsible for implementing each intervention. This could include the social worker, the client, external agencies, or a combination of stakeholders.

Significance of Interventions
Action-Oriented: Interventions transform assessment findings into practical steps that address the client's challenges, promoting proactive and goal-oriented strategies.

Client-Centered: Tailored interventions ensure that the client's individual needs, strengths, and preferences are taken into account, enhancing engagement and motivation.

Collaborative Approach: Involving the client in the development of interventions promotes a collaborative partnership, empowering them to actively participate in their well-being.

Holistic Support: Interventions encompass a range of supports and services that address different aspects of the client's life, promoting holistic growth and change.

Application of Interventions
Interventions are implemented following the problem assessment and are customized to align with the client's unique needs and circumstances. They are an essential component of the client's care plan and are discussed and agreed upon collaboratively with the client. Interventions are regularly reviewed and adjusted as needed to ensure that they remain relevant and effective.

11.6.5 Follow-Up

The "Follow-Up" section of the case record is a critical component that documents the ongoing progress, adjustments, and outcomes of the interventions and services provided to the client. This section ensures that practitioners can track the effectiveness of their interventions, make necessary modifications, and continue to support the client's journey toward positive change. Here's a comprehensive overview of the components and significance of the "Follow-Up" section.

Purpose of Follow-Up
The primary purpose of the follow-up section is to monitor and evaluate the client's progress since the implementation of interventions. It ensures that interventions remain aligned with the client's changing needs and circumstances.

Components of Follow-Up
Follow-Up Dates: Document the dates of follow-up appointments, evaluations, or check-ins. These dates provide a chronological record of the client's journey.

Progress Update: Describe the client's progress since the last intervention or follow-up. Include any positive changes, challenges faced, and any setbacks experienced.

Adjustments: Note any adjustments made to the interventions based on the client's evolving needs or changes in circumstances.

Future Goals: Discuss and set future goals with the client. Outline the steps and interventions that will be implemented to achieve these goals.

Significance of Follow-Up

Continuous Assessment: Follow-up ensures that practitioners have a real-time understanding of the client's progress and can adapt interventions as needed.

Accountability: Practitioners remain accountable for monitoring the impact of interventions and making necessary adjustments to improve outcomes.

Client Engagement: Regular follow-up appointments engage the client in ongoing discussions about their progress, empowering them to actively participate in their growth.

Evidence-Based Practice: Follow-up helps practitioners evaluate the effectiveness of interventions, allowing them to refine their approaches based on evidence and outcomes.

Application of Follow-Up

Follow-up appointments are scheduled at regular intervals to coincide with the timeline of interventions. Practitioners engage in open and honest conversations with the client about their progress, challenges, and achievements. Follow-up appointments provide opportunities for practitioners and clients to collaborate on adjustments to interventions and set new goals.

11.6.6 Evaluation

The "Evaluation" section of the case record provides a reflective assessment of the client's overall progress, the effectiveness of interventions, and the outcomes achieved. This section is crucial for practitioners to gauge the impact of their work, make informed decisions, and continually enhance their practice. Here is a comprehensive breakdown of the components and significance of the "Evaluation" section.

Purpose of Evaluation

The primary purpose of the evaluation section is to critically assess the outcomes of the interventions and services provided to the client. It helps practitioners determine the success of their efforts and informs future decision-making.

Components of Evaluation

Progress Review: Reflect on the client's journey from the initial problem assessment to the present. Summarize the progress made, challenges overcome, and improvements observed.

Outcomes: Evaluate the outcomes achieved about the goals set during the intervention process. Document whether these goals were met and if there were any unexpected positive outcomes.

Intervention Effectiveness: Assess the effectiveness of the interventions implemented. Analyze whether the chosen strategies were appropriate, relevant, and impactful.

Lessons Learned: Reflect on the strengths and limitations of the interventions and the overall approach. Identify lessons learned and insights gained for future practice.

Significance of Evaluation

Informed Decision-Making: Evaluation provides practitioners with evidence-based insights to assess whether the interventions achieved their intended outcomes.

Quality Improvement: Through evaluation, practitioners can identify areas for improvement, refine their intervention strategies, and enhance their practice over time.

Accountability: Evaluation demonstrates accountability to both the client and the larger systems by showing the value and impact of social work interventions.

Client-Centered Approach: Evaluation ensures that interventions remain client-centered, adaptive, and responsive to the client's evolving needs.

Application of Evaluation

Evaluation occurs at various points throughout the intervention process, including at the end of each intervention cycle or when goals are achieved. Practitioners collaborate with clients to assess their perception of progress and outcomes, aligning evaluation with the client's perspective. Lessons learned from evaluation contribute to practitioners' professional growth and inform their approach to future cases.

11.7 How to Write a Referral Letter in Field Work

Writing a referral letter is a vital skill for social work practitioners as it facilitates effective communication and collaboration between different service providers and agencies. This section provides a step-by-step example of how to write a referral letter, including when, why, and how to initiate the process.

When to Write a Referral Letter

Referral letters are written when the client's needs extend beyond the scope of the practitioner's expertise or the agency's services. A referral is warranted when the client requires specialized assistance, resources, or interventions that another agency or professional can provide more effectively.

Why Write a Referral Letter

- Referral letters ensure that the client receives appropriate and targeted support from professionals who possess the required expertise.
- Collaboration through referral letters enhances the client's well-being by addressing their unique needs and challenges comprehensively.
- Referral letters contribute to a coordinated and holistic approach to client care within the larger systems of support.

How to Write a Referral Letter: An Example

Date: [Date of writing the letter]

To: [Name of the Receiving Agency/Professional]

Address: [Address of the Receiving Agency/Professional]

Dear [Recipient's Name],

Introduction

I am writing to refer one of my clients, [Client's Name], to your esteemed agency/professional practice. I have been working with [Client's Name] for [duration of working relationship], and based on our assessments, I believe that their current needs require specialized expertise that your agency/professional practice can provide.

Background

[Provide a brief overview of the client's situation and challenges that have prompted the need for a referral. Include any relevant background information that helps the recipient understand the context.]

Specific Needs

Based on my assessment, [Client's Name] is facing challenges related to [describe the specific challenges, needs, or issues]. I believe that your agency/professional practice's expertise in [mention the specific area of expertise] will be instrumental in addressing these challenges effectively.

Why Referral is Appropriate

It is my professional opinion that [Client's Name] would benefit greatly from the specialized services and interventions that your agency/professional practice offers. Your expertise in [mention the relevant expertise, e.g., trauma therapy, addiction counseling, and financial planning] aligns well with the specific challenges that [Client's Name] is facing.

Client Consent

I have discussed the potential referral with [Client's Name] and they have expressed openness to exploring the support and resources that your agency/professional practice can provide.

Request for Collaboration

I kindly request your agency/professional practice's assistance in providing [Client's Name] with the appropriate interventions and support to address their unique challenges. I believe that our collaboration will contribute significantly to [Client's Name]'s overall well-being and progress.

Contact Information

Please feel free to contact me at [Your Contact Information] if you require any additional information or clarification regarding the referral. I look forward to our collaboration in supporting [Client's Name]'s journey toward positive change.

Thank you for your dedication to providing valuable services to our community.

Sincerely,

[Your Name]

[Your Title]

[Your Contact Information]

A well-written referral letter is a key tool for social work practitioners to ensure that clients receive the specialized support they need. By adhering to this example and tailoring the letter to the specific circumstances of the client and receiving agency/professional, practitioners can facilitate effective collaboration, seamless communication, and comprehensive care within the broader systems of support.

11.8 How to Write a Termination Letter in Field Work

Writing a termination letter is a crucial step in the social work process when the professional relationship between the practitioner and the client is coming to an end. This section provides a step-by-step guide on how to write a termination letter, including when, why, and how to initiate the process.

When to Write a Termination Letter

Termination letters are written when the goals of the intervention have been met and the client's needs have been addressed effectively.

The termination process may also be initiated when the client is transitioning to another level of care, relocating, or no longer requires the services provided by the current practitioner.

Why Write a Termination Letter

Termination letters serve as a formal and respectful way to conclude the professional relationship between the social worker and the client.

These letters provide closure and celebrate the progress made by the client, emphasizing their strengths and accomplishments.

Termination letters ensure that the client understands the reasons for the conclusion of the intervention and is reminded of available resources if needed in the future.

How to Write a Termination Letter

Date: [Date of writing the letter]

To: [Client's Name]

Address: [Client's Address]

Dear [Client's Name],

Introduction

I hope that this letter finds you well. It has been a privilege to work with you during our time together, and I am writing to formally communicate the conclusion of our professional relationship.

Acknowledgment of Progress

I want to take a moment to acknowledge the progress and growth you have made since we began working together. Your dedication, resilience, and commitment to change have been truly inspiring. I have witnessed your hard work and determination, and I want to congratulate you on the positive steps you have taken toward achieving your goals.

Meeting Goals

I am pleased to inform you that the goals we set at the beginning of our journey have been successfully met. The challenges you faced and the progress you achieved have demonstrated your capacity for personal growth and transformation. Your ability to overcome obstacles and embrace change is a testament to your strength.

Transitioning Forward

As we conclude our time together, please know that the termination of our professional relationship does not mean the end of the support available to you. You have developed a toolbox of skills and strategies that you can continue to rely on as you navigate your journey. Additionally, if you find yourself needing further assistance in the future, please do not hesitate to reach out to [mention relevant resources, agencies, or contact information].

Closure and Gratitude

I want to express my heartfelt gratitude for allowing me to be a part of your journey. It has been an honor to work alongside you as you pursue your goals and aspirations. Your dedication to personal growth and your commitment to positive change have left a lasting impression on me.

Contact Information

While our formal relationship is coming to an end, I want to assure you that my support and encouragement remain with you. Please feel free to contact me at [Your Contact Information] if you ever wish to reconnect, provide updates, or seek further guidance.

Conclusion

As you move forward, remember that you possess the strength and resilience to overcome any challenges that come your way. I believe in your capacity to continue making meaningful progress and achieving your dreams. Thank you again for the privilege of working with you, and I wish you all the best in your future endeavors.

Sincerely,

[Your Name]

[Your Title]

[Your Contact Information]

A well-crafted termination letter ensures that the closure of the professional relationship is handled with sensitivity and professionalism. By following this example and adapting it to the specific circumstances of the client, social work practitioners can conclude their work with dignity, respect, and encouragement for the client's continued growth and well-being.

11.9 Collaborating Within Multi-disciplinary Teams

Understanding Multi-disciplinary Teams: Collaboration within multi-disciplinary teams is an integral facet of social work practice, bringing together professionals from diverse disciplines to address complex client needs. These teams comprise experts such as social workers, psychologists, counselors, medical professionals, and educators, each contributing unique skills to create a comprehensive support system.

Benefits of Multi-disciplinary Collaboration: The collaborative approach ensures that clients receive a spectrum of specialized services, addressing various aspects of their well-being. By incorporating diverse perspectives, it facilitates a holistic assessment, considering physical, emotional, psychological, and social factors. Informed decision-making is a key outcome, where the synergy of combined skills enhances intervention effectiveness, leading to positive client outcomes. The collaborative environment also promotes continuous learning, as practitioners expose themselves to various approaches and expand their knowledge base.

Strategies for Effective Collaboration: Effective collaboration relies on open communication, with regular and transparent exchanges among team members. Clearly defined roles, responsibilities, and contributions prevent duplication and ensure a coordinated approach. Fostering an environment of respect and recognition for each team member's expertise is essential. Information sharing, regular meetings, flexibility, and adaptability to changing circumstances, as well as constructive conflict resolution, contribute to the success of collaborative efforts.

Application of Multi-disciplinary Collaboration: The collaborative process begins with case discussions, where team members share perspectives and contribute insights. Intervention plans are crafted based on collective input, addressing the diverse needs identified by the team. Regular updates and feedback loops ensure ongoing tracking of the client's progress, allowing for adjustments to interventions as needed.

Collaborating within multi-disciplinary teams is a hallmark of effective social work practice. Embracing diverse expertise ensures that clients receive holistic support, extending beyond the client to foster professional growth, learning, and a shared commitment to positive change. Effective collaboration not only contributes to improved client outcomes but also promotes a more inclusive and client-centered approach to care. Social work practitioners engaging in collaborative efforts play a pivotal role in shaping a supportive and comprehensive environment for clients.

11.10 Navigating Bureaucracy and Policy Implementation

Understanding Bureaucracy and Policy Implementation: Navigating bureaucracy involves grappling with intricate administrative structures, regulations, and procedures governing the provision of services and resources. Policy implementation, on the other hand, is the translation of laws and regulations into practical actions impacting individuals and communities.

Challenges in Navigating Bureaucracy: Bureaucratic systems' complexity poses challenges, leading to confusion and delays. Clients may face barriers such as limited access to information, language hurdles, or unawareness about available resources. Inequities within bureaucratic systems can disproportionately affect marginalized and vulnerable populations, and the time constraints involved can hinder timely access to support.

Strategies for Effective Navigation: Practitioners must stay informed about policies, regulations, and available resources. Empowering clients through education about their rights and available services is crucial. Advocacy on behalf of clients, building networks, meticulous documentation, persistence in pursuing resources, and cultural competence are key components of effective navigation.

Policy Implementation Strategies: Understanding policies relevant to client's needs, assessing their impact, advocating for necessary changes, collaborating with stakeholders, and providing feedback to policymakers based on real-world experiences are essential in effective policy implementation.

Application of Navigating Bureaucracy and Policy Implementation: Practitioners apply these skills by assessing clients' needs, identifying relevant policies, and guiding them through accessing services. Advocacy efforts may involve engaging in policy discussions, providing data-driven insights, and collaborating with stakeholders. Navigating bureaucracy and policy implementation is integral to social work practice, empowering clients to access resources and services while advocating for their rights and well-being. Practitioners play a vital role in shaping policies by providing real-world insights and advocating for changes that better support the populations they serve, ensuring that social work remains a powerful force for positive change within larger systems.

Review Questions

1. How does effective engagement with clients and their families contribute to successful social work practice?
2. Discuss the importance of community engagement in addressing social issues and promoting positive change.
3. How can an understanding of political systems enhance a social worker's ability to advocate for policy changes?
4. Explain the significance of maintaining a comprehensive case record in social work field practice.
5. What challenges might social workers face when collaborating within multidisciplinary teams, and how can these be addressed?
6. In what ways does policy assessment contribute to effective social work interventions?

Multiple Choice Questions

1. What is the primary purpose of engaging with clients and their families in social work practice?

   (a) Administrative documentation
   (b) Establishing rapport and understanding client needs

(c) Fulfilling bureaucratic requirements
(d) Conducting research on family dynamics

2. Why is community engagement considered a crucial aspect of social work?

(a) To promote positive change and address social issues
(b) To increase paperwork for social workers
(c) To create administrative hurdles
(d) To add complexity to interventions

3. How does an understanding of political systems benefit social workers?

(a) By adding unnecessary bureaucracy
(b) By hindering advocacy efforts
(c) By avoiding engagement with policymakers
(d) By informing advocacy strategies and policy change initiatives

4. What is the primary purpose of maintaining a comprehensive case record in social work?

(a) To create unnecessary paperwork
(b) To track intervention outcomes and client progress
(c) To increase the workload for social workers
(d) To ignore the client's history

5. What is a potential challenge when collaborating within multi-disciplinary teams?

(a) Increased efficiency
(b) Enhanced decision-making
(c) Communication barriers and conflicts
(d) Improved client outcomes

References

Delgado, M. (1999). *Community social work practice in an urban context: The potential of a capacity-enhancement perspective*. Oxford University Press.

Morley, C., Ablett, P., & Macfarlane, S. (2019). *Engaging with social work*. Cambridge University Press.

Chapter 12
Supervision of Fieldwork Students

Learning Objectives
After reading this chapter, you will be able to:

- Understand the fundamental principles and significance of fieldwork supervision in the context of social work practice.
- Explore the theoretical foundations that underpin effective supervision, providing a theoretical framework for guiding supervisory practices.
- Identify and comprehend the diverse roles and responsibilities that supervisors undertake in supporting and guiding fieldwork students.
- Acquire knowledge of various supervision techniques and approaches, including the utilization of a template for structured and effective supervision sessions.
- Develop cultural competence in the supervisory role, recognizing and addressing the cultural dynamics that may impact the fieldwork experience.
- Learn strategies for addressing challenges that may arise in the supervisory relationship, fostering a positive and supportive learning environment for fieldwork students.

12.1 Introduction to Fieldwork Supervision

Fieldwork supervision is a cornerstone of social work education, providing a crucial bridge between theoretical learning and practical application (Dimo, 2013; Kadushin & Harkness, 2014). This introductory section seeks to illuminate the foundational concepts and significance of fieldwork supervision. At its core, fieldwork supervision involves a dynamic relationship between a seasoned social work professional, the supervisor, and a fieldwork student, fostering a supportive environment for learning, reflection, and professional growth.

M. R. Islam, *Fieldwork in Social Work*,
https://doi.org/10.1007/978-3-031-56683-7_12

The role of fieldwork supervision extends beyond a mere oversight of student activities; it is a collaborative and developmental process. As fieldwork students engage in real-world social work practice, the supervisor assumes the responsibility of guiding, mentoring, and facilitating a transformative learning experience. This relationship is distinctly different from evaluation, as its primary focus lies in the student's skill enhancement, self-awareness, and ethical decision-making.

Historically, fieldwork supervision has evolved to meet the changing demands of the social work profession. Early supervisory approaches were often hierarchical, emphasizing a top-down model. However, contemporary perspectives recognize the importance of a more egalitarian and participatory relationship. This evolution aligns with the broader paradigm shift in social work toward client-centered, strengths-based, and culturally competent practices.

Theoretical foundations underpin the practice of fieldwork supervision, drawing from diverse frameworks such as psychodynamic, behavioral, and developmental theories. The introduction of these theories provides supervisors with a conceptual toolbox to understand the complexities of human behavior, organizational dynamics, and the unique challenges within various practice settings. Theoretical grounding is instrumental in tailoring supervision approaches to the individualized needs of fieldwork students.

In the contemporary landscape of social work education, the introduction of fieldwork supervision acknowledges the importance of blending academic knowledge with experiential learning. The reciprocal nature of the supervisory relationship becomes a key enabler for students to integrate classroom theories into their direct practice. Furthermore, it serves as a platform for students to grapple with the ethical dilemmas, cultural nuances, and systemic challenges inherent in the profession.

This introduction sets the stage for an exploration of the multifaceted dimensions of fieldwork supervision, inviting both novice and seasoned professionals to reflect on their roles, responsibilities, and the transformative potential of this dynamic educational process. As we delve deeper into the subsequent sections, we will unravel the theoretical underpinnings, practical strategies, and ethical considerations that shape effective fieldwork supervision in the ever-evolving landscape of social work education.

12.2 Theoretical Foundations of Supervision

Supervision in social work is enriched by a variety of theoretical foundations that inform its structure, purpose, and dynamics. This section delves into key theoretical frameworks that underpin effective fieldwork supervision, recognizing that a well-grounded theoretical approach enhances the quality of the supervisory relationship and contributes to the professional development of fieldwork students.

Psychodynamic Supervision: Rooted in psychodynamic theories, this approach emphasizes the exploration of unconscious processes and dynamics within the supervisory relationship. The supervisor, drawing from psychoanalytic principles, assists the students in understanding their emotional responses, relational patterns, and the impact of personal history on their practice.

Cognitive-Behavioral Supervision: Informed by cognitive-behavioral theories, this supervisory approach focuses on observable behaviors, thoughts, and interventions. The supervisor collaborates with the student to identify and modify specific behaviors and thought patterns, emphasizing skill-building and the application of evidence-based practices.

Developmental Supervision: Borrowing from developmental theories, this approach recognizes that professional growth is a gradual and evolving process. The supervisor assesses the student's competence and developmental stage, tailoring supervision to meet their specific needs and challenges as they progress through various stages of skill acquisition.

Strengths-Based Supervision: Aligned with the strengths-based perspective in social work, this approach accentuates the identification and utilization of the student's strengths and assets. The supervisor fosters a positive and empowering environment, encouraging the students to build on their existing skills and capacities.

Systemic Supervision: Grounded in systems theory, this approach views social work practice within the broader context of interconnected systems. The supervisor helps the student comprehend the systemic influences on their work, including organizational dynamics, community structures, and societal factors, fostering a holistic understanding of social work practice.

Reflective Supervision: Rooted in reflective practice theories, this approach places a premium on critical self-reflection. The supervisor guides the students in exploring their values, assumptions, and reactions, promoting a deeper understanding of their professional identity and enhancing their capacity for ethical decision-making.

These theoretical foundations are not mutually exclusive, and supervisors often integrate elements from multiple approaches based on the unique needs and circumstances of the student and the practice setting. Theoretical diversity in supervision enriches the learning experience, offering a comprehensive framework for understanding the intricacies of social work practice and promoting continuous professional development. As we navigate through the theoretical foundations, it becomes evident that the choice of a supervisory approach is a thoughtful and dynamic process, tailored to optimize the growth and competence of fieldwork students.

12.3 Roles and Responsibilities of Supervisors

Effective fieldwork supervision entails a complex set of roles and responsibilities that go beyond overseeing day-to-day tasks (Briggs, 2020). This section elucidates the multifaceted nature of the supervisor's role and the corresponding responsibilities they bear in shaping the learning and professional development of fieldwork students.

Educator: As educators, supervisors facilitate a learning environment where students acquire knowledge, skills, and values essential for competent social work practice. They guide theoretical frameworks, evidence-based interventions, and ethical considerations, fostering a comprehensive understanding of the profession.

Mentor: The role of a mentor involves nurturing the personal and professional growth of fieldwork students. Supervisors offer insights from their own experiences, share practical wisdom, and serve as role models, inspiring students to navigate the complexities of social work with resilience and integrity.

Evaluator: Supervisors play a crucial role in assessing the performance and progress of fieldwork students. Through regular feedback and evaluations, they identify strengths, areas for improvement, and learning objectives. This evaluative function aims to ensure that students meet competency standards and are prepared for professional practice.

Advocate: Advocacy is inherent in the supervisory role, involving the support and promotion of students' rights, well-being, and professional interests. Supervisors advocate for a conducive learning environment, address challenges faced by students, and encourage their active engagement in advocating for clients.

Clinical Supervisor: In clinical supervision, the focus extends to the emotional and interpersonal aspects of social work practice. Supervisors navigate discussions on challenging cases, explore countertransference issues, and guide students in managing the emotional demands of their work, contributing to the development of effective therapeutic relationships.

Gatekeeper: As gatekeepers, supervisors ensure that fieldwork students are ethically and professionally prepared for social work practice. They monitor adherence to ethical standards, intervene when necessary, and make informed decisions regarding the readiness of students to progress in their fieldwork.

Coordinator: Supervisors often take on a coordinating role, aligning fieldwork experiences with educational objectives. They liaise with educational institutions, agencies, and other stakeholders to create a coherent and meaningful learning experience for students.

Cultural Competence Facilitator: Recognizing the importance of cultural competence, supervisors guide students in navigating diverse cultural contexts. They facilitate discussions on cultural humility, challenge biases, and promote an inclusive approach to social work practice.

Resource Provider: Supervisors act as a valuable resource by offering information, tools, and support to enhance students' practice. They provide access to relevant literature, training opportunities, and networking connections that contribute to the student's professional development.

Feedback Provider: Providing constructive feedback is integral to the supervisory process. Supervisors offer timely, specific, and actionable feedback that helps students reflect on their practice, identify areas for improvement, and refine their skills.

Evaluator of Competencies: Supervisors assess the development of competencies outlined by professional standards. They gauge a student's ability to apply theoretical knowledge, employ ethical decision-making, engage in culturally competent practice, and collaborate effectively within multidisciplinary teams.

The effectiveness of fieldwork supervision hinges on the dynamic and adept navigation of these roles and responsibilities. A skilled supervisor integrates these facets, creating a supportive and challenging learning environment that fosters the growth and professional identity of fieldwork students. The evolving nature of social work practice necessitates supervisors who are responsive, knowledgeable, and attuned to the unique needs of each student under their guidance.

12.4 Supervision Techniques and Approaches

Supervision in social work encompasses a diverse range of techniques and approaches tailored to the dynamic needs of fieldwork students (see Table 12.1).

Reflective Supervision: Encouraging reflective practice is a cornerstone of supervision. Through reflective supervision, supervisors create a space for fieldwork students to critically analyze their experiences, explore emotions, and gain deeper insights into their practice. This approach fosters self-awareness and enhances decision-making skills.

Process-Oriented Supervision: In process-oriented supervision, the focus is on the ongoing dynamics of the client–supervisee relationship. Supervisors examine the interactive processes, communication styles, and therapeutic interventions employed by fieldwork students. This approach aims to refine interpersonal skills and enhance the effectiveness of interventions.

Task-Centered Supervision: Task-centered supervision emphasizes goal-setting and task accomplishment. Supervisors collaboratively set specific, measurable, achievable, relevant, and time-bound (SMART) objectives with fieldwork students. Regular reviews of progress toward these goals provide a structured framework for learning and development.

Strengths-Based Supervision: Rooted in the strengths perspective, this approach accentuates the identification and utilization of the inherent strengths and capacities of fieldwork students. Supervisors emphasize empowering students to leverage their strengths in addressing challenges, promoting a positive and resilient mindset.

Psychoeducational Supervision: Psychoeducational supervision integrates educational components into the supervisory process. Supervisors provide didactic instruction, training modules, and resources to enhance the theoretical knowledge and practical skills of fieldwork students. This approach contributes to a comprehensive understanding of social work practice.

Live Supervision: Live supervision involves the observation of fieldwork sessions by the supervisor in real time. This approach allows supervisors to provide immediate feedback, model effective interventions, and address challenges as they unfold. Live supervision enhances skill development and promotes experiential learning.

Table 12.1 Supervision techniques and approaches

Supervision technique	Explanation
Reflective supervision	Encourages reflective practice, providing a space for critical analysis of experiences, emotions, and practice insights, enhancing self-awareness.
Process-oriented supervision	Focuses on client–supervisee dynamics, refining interpersonal skills and intervention effectiveness through examination of interactive processes.
Task-centered supervision	Emphasizes goal-setting and task accomplishment, with regular reviews to track progress and provide a structured framework for learning.
Strengths-based supervision	Identifies and utilizes inherent strengths of fieldwork students, promoting a positive and resilient mindset to address challenges effectively.
Psychoeducational supervision	Integrates educational components to enhance theoretical knowledge and practical skills, contributing to a comprehensive understanding of practice.
Live supervision	Involves real-time observation of sessions, facilitating immediate feedback and skill development through modeling effective interventions.
Group supervision	Engages multiple students for collective learning, fostering collaboration and diverse perspectives through group discussions and peer feedback.
Task review and feedback	Examines specific tasks, assessing documentation quality and intervention effectiveness and providing feedback to enhance clarity and ethical considerations.
Video-based supervision	Utilizes recorded sessions for self-reflection and skill enhancement, offering insights into actual practice and areas for improvement.
Integrative supervision	Combines elements from various models to create a flexible supervisory process, accommodating diverse learning styles and needs.
Crisis intervention supervision	Equips students with strategies to manage urgent situations effectively and prioritize safety, ensuring competence in crisis intervention.
Competency-based supervision	Focuses on assessing and developing specific competencies required for practice, setting performance expectations, and guiding proficiency.
Narrative supervision	Explores fieldwork experiences through storytelling, gaining insights into unique professional journeys and enhancing understanding.

Source: Author

Group Supervision: Group supervision brings together multiple fieldwork students for collective learning and support. Supervisors facilitate group discussions, case consultations, and peer feedback sessions. Group dynamics foster a collaborative learning environment and provide diverse perspectives on social work practice.

Task Review and Feedback: Task review involves the examination of specific tasks performed by fieldwork students. Supervisors assess the quality of written documentation, intervention strategies, and case management. Feedback is provided to enhance the clarity, effectiveness, and ethical considerations of these tasks.

Video-Based Supervision: Utilizing recorded sessions, video-based supervision allows supervisors and fieldwork students to review and analyze actual practice.

This method offers a unique opportunity for self-reflection, skill enhancement, and the identification of areas for improvement.

Integrative Supervision: Drawing from various theoretical frameworks and approaches, integrative supervision combines elements of different models to create a customized and flexible supervisory process. This approach accommodates the diverse needs and learning styles of fieldwork students.

Crisis Intervention Supervision: In situations involving crises or high-stakes interventions, supervisors employ crisis intervention supervision. This approach equips fieldwork students with strategies to manage urgent situations, prioritize safety, and engage in effective crisis intervention.

Competency-Based Supervision: Aligned with professional competency standards, this approach focuses on assessing and developing specific competencies required for social work practice. Supervisors identify key competencies, set performance expectations, and guide students in achieving proficiency (Kadambari & Lama, 2022).

Narrative Supervision: Narrative supervision involves the exploration of fieldwork experiences through storytelling. Fieldwork students share narratives of their encounters, challenges, and successes, allowing supervisors to gain a deeper understanding of their unique professional journeys.

The selection of supervision techniques and approaches depends on the goals of supervision, the developmental stage of the fieldwork student, and the nature of the social work practice setting. Effective supervisors often integrate multiple approaches, adapting their methods to best meet the evolving needs of their supervisees. The diverse array of supervision techniques ensures a rich and tailored learning experience for fieldwork students as they navigate the complexities of social work practice.

12.5 A Template for Supervision

Supervising social work students at both the agency and university levels plays a crucial role in ensuring their progress and continuity in the field. This dual supervision approach provides a comprehensive framework that integrates academic knowledge with real-world application, fostering a holistic and enriching learning experience for the students. By synergizing agency-based experiences with theoretical insights gained through university coursework, students can navigate the complexities of social work practice more effectively. This collaborative supervision model aims to nurture not only their professional competencies but also their personal growth, equipping them with the skills and insights needed for a successful career in social work. Here is a brief template for supervision:

Supervision Session Details:
Date:
Time:
Location:
Duration:
Student Name:
Educational Institution:
Field Placement Agency:
Field Instructor:

Agenda: Review of Previous Assignments: Discuss the progress and challenges encountered in the student's previous assignments.

Current Fieldwork Activities: Overview of the student's ongoing tasks and responsibilities in the field placement.

Reflective Practice: Encourage the student to reflect on their experiences, challenges, and personal growth.

Client Cases: Discuss specific client cases, addressing ethical considerations, interventions, and outcomes.

Supervisory Challenges: Explore any challenges the student may be facing in the field and provide guidance.

Learning Goals and Objectives: Review and update the student's learning goals and objectives for the field placement.

Professional Development: Discuss opportunities for the student's professional development and growth.

Feedback: Offer constructive feedback on the student's performance and areas for improvement.

Supervisory Support: Discuss how the supervisor can provide support and resources to enhance the student's experience.

Administrative Updates: Address any administrative matters, such as documentation, reporting, or scheduling.

Next Steps: Set goals and action items for the student before the next supervision session.

Student's Reflection and Input: Allow the student to share their reflections on the supervision process and any concerns.

Student Input: Provide an opportunity for the student to express their needs, goals, and expectations.

Action Plan:

Action Items: Clearly outline the tasks, assignments, or activities the student should focus on before the next supervision.

Follow-Up: Determine the date and time for the next supervision session and any follow-up tasks.

Supervisor Signature: ______________________
Student Signature: ______________________
Date: ______________________

[This template provides a structured framework for conducting supervision sessions with fieldwork students in social work, ensuring a comprehensive review of their progress, challenges, and professional development.]

12.6 Cultural Competence in Supervision

Cultural competence in supervision is imperative to ensure that fieldwork students receive guidance that respects, acknowledges, and integrates diverse cultural perspectives (Janus & Smythe, 2011). This section explores the significance of cultural competence in supervision, addressing the dynamics of cross-cultural interactions and the role of supervisors in fostering an inclusive and culturally sensitive learning environment.

Cultural Humility: Cultural humility is foundational to effective supervision. Supervisors cultivate humility by acknowledging their own cultural biases, continuously learning about diverse cultures, and maintaining a genuine openness to different worldviews. This creates a safe space for fieldwork students to explore their own cultural identities and biases.

Intersectionality Awareness: Recognizing the intersectionality of identities is crucial in culturally competent supervision. Fieldwork students often embody multiple intersecting identities, such as race, gender, socioeconomic status, and sexual orientation. Supervisors consider these intersections to better understand the nuanced experiences and challenges faced by their supervisees.

Culturally Tailored Feedback: Supervisors provide feedback that considers the cultural context of social work practice. This involves recognizing culturally specific strengths, acknowledging cultural nuances in communication styles, and offering constructive feedback that aligns with the cultural backgrounds of fieldwork students.

Cultural Responsiveness in Skill Development: Cultural competence is interwoven with skill development in supervision. Supervisors actively guide fieldwork students in developing culturally responsive intervention strategies, communication skills, and assessment techniques. This ensures that social work practice is sensitive to the diverse needs of clients from various cultural backgrounds.

Addressing Microaggressions: Supervisors play a pivotal role in addressing and preventing microaggressions within the supervisory relationship and the broader social work practice setting. They create an environment where fieldwork students feel empowered to discuss instances of microaggressions and collaboratively work toward eliminating them.

Promoting Diversity in Learning Resources: In culturally competent supervision, supervisors curate learning resources that reflect diverse perspectives and authors. This includes literature, case studies, and educational materials that showcase the experiences and contributions of individuals from various cultural backgrounds.

Cultural Competence in Evaluation and Assessment: Supervisors integrate cultural competence into the evaluation and assessment of fieldwork students. This involves considering how cultural factors may influence performance, acknowledging diverse learning styles, and adapting assessment methods to ensure fairness and inclusivity.

Promoting Cross-Cultural Communication: Supervisors actively foster cross-cultural communication skills in fieldwork students. This includes addressing language barriers, promoting effective communication across cultural differences, and providing guidance on adapting communication styles to align with the cultural preferences of clients.

Creating a Culturally Inclusive Learning Environment: Supervisors are intentional about creating a culturally inclusive learning environment. This involves celebrating cultural diversity, organizing cultural competency workshops, and promoting discussions that explore the intersectionality of identities in social work practice.

Cultural Competence as an Ongoing Process: Cultural competence is viewed as a continuous and evolving process in supervision. Supervisors engage in ongoing self-reflection, seek additional training on cultural competence, and model a commitment to lifelong learning. This sets the expectation that fieldwork students also embrace cultural competence as a dynamic and evolving aspect of their professional journey.

Cultural competence in supervision enhances the quality of social work education and practice by preparing fieldwork students to navigate the complexities of diverse and multicultural settings. It ensures that social work professionals are equipped to provide ethical, inclusive, and effective services to clients from various cultural backgrounds. Supervisors, through their commitment to cultural competence, contribute significantly to the development of socially conscious and culturally sensitive social workers.

12.7 Addressing Challenges in Supervision

Supervision in social work field practices is a dynamic process that, despite its many benefits, may encounter challenges that necessitate thoughtful consideration and proactive resolution. Addressing these challenges is essential for maintaining a supportive and constructive supervisory relationship. This section explores common challenges in fieldwork supervision and strategies for addressing them.

Communication Barriers: Effective communication is foundational to successful supervision, yet various barriers can impede it. Differences in communication styles, cultural nuances, or language barriers between supervisors and students may lead to misunderstandings. To address this challenge, it is crucial to establish open and transparent communication channels. Regular check-ins, clarifying expectations, and actively seeking feedback help overcome communication barriers.

Power Dynamics: The inherent power differential in the supervisor–student relationship can pose challenges. Students may feel hesitant to express concerns or disagree with their supervisors, impacting the quality of supervision. Supervisors need to create an inclusive and empowering environment that encourages open dialogue. Emphasizing mutual learning and acknowledging the value of diverse perspectives help mitigate power imbalances.

Cultural Competence and Diversity: Cultural differences between supervisors and students may present challenges related to understanding diverse perspectives. Supervisors must be aware of their own cultural biases and continuously strive for cultural competence. Training on cultural humility, creating an inclusive environment, and addressing cultural nuances in supervision contribute to overcoming these challenges.

Time Constraints: Both supervisors and students often face time constraints due to heavy workloads. Finding dedicated time for supervision amidst busy schedules can be challenging. Establishing a regular and protected supervision schedule, prioritizing key discussion points, and leveraging technology for virtual meetings can help optimize the use of limited time.

Balancing Support and Evaluation: Supervisors must strike a delicate balance between providing support and evaluating students' performance. If supervision leans too heavily toward evaluation, it may hinder the student's ability to openly discuss challenges and seek guidance. Emphasizing formative feedback, goal-setting, and a developmental approach to evaluation promotes a supportive supervisory relationship.

Professional Boundaries: Maintaining appropriate professional boundaries is critical in supervision. Challenges may arise when students disclose personal issues, and supervisors must navigate these situations ethically. Establishing clear guidelines on confidentiality, discussing potential ethical dilemmas, and providing guidance on appropriate disclosure contribute to maintaining professional boundaries.

Addressing these challenges requires ongoing reflection, flexibility, and a commitment to the growth and well-being of both students and supervisors. By fostering an environment of trust, open communication, and cultural humility, fieldwork supervision can navigate challenges effectively, enhancing the overall learning experience for students and contributing to their professional development.

12.8 Evaluation and Feedback in Supervision

Evaluation and feedback are integral components of fieldwork supervision, playing a pivotal role in shaping the professional development of social work students. This section explores the principles, methods, and considerations associated with evaluation and feedback in the supervisory context.

Formative and Summative Evaluation: Supervisors employ both formative and summative evaluation approaches. Formative evaluation occurs throughout the field placement, focusing on ongoing development, skill enhancement, and addressing challenges. Summative evaluation, typically conducted at the end of the placement, provides an overall assessment of the student's performance. Balancing these approaches ensures a comprehensive understanding of the student's progress.

Goal Setting and Competency-Based Evaluation: Effective supervision involves collaboratively setting goals that align with the student's learning objectives and competencies. Competency-based evaluation frameworks, outlining expected skills and behaviors, guide the assessment process. Supervisors work with students to identify specific competencies, providing targeted feedback to enhance skill acquisition and professional growth.

Feedback Delivery Techniques: Feedback should be constructive, specific, and geared toward fostering growth. Supervisors employ various techniques, such as the "sandwich" method (positive feedback, constructive critique, and positive reinforcement), to ensure a balanced and supportive approach. Regular feedback sessions, allowing students to reflect on their experiences, contribute to a dynamic and responsive supervisory process.

Self-Assessment and Reflection: Encouraging students to engage in self-assessment and reflection enhances their ownership of the learning process. Supervisors guide students in critically evaluating their performance, identifying strengths and areas for improvement, and formulating action plans. This reflective practice cultivates a habit of continuous learning and self-awareness.

Cultural Sensitivity in Evaluation: Cultural competence is vital in evaluating students and recognizing diverse perspectives and experiences. Supervisors must consider cultural nuances when assessing competencies and providing feedback. Creating an inclusive evaluation framework that acknowledges and values cultural diversity contributes to fair and equitable assessment practices.

Timely and Regular Feedback: Timely feedback is crucial for students to make real-time adjustments to their practice. Regular check-ins and scheduled feedback sessions ensure ongoing communication and support. Supervisors prioritize creating an environment where students feel comfortable seeking feedback and discussing challenges, fostering a collaborative and responsive supervisory relationship.

Documentation and Record-Keeping: Accurate and comprehensive documentation of evaluation and feedback sessions is essential for accountability and future reference. Supervisors maintain records of students' achievements, areas for growth, and strategies for improvement. Clear documentation supports students in tracking their progress and serves as a valuable resource for future supervisory discussions.

Effective evaluation and feedback in supervision contribute significantly to the professional development of social work students. By employing thoughtful and culturally sensitive approaches, supervisors facilitate a learning environment that empowers students to thrive in their fieldwork experiences and prepares them for successful social work practice.

12.9 Supervision Across Different Fieldwork Settings

Supervision in social work extends across various fieldwork settings, each presenting unique challenges and opportunities. This section explores the nuances and considerations associated with providing effective supervision in diverse fieldwork settings.

Agency-Based Supervision: In agency-based settings, supervisors navigate the organizational structure, policies, and dynamics specific to the agency. Balancing administrative expectations with the educational needs of the student requires a collaborative approach. Supervisors guide students in integrating theoretical knowledge into practical skills within the agency's framework.

Community-Based Supervision: Supervision in community-based settings involves addressing the challenges of working directly within diverse communities. Effective supervisors facilitate an understanding of community dynamics, cultural nuances, and the impact of social issues. Collaborative efforts focus on empowering students to engage authentically with community members and navigate complex social landscapes.

School-Based Supervision: In educational settings, supervisors guide students in navigating the complexities of school environments. Collaboration with educators, administrators, and other professionals is crucial. Supervisors address the intersectionality of education and social work, emphasizing the importance of advocacy, support services, and a student-centered approach.

Healthcare Settings Supervision: Supervision in healthcare settings requires an understanding of the medical context and interdisciplinary collaboration. Supervisors support students in navigating the healthcare system, addressing the psychosocial aspects of health, and integrating social work principles into the medical team's collaborative efforts.

International Fieldwork Supervision: In the context of international fieldwork, supervisors grapple with cross-cultural dynamics, diverse social systems, and varying ethical considerations. Supervising students in global contexts involves addressing cultural humility, and ethical dilemmas unique to international settings, and ensuring the integration of social work principles within diverse cultural frameworks.

Macro-Level Supervision: Supervision at the macro level involves guiding students in systemic and policy-focused work. Supervisors in this setting collaborate with students to understand the broader social, political, and economic forces influencing social issues. The focus extends beyond direct client interactions to macro-level interventions and advocacy.

Technology-Mediated Supervision: With the advancement of technology, supervisors may engage in remote or virtual supervision. Navigating technology-mediated supervision requires addressing challenges related to digital communication, maintaining confidentiality, and ensuring the continued development of practical skills despite physical distance.

Integrated Supervision Models: Recognizing the interdisciplinary nature of social work, supervisors may adopt integrated supervision models. These models involve collaboration with professionals from various disciplines to provide holistic support to clients. Integrated supervision emphasizes the intersectionality of social work within broader systems of care.

Supervision across different fieldwork settings demands a versatile and adaptable approach from supervisors. By acknowledging the unique demands of each setting, supervisors can tailor their guidance to ensure that students are well-equipped to navigate the complexities of diverse social work practice environments. The ability to adapt supervision strategies to specific settings contributes to the overall competence and preparedness of social work students across a range of professional contexts.

12.10 Professional Development and Continuing Education for Supervisors

Professional development and ongoing education for supervisors play a critical role in ensuring the effectiveness and adaptability of fieldwork supervision. This section explores the significance of continuous learning for supervisors, emphasizing its impact on enhancing supervision quality and student outcomes.

Importance of Professional Development: Continuous learning is essential for supervisors to stay abreast of evolving social work theories, methodologies, and ethical standards. Engaging in professional development fosters a commitment to excellence and ensures that supervisors provide relevant, evidence-based guidance to fieldwork students.

Adapting to Changing Social Work Landscape: The field of social work is dynamic, with constant changes in policies, best practices, and societal dynamics. Professional development equips supervisors with the knowledge and skills needed to navigate these changes, fostering adaptability in the face of evolving challenges and opportunities.

Staying Informed about Supervision Models: Ongoing education allows supervisors to explore and integrate new supervision models and approaches. This includes staying informed about best practices in supervision, emerging theoretical frameworks, and innovative strategies for supporting students in diverse fieldwork settings.

Cultural Competence and Diversity Training: Social work is inherently diverse, and supervisors need continuous training in cultural competence. Professional development in this area ensures that supervisors are equipped to address issues related to diversity, equity, and inclusion, providing culturally responsive supervision to students.

Ethical Considerations and Legal Updates: Continuing education is crucial for staying informed about changes in ethical standards and legal requirements in social work. Supervisors must model ethical behavior and provide students with guidance that aligns with the latest ethical considerations and legal obligations.

Incorporating Technology in Supervision: As technology continues to shape the landscape of social work practice, supervisors benefit from ongoing training in utilizing technology for remote supervision, virtual communication, and the ethical considerations associated with technology-mediated interactions.

Mental Health and Trauma-Informed Supervision: Given the prevalence of mental health issues and trauma in clients, supervisors should engage in professional development focused on trauma-informed supervision. This includes understanding the impact of trauma, incorporating trauma-sensitive approaches, and supporting students in trauma-responsive practice.

Peer Collaboration and Learning Communities: Participation in peer collaboration and learning communities enhances supervisors' professional growth. Opportunities for sharing experiences, discussing challenges, and exchanging insights with fellow supervisors contribute to a supportive professional network.

Continued professional development for supervisors is a commitment to the ongoing improvement of fieldwork supervision. It ensures that supervisors remain informed, adaptable, and equipped to provide high-quality guidance to social work students. As the social work landscape evolves, supervisors who engage in continuous education contribute to the development of a resilient and competent social work workforce.

12.11 Supervision Case Studies: Learning from Real-Life Experiences

Supervision case studies serve as invaluable tools for enhancing the practical skills and decision-making capabilities of fieldwork supervisors. This section delves into the importance of utilizing case studies in supervision and presents a real-life example from social work practice in Australia:

Utilizing Case Studies in Supervision: Case studies offer a structured and reflective approach to learning from real-life experiences. They provide supervisors and students with the opportunity to analyze complex scenarios, explore various perspectives, and develop a deeper understanding of the decision-making processes in social work practice.

Learning from Diverse Situations: Supervision case studies encompass a range of situations, allowing supervisors to address diverse challenges encountered by students in the field. From complex client interactions to ethical dilemmas and cultural considerations, case studies provide a comprehensive view of the multifaceted nature of social work practice.

Facilitating Critical Thinking: Case studies encourage critical thinking skills among fieldwork students. Supervisors guide students in analyzing the presented scenarios, identifying key issues, considering alternative approaches, and making informed decisions. This process enhances students' ability to navigate complex situations independently.

Real-Life Example: Social Work Practice in Australia: In a case study from Australia, a fieldwork student faced a challenge in working with an Indigenous client within a healthcare setting. The student grappled with cultural nuances, historical sensitivities, and the need for collaborative engagement. The supervisor, drawing on their expertise and cultural competence, guided the student through a process of cultural humility, emphasizing the importance of building rapport, understanding historical contexts, and collaborating with Indigenous community resources. This case study not only addressed the immediate challenge but also enriched the student's cultural competence and laid the foundation for continued learning.

Enhancing Decision-Making Skills: Supervision case studies contribute to the development of effective decision-making skills. Through guided discussions, supervisors help students explore the consequences of different interventions, consider ethical implications, and refine their ability to make sound judgments in complex situations.

Promoting Reflective Practice: Case studies encourage reflective practice, prompting both supervisors and students to examine their assumptions, biases, and emotional responses. Reflective discussions within the supervision context contribute to ongoing professional development and self-awareness.

Integration of Theory and Practice: Case studies bridge the gap between theoretical knowledge and practical application. They allow supervisors to connect theoretical frameworks with the realities of social work practice, fostering an integrated approach that aligns with best practices and evidence-based interventions.

Application of Supervision Case Studies: The insights gained from case studies are applied in shaping future interventions, refining practice approaches, and preparing students for a diverse range of challenges they may encounter in their social work careers. The process contributes to a well-rounded and competent social work workforce.

Supervision case studies provide a platform for experiential learning, allowing both supervisors and students to draw upon real-life examples to enhance their skills, deepen their understanding, and cultivate a reflective and informed approach to social work practice.

12.12 Emerging Trends and Innovations in Fieldwork Supervision

Fieldwork supervision is a dynamic and evolving aspect of social work education and practice. This section explores emerging trends and innovations that are shaping the landscape of fieldwork supervision, reflecting advancements in technology, pedagogy, and the broader field of social work:

Technology-Enhanced Supervision: With the increasing integration of technology in social work education, supervision is adapting to leverage digital tools. Virtual supervision platforms, video conferencing, and online collaboration tools enable supervisors and students to connect seamlessly, overcoming geographical constraints and enhancing accessibility.

Pedagogical Innovations: Innovations in pedagogy are influencing how fieldwork supervision is conceptualized and delivered. Problem-based learning, simulation exercises, and collaborative online spaces are being integrated to create interactive and engaging supervision experiences that mimic real-world challenges.

Cultural Competence and Diversity Focus: There is a growing recognition of the need for culturally competent supervision. Emerging trends emphasize incorporating diversity, equity, and inclusion considerations into supervisory practices. Supervisors are encouraged to explore their cultural competence and adapt their approaches to meet the diverse needs of students and clients.

Trauma-Informed Supervision: The trauma-informed approach, gaining prominence in social work, is extending to fieldwork supervision. Supervisors are exploring ways to create safe and supportive spaces for students who may have experienced trauma, emphasizing sensitivity, empowerment, and resilience in the supervisory relationship.

Feedback and Evaluation Refinement: There is a shift toward more nuanced approaches to feedback and evaluation. Emerging trends focus on constructive feedback, self-assessment, and collaborative goal-setting. Supervisors are encouraged to adopt strengths-based approaches that highlight accomplishments and provide guidance for continuous improvement.

Integration of Macro-Level Practice: Fieldwork supervision is increasingly recognizing the importance of macro-level practice. Emerging trends emphasize the integration of macro perspectives, including policy analysis, advocacy, and community engagement, into the fieldwork experience. This reflects the evolving landscape of social work and the need for well-rounded practitioners.

Interdisciplinary Collaboration: The trend of interdisciplinary collaboration is expanding into fieldwork supervision. Collaborative supervision models involving professionals from diverse disciplines, such as psychology, nursing, and education, are emerging. This approach mirrors the interdisciplinary nature of social work practice in various settings.

Global Perspectives and Exchanges: Recognizing the interconnectedness of social issues, some fieldwork supervision programs are exploring global perspectives. Initiatives include international field placements, virtual exchanges with students from different countries, and the incorporation of diverse cultural contexts into the supervisory dialogue.

Self-Care Emphasis: Emerging trends underscore the importance of self-care in fieldwork supervision. Supervisors are encouraged to model and promote self-care practices, recognizing that supporting students' well-being contributes to their overall professional development.

Continuing Education for Supervisors: Acknowledging the evolving nature of social work practice, there is an emphasis on continuous professional development for supervisors. Opportunities for ongoing education, training, and engagement in emerging research contribute to the enhancement of supervisory skills.

Inclusive and Anti-oppressive Supervision: A focus on inclusivity and anti-oppressive practices is gaining prominence in fieldwork supervision. Supervisors are exploring ways to create environments that challenge systemic oppression, address power differentials, and promote social justice in both the supervisory relationship and the broader field.

The landscape of fieldwork supervision is undergoing transformative shifts driven by innovation, responsiveness to societal changes, and a commitment to enhancing the quality of social work education. These emerging trends reflect a dynamic field that continues to evolve in response to the complex needs of clients, students, and communities.

Review Questions

1. What is the role of theoretical foundations in shaping effective fieldwork supervision practices?
2. How does cultural competence contribute to a positive supervisory relationship in social work field placement?
3. What are the key responsibilities of supervisors in supporting and guiding fieldwork students?
4. Discuss the importance of having a structured template for supervision sessions. How does it enhance the supervisory process?
5. What challenges might arise in the supervisory relationship, and how can they be effectively addressed to ensure a positive learning experience for fieldwork students?
6. Explore the significance of ongoing professional development and continuing education for supervisors in the field of social work.

Multiple-Choice Questions

1. What is the primary purpose of having a template for fieldwork supervision sessions?

   (a) To restrict the conversation
   (b) To provide structure and guidance
   (c) To limit cultural competence
   (d) To discourage feedback

2. Why is cultural competence essential in the context of fieldwork supervision?

   (a) It adds unnecessary complexity
   (b) It fosters a positive supervisory relationship

(c) It limits communication
(d) It isolates diverse perspectives

3. What is the key responsibility of supervisors in supporting fieldwork students?
   (a) Discouraging advocacy
   (b) Restricting access to resources
   (c) Providing guidance and support
   (d) Avoiding feedback
4. How can supervisors address challenges in the supervisory relationship?
   (a) By ignoring them
   (b) By avoiding communication
   (c) By blaming the fieldwork student
   (d) By addressing them effectively
5. Why is ongoing professional development important for fieldwork supervisors?
   (a) It hinders the learning process
   (b) It limits exposure to new ideas
   (c) It ensures supervisors stay updated and informed
   (d) It discourages collaboration

References

Briggs, L. (Ed.). (2020). *Fieldwork in the human services: Theory and practice for field educators, practice teachers and supervisors*. Routledge.

Dimo, P. M. (2013). *Evaluation of fieldwork practice in social work education at the University of Limpopo (Turfloop campus) aligning theory and practice*. Doctoral dissertation, University of Limpopo (Turfloop Campus).

Janus, K. K., & Smythe, D. (2011). Navigating culture in the field: Cultural competency training lessons from the international human rights clinic. *New York Law School Law, 56*, 445.

Kadambari, P., & Lama, N. (2022). Impact of the competency-based field work practicum on students' learning. In R. Baikady, S. M. Sajid, V. Nadesan, & M. R. Islam (Eds.), *The Routledge handbook of social work field education in the global south* (pp. 39–53). Routledge.

Kadushin, A., & Harkness, D. (2014). *Supervision in social work, 5e*. Columbia University Press.

Chapter 13
Challenges and Opportunities in Fieldwork Practice

Learning Objectives
After reading this chapter, you will be able to:

- Identify and analyze challenges inherent in social work fieldwork practices.
- Apply ethical principles to navigate and resolve complex dilemmas encountered in the field.
- Recognize the importance of managing personal boundaries and emotional well-being for practitioners.
- Enhance cross-cultural communication skills to address diversity challenges in social work.
- Develop strategies for advocating systemic change and overcoming barriers in client and community contexts.
- Navigate client resistance and handle difficult situations with professionalism and sensitivity.
- Understand the significance of supervisory support, recognizing challenges and opportunities for growth in fieldwork practice.

13.1 Introduction to Challenges in Fieldwork Practices

Fieldwork in social work is a dynamic and transformative experience that bridges theoretical knowledge with real-world applications. However, this journey is not without its complexities and hurdles. The introduction to challenges in fieldwork practices serves as a compass, guiding social work practitioners and students through the diverse and intricate terrain they may encounter (Dhema, 2012; Sunirose, 2013; Shokane et al., 2016). It is essential to set the stage for understanding that challenges are inherent in the fieldwork process, but they also present invaluable opportunities for growth, learning, and the development of resilience.

M. R. Islam, *Fieldwork in Social Work*,
https://doi.org/10.1007/978-3-031-56683-7_13

The introduction begins by acknowledging that challenges are an integral part of social work practice. These challenges may manifest in various forms, such as ethical dilemmas, cultural conflicts, systemic barriers, and personal emotional strains (Clarke, 1993; Payne & Askeland, 2016). By recognizing the multifaceted nature of challenges, practitioners are better prepared to navigate the complexities that arise during fieldwork.

Fieldwork challenges are not obstacles to success but opportunities for learning and professional development. The introduction encourages a mindset that views challenges as crucial components of the educational process, providing practitioners with hands-on experiences that contribute to their growth as competent and resilient professionals.

Ethical considerations are at the forefront of social work practice, and the introduction underscores the importance of ethical decision-making in the face of challenges. It highlights the ethical responsibility of practitioners to uphold the principles of social justice, dignity, and integrity, even when confronted with difficult situations.

An essential aspect of addressing challenges in fieldwork involves reflective practice. The introduction introduces the concept of self-reflection as a powerful tool for social work practitioners to critically examine their experiences, emotions, and reactions. By engaging in reflective practice, practitioners can glean insights from challenges and use them as catalysts for continuous improvement.

Rather than viewing challenges as insurmountable roadblocks, the introduction encourages a proactive and problem-solving approach. It emphasizes the importance of developing strategies, seeking support, and leveraging available resources to navigate challenges effectively. This proactive mindset fosters resilience and adaptability in the ever-evolving landscape of social work practice.

Acknowledging that challenges vary across different cultural and global contexts, the introduction sets the stage for exploring diverse perspectives on fieldwork challenges. It recognizes that the challenges faced by social workers in one part of the world may differ from those encountered in another, highlighting the need for a nuanced understanding of global social work practices.

In essence, the introduction to challenges in fieldwork practices serves as a foundational guide, preparing social work practitioners and students to approach their field experiences with an open mind, a commitment to ethical practice, and a proactive stance toward overcoming obstacles.

13.2 Navigating Ethical Dilemmas

Navigating ethical dilemmas is a central aspect of social work practice, requiring practitioners to engage in thoughtful and principled decision-making. This section delves into the complexities of ethical challenges encountered during fieldwork, offering insights, strategies, and a framework for ethical navigation.

Identifying Ethical Dilemmas: The exploration begins with an acknowledgment that ethical dilemmas can manifest in various forms, such as conflicts of interest, boundary issues, confidentiality concerns, and moral quandaries. Social work practitioners are encouraged to develop a keen awareness of situations that present ethical challenges to effectively address them.

Principles of Ethical Decision-Making: Understanding the core principles of ethical decision-making is crucial. The section outlines key ethical principles, including respect for autonomy, beneficence, non-maleficence, justice, and fidelity. Social workers are guided to apply these principles systematically when confronted with ethical dilemmas, ensuring a comprehensive and principled approach.

Utilizing Ethical Decision-Making Models: Ethical decision-making models provide a structured framework for resolving dilemmas. The section introduces widely recognized models such as the NASW Code of Ethics and other decision-making frameworks. These models guide practitioners through a systematic process of identifying, analyzing, and resolving ethical issues, promoting consistency and transparency in decision-making.

Balancing Competing Values: Ethical dilemmas often involve the balancing of competing values and interests. Social work practitioners are encouraged to engage in critical reflection to weigh the potential consequences of various courses of action. The section emphasizes the importance of considering the broader impact on clients, communities, and the profession when making ethical decisions.

Seeking Supervision and Consultation: Acknowledging that ethical dilemmas can be complex and emotionally challenging, the section underscores the value of seeking supervision and consultation. Supervisors and colleagues can provide additional perspectives, guidance, and support, fostering a collaborative approach to ethical problem-solving and mitigating the potential for burnout.

Addressing Cultural and Contextual Nuances: Ethical considerations are inherently tied to cultural and contextual factors. The section emphasizes the need for cultural competence and sensitivity when navigating ethical dilemmas in diverse settings. Social workers are encouraged to consider how cultural norms, values, and power dynamics may influence ethical decision-making.

Learning from Ethical Challenges: Every ethical dilemma presents an opportunity for learning and professional growth. Social work practitioners are urged to view challenges as valuable experiences that contribute to their ethical competence. Reflective practice and ongoing education are highlighted as essential components for continually refining ethical decision-making skills.

Global Perspectives on Ethical Dilemmas: Recognizing that ethical dilemmas vary across cultural and global contexts, the section introduces global perspectives on navigating ethical challenges. It emphasizes the importance of understanding how ethical principles may be interpreted differently in diverse societies, promoting cultural humility and adaptability.

Navigating ethical dilemmas in social work fieldwork is a nuanced and ongoing process that requires a commitment to ethical principles, reflective practice, and continuous learning. By providing practitioners with a robust framework and strategies, this section aims to equip social workers with the tools necessary to address ethical challenges ethically, responsibly, and with a global perspective.

13.3 Managing Personal Boundaries and Emotional Well-being

Maintaining personal boundaries and safeguarding emotional well-being are paramount for social work practitioners engaged in fieldwork. This section explores the intricacies of managing boundaries and emotional health, providing insights and strategies to foster resilience and professional sustainability.

Establishing and Communicating Boundaries: The exploration begins with an emphasis on the importance of clearly establishing and effectively communicating boundaries. Social work practitioners are encouraged to delineate professional boundaries with clients, colleagues, and other stakeholders, promoting clarity and preventing potential ethical pitfalls.

Recognizing Warning Signs of Boundary Issues: Social work professionals are guided to recognize warning signs indicating potential boundary issues. These may include blurred professional–personal boundaries, overidentification with clients, or discomfort in navigating dual relationships. Awareness of these signs is crucial for timely intervention and maintaining ethical practice.

Self-Care Strategies for Emotional Well-Being: Practitioners are advised to cultivate self-awareness, engage in regular supervision, establish a support network, and practice mindfulness. These strategies contribute to emotional resilience, enabling social workers to navigate challenging situations more effectively.

Supervision and Peer Support: Recognizing that fieldwork can be emotionally demanding, the section underscores the importance of supervision and peer support. Regular supervision sessions provide a space for reflective dialogue, guidance, and validation. Peer support networks offer additional avenues for sharing experiences, seeking advice, and fostering a sense of community.

Setting Realistic Expectations: Managing personal boundaries involves setting realistic expectations for oneself. Social work practitioners are encouraged to acknowledge the limitations of their capacity, recognize when to seek additional support, and refrain from taking on excessive responsibilities. Setting boundaries with clients and agencies is essential for maintaining a sustainable and healthy workload.

Addressing Vicarious Trauma and Compassion Fatigue: Social work inherently involves exposure to trauma and challenging life circumstances. The section addresses the impact of vicarious trauma and compassion fatigue on practitioners' emotional well-being. Strategies for mitigating these effects include regular self-assessment, seeking therapeutic support, and engaging in activities that promote rejuvenation.

Promoting a Culture of Well-Being in Agencies: The responsibility for managing personal boundaries and emotional well-being extends beyond individual practitioners. Agencies play a crucial role in fostering a culture of well-being. This involves creating supportive work environments, providing resources for self-care, and promoting open discussions about the challenges associated with fieldwork.

Global Perspectives on Well-Being in Social Work: Recognizing that well-being is influenced by cultural and global contexts, the section introduces global perspectives on managing personal boundaries and emotional health. It emphasizes the need for culturally sensitive approaches and highlights how different societies may perceive and address well-being differently.

Managing personal boundaries and emotional well-being is a foundational aspect of ethical and sustainable social work practice. This section aims to equip practitioners with the knowledge and strategies needed to navigate the complexities of fieldwork while safeguarding their health and promoting a culture of well-being within the profession.

13.4 Cultural and Diversity Challenges

Addressing cultural and diversity challenges is integral to effective social work fieldwork. For example, fieldwork education continues to pose challenges in India, primarily attributed to the diverse ideologies and the varying nature of work undertaken by different schools of social work (Carpenter, 2022). This section explores the nuances of navigating cultural diversity, promoting cultural competence, and overcoming challenges to ensure equitable and inclusive practice.

Understanding Cultural Sensitivity: The exploration begins with an emphasis on understanding cultural sensitivity. Social work practitioners are guided to recognize the significance of cultural competence in their interactions with clients from diverse backgrounds. This includes an appreciation for cultural norms, values, and belief systems that shape clients' worldviews.

Addressing Intersectionality in Client Situations: The intersectionality recognized that clients embody multiple identities and may face intersecting forms of oppression. Through real-world examples from countries such as China and the UK, practitioners gain insights into how intersectionality influences clients' experiences and informs culturally competent interventions.

Integrating Anti-Oppressive Practices: To navigate cultural challenges, social work professionals are encouraged to integrate anti-oppressive practices. This involves critically examining power dynamics, advocating for social justice, and challenging systemic inequalities. Examples from different countries highlight how anti-oppressive approaches contribute to more inclusive and equitable social work practice.

Enhancing Cross-Cultural Communication Skills: Effective communication is foundational in addressing cultural challenges that explore strategies for enhancing cross-cultural communication skills. Practitioners learn how to navigate language barriers, employ active listening, and adapt communication styles to ensure meaningful and respectful interactions with clients from diverse cultural backgrounds.

Fostering Inclusive and Culturally Competent Interventions: Promoting inclusive and culturally competent interventions is central to overcoming cultural challenges. Through global examples, practitioners gain insights into how interventions tailored to specific cultural contexts can enhance the effectiveness of social work practice. This involves collaborative goal setting that respects clients' cultural values and preferences.

Evaluating Personal Biases and Cultural Assumptions: Acknowledging and evaluating personal biases is crucial for social work practitioners. The section explores self-reflection as a tool to identify and address biases that may impact interactions with clients. Practitioners are encouraged to engage in continuous learning to challenge stereotypes and assumptions.

Collaborating with Diverse Stakeholders: The collaborative nature of social work extends to engaging with diverse stakeholders. Through seven paragraphs, practitioners learn how collaborating with stakeholders from different cultural backgrounds contributes to more comprehensive and culturally sensitive interventions. Real-world examples underscore the importance of collaboration in achieving positive outcomes.

Navigating Ethical Challenges in Cross-Cultural Settings: The intersection of cultural diversity and ethics is explored in this section. Social work practitioners are guided in navigating ethical challenges within cross-cultural settings, emphasizing the importance of cultural competence in ethical decision-making. Global perspectives shed light on how ethical considerations may vary across cultures.

This section equips social work practitioners with the knowledge and skills needed to navigate cultural and diversity challenges in fieldwork. By fostering cultural competence, addressing intersectionality, and embracing anti-oppressive practices, social workers can contribute to more equitable and inclusive outcomes for clients from diverse backgrounds. Real-world examples provide practical insights, enhancing the cultural responsiveness of social work practice.

13.5 Overcoming Systemic Barriers

In the dynamic landscape of social work fieldwork, practitioners often encounter systemic barriers that impede the effective delivery of services to clients. This section explores the multifaceted nature of systemic challenges, providing insights into understanding, addressing, and ultimately overcoming these barriers.

Identifying Systemic Barriers: Understanding systemic barriers begins with identifying the various structural obstacles that exist within societal frameworks. This part delves into the nuanced aspects of systemic challenges, ranging from institutional policies and procedures to broader socio-economic factors that impact the well-being of individuals and communities. Social work practitioners are encouraged to critically examine these systemic issues to better comprehend their implications for clients.

Analyzing the Impact on Clients: The next step involves analyzing how systemic barriers directly impact clients. By examining real-world examples from different countries, practitioners gain insights into how systemic challenges exacerbate social inequalities and contribute to disparities in access to resources and opportunities.

This analysis is essential for social workers to tailor interventions that address the specific needs and challenges faced by clients within these systemic constraints.

Advocacy and Systemic Change: A central theme in overcoming systemic barriers is the role of advocacy and the pursuit of systemic change. This part emphasizes the proactive stance that social work practitioners can take in advocating for policy reforms, challenging discriminatory practices, and working toward creating more inclusive and equitable systems. Global examples illustrate successful advocacy efforts that have led to tangible systemic changes, demonstrating the impact of collective action.

Collaboration with Community Partners: Addressing systemic barriers requires collaborative efforts with community partners. By forging alliances with community-based organizations, advocacy groups, and other stakeholders, social work practitioners can amplify their impact. Case studies from various countries showcase successful collaborations that have effectively dismantled systemic barriers, highlighting the power of collective and community-led initiatives.

Policy Analysis and Reform: A crucial aspect of overcoming systemic barriers involves engaging in policy analysis and advocating for reform. Social work practitioners are guided through the process of critically analyzing existing policies, understanding their implications, and actively participating in initiatives aimed at reforming policies that perpetuate systemic inequalities. Practical strategies for engaging with policymakers and contributing to policy changes are explored.

Capacity Building and Empowerment: Empowering individuals and communities to navigate and challenge systemic barriers is integral to social work practice. This part explores capacity-building approaches that enable clients to advocate for their rights, access available resources, and actively participate in the decision-making processes that shape their lives. Real-world examples highlight successful empowerment initiatives from different cultural contexts.

Evaluation and Continuous Improvement: The journey of overcoming systemic barriers is an ongoing process that requires evaluation and continuous improvement. Social work practitioners are encouraged to assess the impact of interventions, gather feedback from clients and communities, and adapt strategies based on lessons learned. This iterative approach ensures that efforts to overcome systemic barriers remain responsive to evolving challenges.

By understanding, analyzing, and actively engaging with advocacy, collaboration, and policy reform, social workers can contribute to dismantling systemic obstacles that hinder the well-being of clients and communities. Real-world examples enrich the content, offering practical insights and inspiring practitioners to take impactful actions in their respective contexts.

13.6 Handling Client Resistance and Difficult Situations

Navigating client resistance and challenging situations is an inherent aspect of social work fieldwork. This section explores the complexities involved in handling such scenarios and offers practical guidance for social work practitioners to effectively address client resistance and manage difficult situations.

Understanding Systemic Barriers: Systemic barriers are deeply embedded within social, economic, and political structures, limiting access to resources and opportunities for marginalized populations. The intricacies of systemic barriers and how they perpetuate inequality and hinder well-being are explored. Global perspectives illustrate the diverse manifestations of systemic barriers across different countries and cultural contexts.

Advocacy and Systemic Change: Addressing systemic barriers requires a commitment to advocacy and systemic change. Effective advocacy strategies aimed at challenging and dismantling oppressive systems are explored, with case studies from various regions demonstrating successful advocacy initiatives leading to tangible changes in policies and practices.

Community Empowerment and Mobilization: Empowering communities to advocate for their rights is a crucial aspect of overcoming systemic barriers. Community mobilization approaches that strengthen the collective voice of marginalized groups are outlined, with examples from around the world highlighting community-led initiatives challenging systemic inequities.

Intersectionality and Inclusive Practices: Systemic barriers often intersect with various forms of oppression, requiring a nuanced understanding of intersectionality. The adoption of inclusive practices that consider the intersecting factors of race, gender, class, and other dimensions of identity is explored. Global examples showcase initiatives embracing intersectionality and fostering more inclusive and equitable interventions.

Policy Analysis and Advocacy: An essential tool in overcoming systemic barriers is policy analysis and advocacy. Practitioners are guided through the process of critically analyzing policies and advocating for changes that address systemic injustices. Real-world examples demonstrate how policy advocacy has contributed to dismantling barriers and creating more equitable social structures globally.

Collaboration with Stakeholders: Collaboration with diverse stakeholders is key to overcoming systemic barriers. Effective collaboration strategies, emphasizing the importance of engaging with policymakers, community leaders, and advocacy groups, are explored. Case studies showcase successful collaborative efforts resulting in positive systemic changes, highlighting the potential impact of collective action.

Research and Data-Informed Advocacy: Informed advocacy requires a robust understanding of systemic issues through research and data analysis. The role of research in identifying systemic barriers and using data to inform advocacy efforts is discussed. Global perspectives showcase examples where research-driven advocacy has played a pivotal role in challenging and transforming systemic structures.

Cultural Competence in Systemic Advocacy: Advocacy efforts must be culturally competent to effectively address systemic barriers. The integration of cultural competence in systemic advocacy is explored, ensuring that interventions resonate with the cultural contexts of diverse populations. Case studies highlight instances where culturally competent advocacy has led to more impactful and sustainable systemic changes.

By engaging in advocacy, empowering communities, embracing intersectionality, conducting policy analysis, fostering collaboration, leveraging research, and ensuring cultural competence, social workers can contribute to dismantling oppressive systems. Real-world examples from various global contexts enrich the content, offering valuable insights and actionable approaches for practitioners committed to addressing and overcoming systemic barriers in their fieldwork.

13.7 Supervisory Challenges and Support

Supervisory Challenges and Support play a pivotal role in the success and well-being of individuals engaged in fieldwork practices. Supervisors, often experienced professionals, are tasked with guiding, mentoring, and evaluating the performance of fieldwork practitioners. One significant challenge faced by supervisors is striking a balance between providing guidance and allowing autonomy. Finding this equilibrium is crucial to fostering professional growth while ensuring adherence to ethical and procedural standards. Supervisors must navigate the delicate line between offering support and promoting independence, recognizing that practitioners require both to thrive in their roles.

Moreover, the dynamic nature of fieldwork introduces a range of unexpected challenges that supervisors must address. These challenges may include handling crises, addressing client resistance, and managing difficult situations. Supervisors are instrumental in equipping practitioners with the skills and strategies needed to navigate such obstacles effectively. They serve as a source of expertise, offering insights derived from their own experiences and providing valuable perspectives to help practitioners develop the resilience required in demanding fieldwork environments.

In addition to addressing challenges, effective supervision involves providing ongoing support to enhance practitioners' emotional well-being. The nature of fieldwork can be emotionally taxing, as practitioners often encounter sensitive and challenging situations. Supervisors play a crucial role in fostering a supportive environment where practitioners feel comfortable discussing their emotional responses, seeking guidance, and accessing resources for self-care. This support is essential for preventing burnout and promoting the overall mental health of fieldwork practitioners.

Supervisory support also extends to the professional development of fieldwork practitioners. Regular supervision sessions offer opportunities for constructive feedback, skill enhancement, and goal setting. Supervisors can identify areas for improvement, facilitate training opportunities, and guide practitioners in setting realistic career objectives. This proactive approach to professional development ensures that fieldwork practitioners continually refine their skills and stay abreast of best practices in their respective fields.

Supervisory Challenges and Support are integral components of effective fieldwork practices. Navigating the balance between guidance and autonomy, addressing unexpected challenges, and fostering emotional well-being are critical aspects of successful supervision. By providing ongoing support and facilitating professional development, supervisors contribute significantly to the growth and resilience of fieldwork practitioners, ultimately enhancing the quality of services delivered in diverse and challenging environments.

13.8 Opportunities for Students in Fieldwork Practice

Fieldwork practice in social work provides a myriad of opportunities for students that extend beyond the conventional classroom setting. As students engage in real-world scenarios, they not only apply theoretical knowledge but also acquire invaluable skills and experiences that shape their professional journey. This section explores the diverse opportunities that fieldwork practice presents for social work students.

Hands-On Application of Theoretical Knowledge: One of the primary opportunities afforded by fieldwork practice is the chance to apply theoretical concepts learned in the classroom to actual situations. Students have the opportunity to see how social work theories translate into tangible interventions, providing a deeper understanding of the complexities and nuances of social work practice.

Skill Development and Enhancement: Fieldwork serves as a laboratory for skill development. Students have the chance to hone their communication, assessment, and intervention skills in real-life situations. The dynamic nature of fieldwork exposes them to a variety of challenges, fostering adaptability and resilience—key attributes for effective social work practice.

Cultural Competence and Diversity Exposure: Engaging with diverse populations during fieldwork exposes students to various cultural contexts and lifestyles. This opportunity enhances their cultural competence, enabling them to navigate different belief systems and value frameworks. Exposure to diversity broadens their perspectives and equips them to work effectively with individuals from various backgrounds.

Professional Networking and Collaboration: Fieldwork allows students to build professional networks by collaborating with agencies, organizations, and professionals in the field. Establishing connections with experienced practitioners provides valuable insights, mentorship opportunities, and a glimpse into the broader landscape of social work practice.

Personal and Professional Growth: Fieldwork is a transformative experience that fosters personal and professional growth. Students confront challenges, make critical decisions, and reflect on their values and biases. This process of self-discovery contributes to their growth as individuals and emerging professionals in the field.

Community Engagement and Advocacy Exposure: Working directly with communities during fieldwork exposes students to the intricacies of community dynamics and the challenges residents face. This experience cultivates a sense of advocacy as students witness firsthand the systemic issues affecting vulnerable populations. It empowers them to become agents of change and advocates for social justice.

Real-Time Problem-Solving: Fieldwork situations often demand quick thinking and adaptive problem-solving. Students encounter real-time challenges that require them to synthesize information, assess priorities, and formulate effective solutions. These experiences enhance their problem-solving skills, preparing them for the unpredictable nature of social work practice.

Integration of Reflective Practices: Fieldwork offers students the opportunity to engage in reflective practices. Regular supervision and reflective exercises encourage them to critically analyze their experiences, identify areas for improvement, and continuously enhance their practice. This reflective component contributes to a lifelong commitment to learning and professional development.

The opportunities presented to social work students during fieldwork practice extend far beyond academic learning. This experiential phase of their education lays the foundation for a successful and impactful career, instilling in them the skills, values, and perspectives essential for effective and ethical social work practice.

13.9 Utilizing Reflective Practices for Continuous Improvement

Utilizing reflective practices in the context of fieldwork is a transformative approach that contributes significantly to continuous improvement for practitioners. Reflection involves a purposeful and thoughtful analysis of one's experiences, actions, and decisions, leading to a deeper understanding of the dynamics at play. This process is particularly valuable in fieldwork settings, where practitioners often encounter complex and dynamic situations. By engaging in reflective practices, fieldwork professionals can enhance their self-awareness, refine their skills, and continuously adapt to evolving challenges.

One key aspect of reflective practices is the encouragement of critical self-examination. Practitioners are prompted to explore the underlying assumptions, biases, and values that shape their decision-making processes. This introspective analysis allows individuals to identify areas for improvement, challenge preconceived notions, and cultivate a more nuanced and adaptable approach to their work. In the field of social work, for instance, reflective practices help practitioners understand the impact of their cultural backgrounds on client interactions, fostering cultural competence and sensitivity.

Moreover, reflective practices contribute to the development of a learning culture within fieldwork settings. By regularly engaging in reflective exercises, practitioners create opportunities for ongoing learning and skill refinement. They can draw insights from both successful interventions and challenges faced, turning each experience into a valuable lesson. This iterative learning process is essential for staying current with best practices, adapting to changing environments, and continuously improving the quality of services provided.

Reflective practices also promote collaboration and knowledge sharing within the fieldwork community. Through group reflections and discussions, practitioners can benefit from diverse perspectives, gaining new insights and alternative approaches to common challenges. This collective reflection not only enriches individual learning but also contributes to the overall improvement of fieldwork practices within a team or an organization.

Utilizing reflective practices in fieldwork is a powerful mechanism for continuous improvement. By fostering self-awareness, encouraging critical examination, and creating a culture of learning and collaboration, reflective practices empower practitioners to navigate challenges more effectively and deliver high-quality services. As an integral part of professional development, these practices contribute to the evolution of fieldwork professionals and the advancement of their respective fields.

13.10 Technology and Ethical Considerations in Fieldwork

The integration of technology and ethical considerations in fieldwork refers to the conscientious and responsible use of technological tools and platforms in professional practices, particularly in fields such as social work, counseling, or mental health services. As technology continues to advance, professionals engaging in fieldwork activities must grapple with the ethical implications of leveraging digital tools. This involves ensuring the privacy and security of client information, addressing issues of technological competence, and upholding cultural sensitivity in the digital realm.

13.10.1 Example: Telehealth Services in Mental Health Counseling

In the United States, mental health practitioners increasingly utilize telehealth services to provide counseling and therapy to clients remotely. This technology-driven approach allows individuals to access mental health care from the comfort of their homes, overcoming geographical barriers. However, ethical considerations come to the forefront in this context.

Privacy and Confidentiality: Mental health professionals must select secure and encrypted telehealth platforms to safeguard client privacy. Ensuring that online sessions are conducted in private locations where clients feel comfortable discussing sensitive issues becomes crucial. For instance, a social worker conducting virtual therapy sessions must take measures to protect the confidentiality of client information as they would in a face-to-face setting.

Informed Consent and Technological Competence: Practitioners need to obtain informed consent from clients regarding the use of technology in their sessions. This includes explaining the potential risks and benefits of telehealth services. Additionally, professionals must assess their technological competence to ensure that they can effectively use digital platforms for therapeutic purposes. For example, a counselor may need to offer training or alternative communication methods if a client faces challenges in using the chosen technology.

Cultural Sensitivity: The ethical use of technology also involves being culturally sensitive in a virtual space. Mental health practitioners must consider how cultural backgrounds influence the perception and utilization of technology. For instance, a therapist may need to offer language-specific telehealth options or adapt their communication style to respect cultural differences in expressing emotions.

This example illustrates how the integration of technology in mental health fieldwork demands thoughtful consideration of ethical principles to maintain the quality, confidentiality, and cultural competence of services provided to clients.

13.11 Resilience and Coping Mechanisms

Resilience and coping mechanisms are integral components of an individual's ability to navigate and adapt to adversity, stress, and challenging circumstances. In the context of fieldwork, which often involves complex and emotionally demanding situations, resilience refers to the capacity to bounce back from setbacks, learn from experiences, and maintain a sense of well-being. Coping mechanisms are the strategies individuals employ to manage stress, emotions, and the demands of their work. Together, resilience and coping mechanisms play a crucial role in sustaining the well-being and effectiveness of professionals engaged in fieldwork.

Fieldwork practitioners encounter a myriad of challenges, from client resistance to systemic barriers, which can impact their emotional well-being. Resilience in this context involves developing the ability to remain emotionally steady and maintain a sense of purpose in the face of adversity. For example, a social worker dealing with a challenging case involving a child in a difficult living situation must draw on resilience to persist in advocating for the child's welfare despite obstacles and setbacks.

Coping mechanisms are the strategies individuals use to manage stress and maintain their mental and emotional well-being. In fieldwork, practitioners often adopt various coping mechanisms to navigate the emotional intensity of their work. This may include seeking social support from colleagues, engaging in self-care activities, or utilizing mindfulness techniques. For instance, a counselor dealing with the emotional toll of supporting individuals through trauma might engage in regular supervision sessions to process challenging cases and ensure personal well-being.

Fieldwork professionals benefit from a holistic approach that integrates resilience-building practices and coping mechanisms into their routines. This involves recognizing and acknowledging the emotional demands of the work, actively developing resilience through training and self-reflection, and implementing healthy coping mechanisms. For example, a healthcare worker in a high-stress environment may participate in resilience workshops to enhance their ability to adapt to the demands of the job while also incorporating regular exercise and mindfulness practices into their routine as coping mechanisms.

Fieldwork organizations and institutions can contribute to the development of resilience by providing training, supervision, and a supportive work environment. Training programs that address stress management, emotional intelligence, and self-care can empower practitioners with the skills to navigate challenges effectively. Supervisors also play a crucial role by offering support, monitoring workload, and creating a culture that prioritizes the well-being of fieldwork professionals.

Resilience and coping mechanisms are indispensable in the fieldwork context, offering professionals the strength and tools needed to navigate the challenges inherent in their roles while maintaining their well-being. The integration of these elements contributes to the overall effectiveness and longevity of individuals engaged in fieldwork professions.

13.12 Global Perspectives on Fieldwork Challenges

Fieldwork challenges vary across the globe, influenced by diverse cultural, social, and economic contexts. Understanding the global perspectives on fieldwork challenges is crucial for practitioners, researchers, and policymakers seeking to enhance the effectiveness of fieldwork practices. This discussion explores challenges faced in Bangladesh, Pakistan, China, and India, shedding light on the unique considerations in each country.

13.12.1 Some Examples from Asia

Bangladesh: In Bangladesh, a densely populated and culturally rich country, fieldwork challenges often revolve around resource constraints and access to remote areas. Social workers conducting community outreach may encounter difficulties in reaching marginalized populations due to infrastructural limitations. For instance, implementing healthcare initiatives in rural areas may be impeded by inadequate transportation infrastructure. Additionally, cultural nuances require fieldwork professionals to navigate diverse ethnic communities, emphasizing the need for cultural sensitivity in interventions.

Pakistan: Pakistan, with its diverse cultural landscape, faces challenges in the realm of security and cultural acceptance. Fieldwork practitioners, especially those involved in conflict resolution or community development, may encounter security concerns in certain regions. Moreover, cultural norms and traditions can influence the acceptance of external interventions. For example, a project aimed at empowering women may face resistance in conservative communities, necessitating careful navigation of cultural sensitivities.

China: In China, rapid urbanization and the coexistence of traditional and modern values present unique challenges for fieldwork practitioners. Social workers addressing issues such as migration, family dynamics, or mental health may grapple with the impact of rapid societal changes. For example, the traditional expectation of filial piety may clash with the aspirations of the younger generation for urban lifestyles, creating tensions that practitioners need to navigate. Moreover, the government's role in regulating social work practices adds another layer of complexity to fieldwork dynamics.

India: India, with its vast diversity and complex social structures, presents multifaceted challenges for fieldwork professionals. The caste system, regional disparities, and linguistic diversity are factors that influence the dynamics of interventions. For instance, a public health campaign may require tailored approaches in different states to address linguistic and cultural variations. Additionally, practitioners addressing issues related to gender inequality may encounter varying degrees of acceptance and resistance based on regional and cultural norms.

13.12.2 Some Common Challenges

Cross-Cutting Themes: While each country has its unique challenges, there are cross-cutting themes that transcend borders. Issues such as poverty, gender inequality, and limited access to education persist across these countries, impacting the effectiveness of fieldwork interventions. Fieldwork professionals must consider these common challenges while tailoring their approaches to specific cultural contexts.

Technology and Innovation: Global perspectives on fieldwork challenges also highlight the role of technology in overcoming barriers. For instance, mobile technology has been used in Bangladesh and India to reach remote communities with health information. In China, innovative technological solutions have been integrated into social work practices to address mental health issues, demonstrating the potential for technology to bridge gaps in service delivery.

Policy and Advocacy: Fieldwork challenges often intersect with policy issues, emphasizing the need for advocacy and policy changes. In Pakistan, advocacy efforts may focus on promoting community acceptance of certain interventions, while in India, addressing systemic issues such as caste-based discrimination requires a concerted policy approach. Fieldwork professionals need to engage in policy dialogue to create an enabling environment for effective interventions.

Capacity Building and Collaboration: Capacity building and international collaboration play vital roles in addressing global fieldwork challenges. Initiatives that focus on training local practitioners, sharing best practices, and fostering cross-cultural collaboration contribute to a more robust and effective fieldwork landscape. For instance, collaborative projects between organizations in China and Bangladesh may involve knowledge exchange on sustainable development practices.

Global perspectives on fieldwork challenges underscore the need for context-specific approaches that consider cultural nuances, policy landscapes, and the role of technology. By recognizing the unique challenges in countries such as Bangladesh, Pakistan, China, and India, and embracing collaborative and innovative solutions, fieldwork practitioners can contribute to meaningful and sustainable change on a global scale.

13.13 Innovative Solutions to Fieldwork Challenges

In the dynamic landscape of fieldwork, practitioners often encounter a myriad of challenges that demand creative and innovative solutions. This discussion explores innovative approaches adopted globally to overcome fieldwork challenges, emphasizing the adaptive strategies employed by professionals to enhance the effectiveness of their interventions.

Technology Integration: One of the most prevalent innovative solutions is the integration of technology to augment fieldwork practices. For example, mobile applications have been leveraged to streamline data collection processes in healthcare initiatives in sub-Saharan Africa. By replacing traditional paper-based methods, practitioners can collect real-time data, improving the accuracy and efficiency of their interventions.

Community Engagement Platforms: In diverse cultural contexts, creating robust community engagement platforms has proven instrumental. In Latin American countries, practitioners have employed online forums and social media platforms to facilitate community discussions on topics such as public health and education. These virtual spaces enable practitioners to gather insights directly from the community, fostering a sense of ownership and collaboration in the intervention process.

Collaborative Partnerships: Innovative solutions often emerge through collaborative partnerships between fieldwork organizations, government agencies, and local communities. For instance, in Southeast Asia, collaborative initiatives between non-governmental organizations (NGOs) and government bodies have successfully addressed environmental challenges. By pooling resources and expertise, these partnerships have resulted in more comprehensive and sustainable solutions.

Humanitarian Innovation Labs: The establishment of humanitarian innovation labs has emerged as a promising model for addressing fieldwork challenges, particularly in crisis zones. These labs, found in regions such as the Middle East, provide a space for interdisciplinary collaboration, encouraging the development of creative solutions to complex challenges, ranging from water scarcity to refugee support programs.

Remote Sensing Technologies: In addressing environmental and agricultural challenges, remote sensing technologies have proven invaluable. In parts of Southeast Asia, satellite imagery and drones are used to monitor crop health, assess deforestation, and manage natural resources. This not only enhances the efficiency of fieldwork but also provides a data-driven foundation for sustainable environmental practices.

Artificial Intelligence (AI) and Data Analytics: The integration of AI and data analytics is transforming fieldwork practices globally. In regions like Europe, AI-driven predictive modeling is applied to public health data to anticipate disease outbreaks and allocate resources efficiently. Such innovations not only enhance the precision of interventions but also contribute to proactive and preventive approaches.

Cultural Competence Training: Recognizing the importance of cultural competence in fieldwork, innovative solutions include the incorporation of specialized training programs. In the United States, for example, social work practitioners undergo immersive cultural competence training to better understand and engage with diverse communities. This approach ensures that interventions are culturally sensitive and tailored to the unique needs of each population.

Eco-Friendly and Sustainable Solutions: In the face of environmental challenges, fieldwork practitioners are increasingly adopting eco-friendly and sustainable solutions. This is exemplified by initiatives in Scandinavian countries, where eco-friendly technologies are employed in waste management and renewable energy projects. By prioritizing sustainability, practitioners contribute not only to immediate problem-solving but also to the long-term resilience of communities.

Innovative solutions to fieldwork challenges are essential for staying ahead of evolving issues and creating meaningful impact. Whether through technological advancements, community engagement platforms, collaborative partnerships, or a focus on sustainability, fieldwork practitioners are embracing innovative approaches to address complex problems. By fostering a culture of creativity, adaptability, and continuous learning, the fieldwork community can contribute to more effective, sustainable, and socially responsible interventions worldwide.

Review Questions

1. What are the key considerations when navigating ethical dilemmas in social work fieldwork?
2. How can social work practitioners effectively manage personal boundaries and prioritize emotional well-being?
3. Discuss the importance of cultural competence in addressing diversity challenges during fieldwork.

4. Explore strategies for overcoming systemic barriers in social work fieldwork practice.
5. How can practitioners handle client resistance and navigate difficult situations in a client-centered manner?
6. In what ways can supervision contribute to addressing challenges and fostering professional growth in fieldwork?
7. Reflect on the opportunities for students in fieldwork practice, considering both personal and professional development.
8. Discuss the ethical considerations associated with technology use in social work fieldwork, highlighting potential benefits and challenges.

Multiple-Choice Questions

1. What is a crucial consideration when navigating ethical dilemmas in social work fieldwork?
   (a) Avoiding difficult conversations
   (b) Prioritizing personal interests
   (c) Ignoring ethical principles
   (d) Seeking guidance from colleagues
2. How can practitioners best manage personal boundaries in fieldwork?
   (a) Isolating themselves from clients
   (b) Establishing flexible boundaries
   (c) Ignoring ethical guidelines
   (d) Overidentifying with clients
3. Why is cultural competence important in addressing diversity challenges during fieldwork?
   (a) It enhances effective communication and interventions
   (b) It is optional and does not impact client outcomes
   (c) It leads to exclusionary practices
   (d) It is unrelated to social work ethics
4. What is a key strategy for overcoming systemic barriers in social work fieldwork?
   (a) Ignoring systemic issues
   (b) Advocating for policy change
   (c) Maintaining the status quo
   (d) Avoiding collaboration with other professionals
5. How should practitioners approach client resistance and difficult situations?
   (a) By avoiding challenges and conflict
   (b) By imposing solutions on clients

   (c) By embracing a client-centered approach
   (d) By prioritizing personal opinions over client needs

6. What is the primary purpose of supervision in social work fieldwork?

   (a) To micromanage practitioners
   (b) To create a hierarchical relationship
   (c) To impose rigid rules and regulations
   (d) To address challenges and foster professional growth

7. What opportunities can fieldwork practice offer to students?

   (a) Limited opportunities for growth
   (b) Stagnation in professional development
   (c) Opportunities for both personal and professional development
   (d) Exclusively personal development opportunities

References

Carpenter, D. (2022). Challenges faced in field work. In Baikady, R., Sajid, S. M., Nadesan, V., & Islam, M. R. (Eds.). *The Routledge handbook of social work field education in the global south* (pp. 53-64), Taylor & Francis.

Clarke, J. (Ed.). (1993). *A crisis in care?: Challenges to social work.* Sage.

Dhemba, J. (2012). Fieldwork in social work education and training: Issues and challenges in the case of Eastern and Southern Africa. *Social Work and Society: International Online Journal, 10*(1), n. p.

Payne, M., & Askeland, G. A. (2016). *Globalization and international social work: Postmodern change and challenge.* Routledge.

Shokane, A. L., Nemutandani, V., & Budeli, N. J. (2016). Challenges faced by fourth year social work students during fieldwork practice at a rural-based university. *AFFRIKA Journal of Politics, Economics and Society, 6*(1), 133–163.

Sunirose, I. P. (2013). Fieldwork in social work education: Challenges, issues and best practices. *Rajagiri Journal of Social Development, 5*(1), 48–56.

Chapter 14
Fieldwork Report Writing Format

Learning Objectives
After reading this chapter, you will be able to:

- Develop an understanding of the purpose and significance of fieldwork reports in social work.
- Recognize and articulate the specific objectives that guide the creation of a fieldwork report.
- Evaluate the essential characteristics that contribute to the quality of a fieldwork report.
- Analyze the typical contents of a fieldwork report through a practical example.

14.1 What Is a Fieldwork Report in Social Work?

A Fieldwork Report in social work is a comprehensive documentation that captures the practical experiences, insights, and reflections of a social work practitioner during their hands-on involvement in the field. This report is a crucial component of social work education and professional development, serving as a means to integrate theoretical knowledge with real-world application. Through the Fieldwork Report, social work professionals articulate the details of their interventions, interactions with clients, and the challenges faced in diverse and dynamic settings (for details, please read Bogo, 2014).

The primary purpose of a Fieldwork Report in social work is to provide a detailed account of the practitioner's activities, observations, and reflections during the fieldwork period (Bogo, 2010). It offers a platform for practitioners to critically analyze their experiences, assess the effectiveness of their interventions, and reflect on the ethical considerations and cultural competence applied in their practice. The report becomes a reflective tool that enables social workers to connect their practical

M. R. Islam, *Fieldwork in Social Work*,
https://doi.org/10.1007/978-3-031-56683-7_14

experiences with the theories learned in the classroom, fostering a deeper understanding of the complexities of social work practice.

The structure of a Fieldwork Report typically includes an introduction that outlines the objectives of the fieldwork, a detailed description of the interventions and activities performed, and a reflective analysis that ties back to social work theories and principles. This documentation not only contributes to the practitioner's personal and professional development but also plays a significant role in advancing the field of social work by sharing valuable insights, best practices, and challenges faced in the pursuit of social justice and well-being.

14.2 Objectives of Fieldwork Report

The primary objective of a fieldwork report is to provide a structured and comprehensive account of an individual's or a group's practical experiences, observations, and activities during a fieldwork placement, internship, or similar practical training program (Maidment, 2000). The specific objectives of a fieldwork report include the following:

Documentation: To record and document the experiences and activities encountered during the fieldwork. This includes details about the work undertaken, interactions with clients or individuals, and the tasks performed.

Reflection: To encourage individuals to reflect on their experiences, learning, and challenges faced during the fieldwork. Reflection is a critical component of the learning process, allowing individuals to make sense of their experiences and extract valuable insights.

Assessment: In educational contexts, fieldwork reports are often used as a means of assessing the individual's performance and understanding of the practical aspects of their field of study. It allows instructors and supervisors to evaluate the student's ability to apply theoretical knowledge in real-world settings.

Communication: To communicate findings, observations, and recommendations to supervisors, instructors, or relevant stakeholders. The report serves as a way to share what was learned during the fieldwork and convey any significant findings or insights.

Professional Development: To aid in the individual's professional development by identifying areas of strength and areas that require improvement. Through self-assessment and reflection, individuals can set goals for further development in their chosen field.

Accountability: To provide a transparent and accountable record of activities and outcomes achieved during the fieldwork. This is important for both the individual and the organization hosting the fieldwork placement.

Knowledge Dissemination: In some cases, fieldwork reports contribute to the dissemination of knowledge and best practices within the field. They may be shared with colleagues, organizations, or the broader community to promote learning and improvement.

Continuous Improvement: To facilitate continuous improvement in the fieldwork process, the report may include recommendations for enhancing the fieldwork experience for future participants or for improving the organization's services or operations.

Documentation of Client Interactions: For professions involving client care, such as healthcare or social work, fieldwork reports serve as a legal and ethical record of client interactions, assessments, and interventions. They help ensure compliance with professional standards and regulations.

Research and Analysis: In research-related fieldwork, the report may contribute to the research process by documenting data collection, analysis, and findings. It may also serve as a reference for future research endeavors.

Overall, the objective of a fieldwork report is to provide a comprehensive and informative account of the fieldwork experience, demonstrating the individual's competency, growth, and contributions while serving as a valuable tool for assessment, reflection, and communication within educational and professional settings.

14.3 Characteristics of a Good Fieldwork Report

A good fieldwork report should possess several key characteristics to effectively convey the individual's or group's experiences, insights, and findings during their fieldwork placement or internship. These characteristics ensure that the report is clear, informative, and valuable for assessment, reflection, and communication (Bogo, 2014). Here are the characteristics of a good fieldwork report:

Clarity and Conciseness:

- The report should be written in clear, straightforward language, avoiding jargon or overly technical terms.
- Information should be presented concisely, with a focus on relevant details and key findings.

Structure and Organization:

- The report should have a logical and well-organized structure, including clear headings and subheadings.
- Each section should flow logically, leading the reader through the report.

Objective and Factual:

- The report should be objective and based on factual information, presenting observations and experiences accurately.
- Personal biases or opinions should be minimized, and any subjective statements should be clearly labeled as such.

Evidence-Based:

- Findings and observations should be supported by evidence, such as case studies, client interactions, or data collected during the fieldwork.
- Use of appropriate references or citations is encouraged when applicable.

Reflective and Critical Analysis:

- The report should include a reflective analysis of experiences, challenges, and lessons learned during the fieldwork.
- Critical analysis should be applied to evaluate the effectiveness of interventions or approaches used.

Relevance and Focus:

- The content of the report should remain focused on the objectives of the fieldwork and the specific tasks undertaken.
- Irrelevant or extraneous information should be avoided.

Objectives and Learning Goals:

- The report should clearly state the objectives and learning goals of the fieldwork placement and assess the extent to which they were achieved.

Client Privacy and Confidentiality:

- Any information related to clients or individuals encountered during the fieldwork should be treated with utmost respect for privacy and confidentiality.
- Pseudonyms or de-identified information should be used to protect client identities.

Professional and Ethical Standards:

- The report should demonstrate adherence to professional and ethical standards relevant to the field of study or practice.
- Ethical dilemmas encountered and their resolution should be discussed transparently.

Recommendations and Future Directions:

- The report should include practical recommendations based on the findings and experiences.
- Suggestions for future actions, improvements, or areas of research should be provided.

Well-Documented:

- Adequate documentation of client interactions, interventions, and any relevant processes should be included, complying with record-keeping standards.

Grammar and Writing Style:

- The report should be free of grammatical errors and written in a professional and coherent style.

Visual Aids (if applicable):

- Charts, graphs, tables, or visual aids may be used to enhance the understanding and presentation of data.
- These aids should be clear, labeled, and relevant to the content.

References and Citations:

- Proper citation of sources, if used, should be provided in a consistent citation style (e.g., APA and MLA) following academic or professional standards.

Feedback and Evaluation:

- The report should invite feedback and evaluation from instructors, supervisors, or relevant stakeholders to foster continuous improvement.

Accessibility and Formatting:

- The report should be formatted in a way that makes it easily accessible to readers, including appropriate fonts, headings, and page numbers.

A well-structured, clear, and informative fieldwork report not only serves its immediate purpose but also becomes a valuable resource for the individual's professional development, assessment, and future reference within academic and professional settings.

14.4 Contents of Fieldwork Report: An Example

Cover/Title Page

Title: Fieldwork Report: Social Work Student in a Hospital Setting
Student Name: [Your Name]
University: [Your University]
Fieldwork Duration: [Start Date]–[End Date]
Supervisors: [Supervisors' Names both in University and Agency]
Use Logos: [If permits) use logos in both University and Agency
Date of Submission: [Submission Date]

Acknowledgments

- The acknowledgments section is an opportunity to express gratitude to individuals or organizations who provided support and guidance throughout the fieldwork experience.
- Begin by expressing sincere gratitude to your fieldwork supervisor, mentioning their name and role.
- Acknowledge the hospital administration, staff, and the social work department for their cooperation and assistance.

- If some specific individuals or colleagues offered valuable insights or mentorship, mention their names and roles.

You can also express appreciation for any resources, materials, or facilities provided by the hospital that contributed to your learning.

Abbreviations

- The abbreviations section provides a list of acronyms or abbreviations used throughout the report, along with their corresponding full forms.
- List each abbreviation in alphabetical order.
- Provide the full form of each abbreviation in parentheses right after the abbreviation.
- If you have used a lot of abbreviations, you might want to consider grouping them by category or subject matter to make the list more organized.
- Include all abbreviations that are used in the report and might not be familiar to readers.
- Do not include common abbreviations that are widely understood (e.g., USA and CEO).
- Keep the list concise but comprehensive enough to assist readers in understanding the report.
- Remember that the acknowledgments section is a way to show appreciation and build professional relationships, while the abbreviations section helps readers navigate your report more easily.

Table of Contents

Abstract
Executive Summary
Chapter 1: Introduction to Fieldwork

1.1 Definition, Objectives, and Importance
1.2 Ethical Values and Principles in Fieldwork
1.3 Duties and Assignments

Chapter 2: Agency as Field Placement

2.1 Agency Background
2.2 Departments of the Agency
2.3 Staff and Administrative Procedures
2.4 Agency Functions
2.5 Budgeting and Sources of Funds
2.6 Resources of the Agency

Chapter 3: Duties and Responsibilities of Fieldwork Student

3.1 Long and Short Cases
3.2 Support for the Agency
3.3 Group Work and Community Engagement
3.4 Collaboration and Partnership

Chapter 4: SWOT Analysis
Chapter 5: Learnings and Achievements
Chapter 6: Conclusion and Recommendations
References
Appendices

Abstract

- The abstract provides a concise overview of the entire report, highlighting its key components, scope, and purpose. It is usually written after the report is completed and should be around 150–250 words.
- Begin by briefly introducing the context of the report, mentioning the hospital setting and the student's role.
- Summarize the main chapters or sections covered in the report, including the key areas of focus.
- Mention the significant findings, conclusions, and recommendations presented in the report.
- Conclude by emphasizing the report's contribution to understanding the fieldwork experience in a hospital setting.

Executive Summary

- The executive summary offers a condensed version of the report, designed to provide a quick overview of the entire document. It is typically written after the report is completed and should be around one to two pages in length.
- Start with a brief introduction, explaining the purpose of the report and the student's role in the hospital.
- Provide a concise summary of the main points covered in each chapter or section of the report. Focus on the most important aspects of each chapter.
- Highlight the key findings, major achievements, and significant challenges faced during the fieldwork.
- Discuss the implications of the findings and their relevance for both the agency and future social work students.
- Conclude with actionable recommendations based on the insights gained during the fieldwork experience. These recommendations should be directed toward the agency and future students.
- Remember that both the abstract and executive summary should be clear, succinct, and engaging. They serve as a preview for readers who may not have the time to read the entire report, so prioritize the most essential information concisely.

Chapter 1: Introduction to Fieldwork

1.1 Definition, Objectives, and Importance

- Define fieldwork in the context of social work practice.
- Explain the objectives of fieldwork, including skill development, practical application of theories, and exposure to real-world scenarios.

- Emphasize the importance of fieldwork in bridging the gap between classroom learning and professional practice.

1.2 Ethical Values and Principles in Fieldwork

- Discuss the ethical values (e.g., confidentiality, respect, and empathy) and principles (e.g., client empowerment and social justice) that guided your actions during fieldwork.
- Reflect on how these ethical considerations influenced your decision-making and interactions with clients.

1.3 Duties and Assignments

- Describe the specific tasks and assignments you were assigned during your fieldwork in the hospital.
- Detail your responsibilities, such as conducting assessments, providing counseling, advocating for clients, and collaborating with the health-care team.

Chapter 2: Agency as Field Placement

2.1 Agency Background

- Provide an overview of the hospital's history, mission, and values.
- Explain how the hospital's mission aligns with the goals of social work practice.

2.2 Departments of the Agency

- Describe the different departments or units within the hospital where you were placed.
- Highlight your involvement in various departments and the diverse experiences you gained.

2.3 Staff and Administrative Procedures

- Discuss the hospital's staff structure, including roles and responsibilities.
- Explain the administrative procedures you encountered, such as intake processes, case management, and interdisciplinary meetings.

2.4 Agency Functions

- Outline the range of services and programs the hospital offers to patients.
- Share your contributions to these services, such as providing emotional support, coordinating discharge plans, and facilitating support groups.

2.5 Budgeting and Sources of Funds

- Explain how the hospital's budgeting and funding sources impact its operations and services.

- Reflect on how financial considerations influenced your approach to service delivery.

2.6 Resources of the Agency

- Detail the resources available to support both clients and staff in the hospital.
- Discuss how you utilized these resources to enhance your practice and support clients effectively.

Chapter 3: Duties and Responsibilities of Fieldwork Student

3.1 Long and Short Cases

- Describe specific cases you worked on, both in short and long terms.
- Discuss the challenges, interventions, and outcomes you experienced in these cases.

3.2 Support for the Agency

- Explain how you contributed to the hospital's programs and initiatives.
- Detail your involvement in planning and executing workshops, campaigns, or other community-oriented projects.

3.3 Group Work and Community Engagement

- Reflect on your participation in group work sessions with clients or community members.
- Discuss the impact of group dynamics on the interventions and support you provided.

3.4 Collaboration and Partnership

- Describe instances where you collaborated with other healthcare professionals, social workers, or external organizations.
- Highlight the benefits of collaboration and the challenges you encountered.

Chapter 4: SWOT Analysis

- Analyze the strengths, weaknesses, opportunities, and threats you identified during your fieldwork experience.
- Provide examples for each category and explain how they influenced your practice and learning.

Chapter 5: Learnings and Achievements

- Reflect on the knowledge and skills you gained during your fieldwork.
- Discuss personal achievements, growth, and areas for further development.

Chapter 6: Conclusion and Recommendations

- Summarize your overall fieldwork experience and the insights you have gained.

- Provide recommendations for the hospital to enhance its collaboration with social work students and improve the fieldwork experience.
- Offer advice and recommendations for future social work students undertaking fieldwork in a hospital setting.

References

- List all the sources and references you consulted and cited in your report. Follow the reference style that your university follows (i.e., APA 6th edition)

Appendices

- Include additional materials such as case notes, assessment tools, community engagement plans, or any other relevant documents that support your narrative.

Review Questions

1. What is the significance of having clear objectives in a fieldwork report?
2. How do the characteristics of a good fieldwork report contribute to effective communication?
3. Can you identify potential challenges in compiling the contents of a fieldwork report, and how might they be addressed?
4. In what ways does a well-structured fieldwork report benefit the social work practitioner, the client, and other stakeholders?

Multiple-Choice Questions

1. What is the primary purpose of a fieldwork report in social work?
   (a) To entertain the reader
   (b) To document personal opinions
   (c) To share personal experiences
   (d) To communicate professional observations and interventions
2. Why are clear objectives important in a fieldwork report?
   (a) They add unnecessary complexity
   (b) They help guide the report's content and focus
   (c) They limit the writer's creativity
   (d) They are not relevant to social work reports
3. What role do characteristics of a good fieldwork report play in the assessment process?
   (a) They hinder the assessment

(b) They have no impact on the assessment
(c) They contribute to a thorough and accurate assessment
(d) They create bias in the assessment

4. When considering the contents of a fieldwork report, what should be prioritized?

(a) Relevant and significant information
(b) Personal opinions
(c) A wide range of unrelated information
(d) Abstract and theoretical concepts

References

Bogo, M. (2010). *Achieving competence in social work through field education*. University of Toronto Press.
Bogo, M. (2014). Field instruction in social work: A review of the research literature. *Supervision in Counseling*, 163–193.
Maidment, J. (2000). *Methods used to teach social work students in the field: A research report from New Zealand* (Vol. 19, p. 145). Social Work Education.

Chapter 15
Reflective Practice and Learning in Fieldwork

Learning Objectives
After reading this chapter, you will be able to:

- Develop a comprehensive understanding of reflective practice in the context of social work agencies.
- Learn to seamlessly integrate reflective practices into the organizational culture of social work agencies.
- Acquire knowledge on establishing structural mechanisms that support reflective learning within social work organizations.
- Develop the skills to measure and evaluate the outcomes of reflective practices, assessing their impact on professional growth and service delivery.
- Explore challenges related to reflective practice and discover effective strategies for overcoming these barriers, ensuring successful implementation in the field of social work.

15.1 Understanding Reflective Practice in Agency Context

Reflective practice within the context of social work agencies is a dynamic and essential component that contributes to organizational learning, professional growth, and the overall enhancement of service delivery (for details, please read Pawar, 2017). This section delves into the nuanced understanding of reflective practice within the agency setting, shedding light on its significance and the unique dynamics it assumes within the organizational framework.

Definition and Significance: Reflective practice, at its core, involves the intentional process of critically examining one's actions, decisions, and experiences to derive meaningful insights and inform future actions. Within social work agencies, this practice takes on added significance as it directly contributes to the

M. R. Islam, *Fieldwork in Social Work*,
https://doi.org/10.1007/978-3-031-56683-7_15

organization's ability to adapt, learn, and continuously improve. It serves as a collective mechanism for staff members to learn from both successes and challenges, ultimately enhancing the agency's effectiveness in meeting the diverse needs of its clientele.

Organizational Learning and Adaptation: Reflective practice at the agency level aligns with the principles of organizational learning. It goes beyond individual reflection, encompassing a collective and shared process where insights gained by one staff member can inform and benefit the entire organization. This shared learning contributes to the agency's capacity for adaptation, allowing it to respond effectively to evolving social issues, changes in client demographics, and shifts in best practices within the field of social work.

Enhancing Professional Development: Within the agency context, reflective practice becomes a cornerstone for professional development. Social work practitioners engage in thoughtful reflection on their interactions with clients, the impact of interventions, and the broader systemic factors at play. This self-reflection contributes to the continuous development of individual practitioners, fostering a culture of ongoing learning and growth within the agency.

Facilitating Open Communication and Collaboration: Reflective practice creates a culture of open communication and collaboration within social work agencies. It encourages staff members to share their experiences, insights, and challenges, fostering a sense of trust and mutual support. This collaborative approach breaks down silos within the organization, promoting a holistic understanding of the agency's operations and the diverse perspectives of its workforce.

Aligning with Organizational Values and Mission: Reflective practice is inherently tied to the values and mission of social work agencies. It provides a structured mechanism for staff members to align their daily practices with the core values of social work, such as empathy, social justice, and client-centered approaches. This alignment ensures that the agency's mission is not only articulated in its documents but also actively reflected in the day-to-day work of its practitioners.

Continuous Quality Improvement: In the agency context, reflective practice serves as a driving force behind continuous quality improvement. By systematically reflecting on the effectiveness of interventions, identifying areas for improvement, and implementing changes based on these reflections, social work agencies enhance the overall quality of their services. This commitment to continuous improvement is foundational for agencies striving to meet the evolving needs of the communities they serve.

Institutionalizing Reflective Practices: Understanding reflective practice at the agency level involves a commitment to institutionalizing these practices. This requires leadership support, the establishment of formalized processes for reflection (such as regular supervision sessions and team meetings), and the integration of reflective practices into organizational policies and procedures. Creating a systemic approach ensures that reflective practice becomes an inherent and sustainable aspect of the agency's culture.

Understanding reflective practice in the agency context is about recognizing its profound impact on organizational learning, professional development, and the quality of services provided by social work agencies. It involves embracing reflective practice as more than an individual endeavor but as a collective and organizational commitment to learning, growth, and the pursuit of excellence in social work practice.

15.2 Integrating Reflective Practices into Organizational Culture

Integrating reflective practices into the organizational culture of social work agencies is a strategic and transformative process that fosters continuous learning, enhances staff development, and contributes to the overall effectiveness of the agency's mission (Gould, 2016; Williams & Graham, 2016). This section explores the key components and strategies involved in successfully embedding reflective practices within the broader organizational culture.

Leadership Commitment and Modeling: The successful integration of reflective practices begins with a commitment from organizational leadership. Leaders play a pivotal role in modeling reflective behaviors and demonstrating the value of self-assessment and continuous learning. Leadership commitment is reflected in both rhetoric and action, emphasizing the importance of reflection in staff meetings, organizational communications, and decision-making processes.

Establishing a Supportive Environment: Creating a supportive environment is essential for the integration of reflective practices. This involves cultivating a culture that values learning from experiences, views mistakes as opportunities for growth, and encourages open communication. Social work agencies can establish channels for staff to express their thoughts and experiences, ensuring that reflective practices are embraced rather than viewed as additional tasks.

Incorporating Reflective Elements into Supervision: Supervision sessions provide a structured platform for integrating reflective practices. Supervisors can guide staff members in reflecting on their experiences, challenging situations, and personal growth. By incorporating reflective elements into regular supervision, agencies create a space for practitioners to share insights, seek guidance, and collectively learn from each other's experiences.

Providing Training and Resources: The successful integration of reflective practices requires providing training and resources to support staff. This includes workshops, seminars, or training sessions focused on the principles and techniques of reflective practice. Additionally, agencies can offer resources such as literature, case studies, and tools that facilitate the development of reflective skills among staff members.

Formalizing Reflective Processes: Formalizing reflective processes involves embedding them into the organizational structure. This may include creating dedicated time during staff meetings for reflection, incorporating reflective components into performance appraisal processes, or establishing regular forums where staff can collectively engage in reflective discussions. By formalizing these processes, reflective practices become ingrained in the day-to-day operations of the agency.

Encouraging Peer Collaboration: Peer collaboration is a powerful strategy for integrating reflective practices. Establishing opportunities for staff members to engage in peer-to-peer reflective discussions, collaborative problem-solving, and knowledge-sharing creates a culture of mutual support. This collaborative approach not only enhances the quality of reflection but also fosters a sense of collective responsibility for continuous learning.

Recognizing and Celebrating Reflective Efforts: Recognition is a key motivator for staff engagement in reflective practices. Social work agencies can create mechanisms for acknowledging and celebrating reflective efforts. This may include commendations, awards, or simply acknowledging individuals and teams during organizational events. Recognizing reflective practices reinforces their importance and encourages a culture of continuous improvement.

Aligning Reflective Practices with Organizational Values: Integration is most effective when reflective practices align with the core values of the organization. By explicitly connecting reflective behaviors with organizational values such as accountability, compassion, and integrity, agencies reinforce the idea that reflection is not a separate activity but an integral part of embodying the organization's ethos.

Emphasizing Inclusivity and Diversity in Reflection: Reflective practices should be inclusive and culturally competent. Organizations should emphasize the importance of considering diverse perspectives and experiences in reflection. Encouraging staff to explore how their cultural background and biases may influence their practice fosters a reflective culture that is sensitive to the diverse needs of the communities served.

Establishing a Feedback Loop for Continuous Improvement: The integration of reflective practices should be accompanied by a feedback loop for continuous improvement. Agencies can establish mechanisms for collecting feedback from staff about the effectiveness of reflective processes, and use this information to refine and adapt reflective practices over time.

Integrating reflective practices into the organizational culture of social work agencies requires a comprehensive approach that involves leadership commitment, a supportive environment, formalized processes, and ongoing training. By fostering a culture that values and celebrates reflective practices, agencies can create an environment where continuous learning, professional growth, and effective service delivery thrive.

15.3 Structural Mechanisms for Reflective Learning

Structural mechanisms for reflective learning provide the organizational framework necessary to cultivate a culture of continuous improvement, professional development, and enhanced service delivery within social work agencies. This section explores the key structural elements that support and facilitate reflective practices at both individual and organizational levels.

Regular Supervision Sessions: Structured and regular supervision sessions serve as a cornerstone for reflective learning. These sessions provide dedicated time for practitioners to discuss their caseloads, challenges faced, and the impact of their interventions. Supervisors play a crucial role in guiding reflective conversations, encouraging self-assessment, and fostering a supportive environment for practitioners to learn from their experiences.

Reflective Team Meetings: Beyond individual reflection, reflective team meetings create a collaborative space for practitioners to collectively explore cases, share insights, and learn from each other. These meetings encourage interdisciplinary collaboration, allowing different perspectives and expertise to contribute to a more comprehensive understanding of complex cases. Reflective team meetings contribute to a shared learning culture within the agency.

Case Conferencing and Consultations: Structuring case conferencing and consultations provides practitioners with opportunities to seek input from colleagues and experts within the organization. These structured discussions not only offer diverse perspectives on challenging cases but also promote a culture of shared learning and mutual support. Case conferences can be scheduled regularly to ensure ongoing opportunities for reflective dialogue.

Formalized Reflective Practices in Workflows: Integrating reflective practices into formal workflows ensures that reflection becomes an integral part of everyday tasks. This can involve incorporating reflection into case documentation processes, creating templates that prompt practitioners to consider the outcomes of their interventions, and embedding reflective elements into organizational protocols. Formalizing these practices ensures their consistent application.

Learning and Development Programs: Establishing structured learning and development programs provides a systematic approach to reflective learning. These programs may include workshops, seminars, or training sessions specifically designed to enhance reflective skills. Topics can range from case analysis to ethical considerations, empowering practitioners with the knowledge and tools needed for effective reflection.

Utilizing Technology for Reflective Platforms: Incorporating technology into reflective learning enhances accessibility and efficiency. Creating online platforms or utilizing existing communication tools allows practitioners to engage in virtual reflective discussions, share insights, and access resources. Technology facilitates ongoing communication and collaboration, particularly in situations where in-person meetings may be challenging.

Actionable Feedback Mechanisms: Establishing actionable feedback mechanisms is crucial for structural reflective learning. Practitioners should receive constructive feedback on their reflections, encouraging a continuous improvement mindset. Feedback can be provided through formal channels, such as performance appraisals, or informally through regular check-ins and discussions.

Integration into Performance Appraisals: Reflective learning should be integrated into the performance appraisal process. This involves assessing practitioners based not only on outcomes but also on their ability to reflect, adapt, and contribute to the learning culture of the organization. Performance appraisals provide a formalized structure for recognizing and rewarding reflective efforts.

Creating a Repository of Best Practices: Establishing a repository of best practices serves as a structural mechanism for sharing successful reflective strategies within the organization. This centralized resource allows practitioners to access case studies, success stories, and lessons learned. It promotes a culture of learning from both successes and challenges, contributing to organizational growth.

Encouraging Cross-Departmental Collaboration: Breaking down departmental silos and encouraging cross-departmental collaboration enhance reflective learning. When practitioners from different departments engage in collaborative reflection, it broadens perspectives, introduces fresh insights, and promotes a holistic understanding of agency operations.

Structural mechanisms for reflective learning create the scaffolding necessary for practitioners to engage in intentional and meaningful reflection. By incorporating reflective practices into formalized structures, social work agencies can foster a culture of continuous learning, adaptability, and excellence in service delivery.

15.4 Measuring and Evaluating Reflective Practice Outcomes

Measuring and evaluating reflective practice outcomes is a critical aspect of ensuring that the integration of reflective practices within social work agencies is effective, impactful, and aligns with the overarching goals of the organization. This section explores the key considerations, methodologies, and indicators involved in assessing the outcomes of reflective practices.

Establishing Clear Objectives and Indicators: Before embarking on the measurement process, agencies must establish clear objectives for reflective practices. These objectives should align with the organization's mission, values, and strategic goals. Additionally, defining measurable indicators that reflect the intended outcomes of reflective practices provides a foundation for evaluation.

Utilizing Key Performance Indicators (KPIs): KPIs serve as quantitative and qualitative metrics that measure the success of reflective practices. These may include indicators related to improved client outcomes, staff satisfaction, reduced turnover rates, and enhanced service delivery. KPIs should be relevant, specific, and aligned with the goals of reflective learning.

Client Feedback and Satisfaction: One crucial outcome of reflective practice is the potential improvement in client satisfaction and outcomes. Agencies can collect client feedback through surveys, interviews, or focus groups to assess whether reflective practices contribute to enhanced client engagement, understanding, and positive outcomes.

Staff Engagement and Well-Being: Reflective practices are expected to positively impact staff engagement and well-being. Assessing staff satisfaction, morale, and perceived work-related stress provides insights into the effects of reflective practices on the overall work environment. Reduced burnout rates and increased job satisfaction may be indicative of successful reflective interventions.

Assessing Changes in Practice: Evaluating changes in practice is a direct measure of the impact of reflective learning. Agencies can examine whether practitioners have altered their approaches, interventions, or decision-making processes as a result of engaging in reflective practices. This may involve reviewing case files, documentation, and reports to identify observable changes.

Case Outcome Improvements: Measuring the impact of reflective practices on individual cases can be indicative of broader success. Assessing improvements in case outcomes, client progress, and resolution rates provides tangible evidence of the efficacy of reflective learning. This may involve comparing outcomes before and after the implementation of reflective practices.

Qualitative Analysis of Reflections: Qualitative analysis of reflective writings, discussions, or reports can offer rich insights into the depth and quality of reflective practices. Analyzing the content of reflections allows agencies to identify patterns, themes, and areas of growth. Qualitative data provide a nuanced understanding of the impact of reflective practices on individual practitioners and the organization as a whole.

Incorporating 360-Degree Feedback: 360-Degree feedback involves collecting input from multiple sources, including supervisors, peers, and subordinates. This comprehensive feedback mechanism can provide a holistic view of the impact of reflective practices on individual practitioners. It captures how reflective learning influences teamwork, communication, and collaboration within the organization.

Adaptation and Innovation: Successful reflective practices should contribute to the adaptation and innovation within the agency. Evaluating the organization's ability to adapt to changing circumstances, integrate new knowledge, and implement innovative solutions can be indicative of the transformative impact of reflective learning.

Continuous Improvement of Reflective Processes: The assessment of reflective practice outcomes should not be a one-time effort but an ongoing process. Agencies should incorporate feedback loops and mechanisms for continuous improvement into their evaluation strategies. This involves regularly reviewing outcomes, gathering input from practitioners, and making adjustments to reflective processes to enhance their effectiveness.

Comparative Analysis Over Time: Conducting a comparative analysis over time allows agencies to track changes in reflective practice outcomes. Comparing data from different periods provides insights into the evolution of reflective practices and their cumulative impact on organizational culture, client outcomes, and staff development.

Measuring and evaluating reflective practice outcomes involve a multifaceted approach that combines quantitative and qualitative measures. By aligning assessment strategies with organizational objectives and utilizing a range of indicators, social work agencies can gauge the effectiveness of reflective practices and make informed decisions to enhance their impact over time.

15.5 Challenges and Strategies for Overcoming Barriers

15.5.1 Challenges

Novice social workers face diverse challenges when they are assigned to field practice at the agency level (Sunirose, 2013). These challenges significantly differ from one country, context, or culture to another. Here, we delve into ten major challenges encountered by social workers as they navigate the complexities of field practice within various organizational settings. Embarking on field practice in social work comes with its set of hurdles, and the nuances of these challenges vary widely based on the geographical location, cultural context, and the specific nature of the social work agency. As social work is inherently dynamic and responsive to local needs, understanding and addressing these challenges become paramount for practitioners striving to make a meaningful impact on individuals and communities.

Navigating the landscape of field practice is a multifaceted journey that involves tackling intricate issues and adapting to the unique demands of different contexts. From communication barriers to cultural disparities, each challenge presents an opportunity for growth and learning, shaping the experiences of social workers as they engage in agency-level field practice. Let us explore these challenges that resonate across borders but manifest in distinct ways. In the realm of global social work, practitioners encounter a myriad of challenges as they engage in field practice at the agency level. These challenges are not only shaped by the unique characteristics of each country but are also deeply influenced by cultural factors, organizational dynamics, and the broader socio-economic context. Here, we explore ten major challenges that social workers navigate, highlighting the diverse and complex nature of field practice on a global scale. Embarking on field practice in social work requires adeptness in navigating challenges that are not only inherent to the profession but also intricately linked to the cultural and contextual nuances of the assigned agency. From communication hurdles to grappling with systemic barriers, social workers encounter a spectrum of obstacles that demand resilience, adaptability, and a deep understanding of the specific challenges embedded in the diverse landscapes of field practice. Here, we examine ten major challenges that encapsulate the varied experiences of social workers engaged in agency-level field practice.

Resistance to Change: Resistance to change poses a significant challenge in implementing reflective practices. This resistance may stem from established norms, traditions, or previous methodologies that practitioners are accustomed to. For instance, in a social work agency where traditional approaches have long been in place, introducing reflective practices may face pushback as staff members may perceive them as additional or unnecessary tasks. Overcoming this challenge involves clear communication about the purpose and benefits of reflective practices, along with involving staff in decision-making processes to foster a sense of ownership.

Time Constraints: Time constraints are a prevalent challenge faced by social work professionals globally. Balancing heavy caseloads, administrative tasks, and the demands of client interactions often leaves practitioners with limited time for reflective activities. This challenge requires strategies that prioritize the importance of reflective practices, emphasizing their potential to enhance efficiency, reduce burnout, and ultimately improve the overall quality of service delivery. Additionally, integrating reflective activities seamlessly into existing workflows can help overcome this time-related hurdle.

Lack of Supervisory Support: The lack of support from supervisors is a significant barrier to the successful implementation of reflective practices. Supervisors play a crucial role in fostering a supportive environment for practitioners to engage in reflective activities. Without their active encouragement and guidance, practitioners may feel unsupported or question the relevance of reflective practices. Addressing this challenge involves providing training for supervisors on the importance of reflective practices and implementing supervision models that explicitly incorporate reflective elements.

Cultural and Linguistic Diversity: Cultural and linguistic diversity poses a challenge in ensuring that reflective practices are inclusive and culturally competent. In multinational or culturally diverse social work settings, practitioners may face difficulties in adapting reflective practices to address the unique cultural nuances and linguistic variations within the team. Overcoming this challenge involves offering cultural competency training to staff and providing reflective resources in multiple languages to accommodate the diverse backgrounds of practitioners.

Lack of Clarity on Reflective Processes: A lack of clarity on the specific steps involved in reflective processes can hinder practitioners from engaging in meaningful reflection. Without a clear understanding of how to approach reflective activities, practitioners may feel uncertain or hesitant. Overcoming this challenge requires the organization to conduct training sessions and workshops to clarify the purpose and process of reflective practices. Providing mentorship for less experienced practitioners can also contribute to building confidence in engaging with reflective activities.

Fear of Judgment: Fear of judgment is a psychological barrier that may inhibit practitioners from engaging openly and honestly in reflective practices. In hierarchical organizational structures, where there is a perceived risk of negative evaluation, practitioners may hesitate to share experiences or insights. Creating a non-judgmental culture and assuring practitioners of the confidentiality of reflective discussions are crucial strategies for overcoming this fear and fostering a supportive environment for reflection.

Limited Resources: Limited resources, including financial constraints, can impede the successful implementation of reflective practices. Social work agencies in resource-limited regions may struggle to allocate funds for training, technology, or materials necessary to support reflective activities. Overcoming this challenge involves prioritizing resource allocation for reflective practices and exploring collaboration opportunities with external organizations or partners to supplement resources.

Sustainability and Institutionalization: Ensuring the sustainability and institutionalization of reflective practices is a long-term challenge. While initial enthusiasm may drive the adoption of reflective practices, maintaining their momentum over time requires ongoing commitment from organizational leadership. Embedding reflective practices into organizational policies and procedures is essential to make them integral to the organizational culture and overcome the challenge of sustainability.

Technology Integration: The integration of technology into reflective practices can be challenging, especially in regions where access to technology is limited. Social work agencies may face difficulties in adopting digital tools and platforms for reflective activities. Overcoming this challenge involves considering alternative methods or low-tech solutions, ensuring that the benefits of reflective practices are accessible to all practitioners, regardless of technological constraints.

Resistance Due to Past Experiences: Resistance due to past experiences represents a challenge rooted in organizational history. Practitioners who have had negative experiences with previous attempts to introduce reflective practices may be hesitant to engage in them again. Addressing this challenge requires acknowledging past failures, learning from them, and actively working to rebuild trust among practitioners. Clear communication about the improvements and benefits of the current reflective initiatives is essential to overcoming resistance based on past experiences.

15.5.2 Strategies for Overcoming Challenges

Addressing the barriers encountered in field practice is crucial for social workers seeking to navigate the complexities of agency-level work. These barriers vary significantly, presenting challenges that are uniquely shaped by the cultural context, organizational dynamics, and specific demands of each social work setting. Here, we delve into ten major strategies designed to empower social workers in overcoming these barriers, fostering resilience, and enhancing the effectiveness of their field practice (for details, please read Arthur & Nazroo, 2003; Matthew & Lough, 2017; Pawar, 2017). As social workers engage in field practice at the agency level, it becomes imperative to develop strategies that effectively overcome the diverse barriers encountered in this dynamic profession. These barriers, ranging from resistance to change to time constraints, demand thoughtful approaches that acknowledge the nuances of each challenge. In this discussion, we explore ten major strategies aimed at equipping social workers with the tools and insights needed to navigate these obstacles, fostering a more impactful and fulfilling field practice experience.

Embarking on field practice at the agency level presents social workers with a myriad of challenges, necessitating the development of effective strategies to overcome these hurdles. These challenges, shaped by cultural nuances, organizational intricacies, and the unique demands of social work settings, call for tailored approaches that address their specific nature. Here, we explore ten major strategies designed to empower social workers in overcoming barriers, fostering resilience, and ensuring a successful journey through the complexities of agency-level field practice. In the realm of global social work, practitioners encounter diverse barriers during field practice at the agency level.

These barriers, shaped by cultural, organizational, and contextual factors, necessitate the development of strategies that transcend geographical boundaries. In this exploration, we discuss ten major strategies designed to empower social workers in overcoming these global barriers, fostering adaptability, and promoting effective field practice across different cultural and organizational contexts. Navigating the intricate landscape of field practice in social work requires the formulation of effective strategies to overcome the diverse barriers inherent in the profession. While varying in nature, these barriers demand thoughtful and context-specific approaches. Here, we delve into ten major strategies aimed at equipping social workers with the tools and insights needed to navigate the challenges, fostering resilience, and ensuring a successful journey through the complexities of agency-level field practice.

Establishing Open Communication Channels: Creating an environment of open communication is foundational to overcoming barriers in social work field practice. By fostering a culture where practitioners feel comfortable expressing concerns and sharing insights, organizations create a collaborative atmosphere. Regular team meetings provide a structured platform for practitioners to discuss challenges faced during field practice, facilitating the exchange of ideas and mutual support.

Providing Comprehensive Training Programs: Empowering social workers with comprehensive training programs is a proactive strategy to enhance their ability to navigate challenges. These programs cover essential skills and knowledge areas, ensuring that practitioners are well-prepared to face diverse obstacles. Workshops on cultural competency, time management, and reflective practices contribute to a well-rounded training approach, equipping practitioners with the complexities of field practice.

Cultivating Cultural Competence: Recognizing and embracing cultural diversity is pivotal for effective social work practice. Cultivating cultural competence within the organization ensures that practitioners are equipped to navigate challenges arising from diverse backgrounds. Integrating cultural competency training into the organizational culture provides practitioners with the understanding and adaptability needed to address the unique needs of the populations they serve.

Developing Flexible Workflow Structures: Creating flexible workflow structures is essential to accommodate the dynamic nature of social work. These structures enable practitioners to adapt to unexpected challenges without compromising the quality of their work. By incorporating flexibility into organizational processes, social workers can respond more effectively to the ever-changing demands of field practice, fostering resilience and adaptability.

Implementing Reflective Practices: Integrating reflective practices into the daily routines of social workers is a powerful strategy for overcoming barriers. This approach allows practitioners to process their experiences, identify challenges, and strategize solutions. Regular reflection fosters a culture of continuous learning, contributing to resilience in the face of obstacles. Encouraging practitioners to maintain reflective journals or participate in regular reflective sessions provides structured opportunities for self-awareness and skill improvement.

Establishing Mentorship Programs: The establishment of mentorship programs is a valuable strategy for overcoming barriers in social work field practice. These programs connect less experienced social workers with seasoned professionals, creating a platform for guidance and shared experiences. The mentor–mentee relationship facilitates knowledge transfer and offers practical insights into navigating complex challenges. Pairing novice practitioners with experienced mentors enables them to benefit from the wisdom and advice of those who have successfully navigated similar hurdles.

Prioritizing Self-Care and Well-Being: Recognizing the demanding nature of social work, organizations should prioritize initiatives that promote self-care and well-being among practitioners. This strategic focus enhances the resilience of social workers and equips them to cope effectively with the stressors inherent in the profession. Implementing wellness programs, offering mental health resources, and encouraging a healthy work–life balance contribute to the overall well-being of practitioners, enabling them to navigate challenges with greater stability.

Fostering a Team-Based Approach: Promoting a team-based approach is a strategic initiative to overcome barriers in social work field practice. Encouraging collaboration among social workers fosters a sense of collective responsibility. By pooling their strengths and expertise, practitioners can address challenges more effectively. Organizing regular team-building activities or collaborative projects strengthens the bonds among practitioners, enhancing their ability to work cohesively in overcoming obstacles.

Advocating for Systemic Change: Advocating for systemic change involves addressing broader organizational or societal issues contributing to barriers in field practice. Social workers can leverage their collective voice to influence policies and practices for a more supportive work environment. Collaborating with advocacy groups and engaging in initiatives to address systemic issues, such as inadequate resources or discriminatory policies, is a powerful strategy to overcome barriers at a systemic level.

Establishing Continuous Professional Development: Establishing opportunities for continuous professional development is essential to ensure that social workers stay updated on best practices and acquire new skills. This strategic approach enhances their overall competence and adaptability, enabling them to navigate evolving challenges in the field. Organizations can facilitate workshops, training sessions, and access to resources that support ongoing learning, contributing to the continuous growth and effectiveness of social workers in their field practice.

Review Questions

1. What is the role of reflective practice in the context of social work agencies, and how does it contribute to professional development?
2. How can reflective practices be effectively integrated into the organizational culture of social work agencies?
3. Discuss the importance of establishing structural mechanisms to support reflective learning within social work organizations.
4. What are the key challenges associated with implementing reflective practices in the field of social work, and what strategies can be employed to overcome these challenges?

Multiple-Choice Questions

1. In the context of social work, reflective practice primarily aims to:

   (a) Enhance administrative tasks
   (b) Facilitate organizational hierarchy
   (c) Promote ongoing learning and professional development
   (d) Establish strict guidelines for fieldwork

2. How can reflective practices be integrated into the organizational culture of social work agencies?

   (a) By avoiding open communication
   (b) By emphasizing rigid procedures
   (c) By fostering an environment that encourages self-reflection
   (d) By limiting feedback channels

3. What is a structural mechanism in the context of reflective learning within social work organizations?

   (a) A formal process for avoiding challenges
   (b) A method to discourage continuous improvement
   (c) An established system that supports reflective practices
   (d) A set of strict rules for reporting

4. When encountering challenges in implementing reflective practices, what is a recommended strategy for overcoming them?

   (a) Avoiding reflection on challenges
   (b) Ignoring the need for adaptation
   (c) Seeking external blame for difficulties
   (d) Developing strategies to address and overcome challenges

References

Arthur, S., & Nazroo, J. (2003). Designing fieldwork strategies and materials. *Qualitative Research Practice: A Guide for Social Science Students and Researchers, 1*, 109–137.

Gould, N. (2016). Introduction: The learning organization and reflective practice – The emergence of a concept. In M. Baldwin (Ed.), *Social work, critical reflection and the learning organization* (pp. 1–10). Routledge.

Matthew, L. E., & Lough, B. J. (2017). Challenges social work students encounter in international field placements and recommendations for responsible management. *Journal of Social Work Education, 53*(1), 18–36.

Pawar, M. (2017). Reflective learning and teaching in social work field education in international contexts. *The British Journal of Social Work, 47*(1), 198–218.

Sunirose, I. P. (2013). Fieldwork in social work education: Challenges, issues and best practices. *Rajagiri Journal of Social Development, 5*(1), 48–56.

Williams, C., & Graham, M. J. (2016). Building transformative practice. In C. Williams & M. J. Graham (Eds.), *Social work in a diverse society* (pp. 3–20). Policy Press.

Chapter 16
Concluding and Future Directions in Social Work Field Practice

Learning Objectives

After reading this chapter, you will be able to:

- Understand the process of transitioning out-of-field placement, including the challenges and opportunities involved.
- Gain insights into celebrating achievements and extracting valuable lessons from your fieldwork experiences, fostering a reflective and growth-oriented approach.
- Comprehend the impact of technological advancements on social work, recognizing the evolving landscape and potential applications for improved practice.

16.1 Transitioning Out-of-Field Placement

The process of transitioning out-of-field placement marks a significant milestone in the journey of social work practitioners. This phase involves a multifaceted approach to bidding farewell to the fieldwork setting, encompassing both emotional and practical dimensions (Chilvers, 2017; Homonoff, 2008).

Understanding the Emotional Landscape: Navigating the culmination of fieldwork involves acknowledging and understanding the emotional landscape practitioners may experience. Recognizing the attachments formed, the gratitude felt toward clients and colleagues, and the potential sadness associated with farewells is essential for a holistic transition.

Expressing Gratitude and Closure: Encouraging practitioners to express gratitude is crucial for a meaningful transition. This involves articulating appreciation to clients, colleagues, and the community. Whether through verbal expressions, heartfelt notes, or symbolic gestures, expressing gratitude fosters a sense of closure and acknowledges the impact of the relationships formed.

M. R. Islam, *Fieldwork in Social Work*,
https://doi.org/10.1007/978-3-031-56683-7_16

Reflective Discussions with Supervisors: Structured reflective discussions with supervisors play a pivotal role in processing the emotional and professional dimensions of concluding fieldwork. These sessions provide a space for practitioners to share experiences, gain insights, and receive guidance for future growth. Supervisors offer support and facilitate a thoughtful reflection on the entire fieldwork experience.

Effective Time Management Strategies: Practical guidance on effective time management during the concluding phase is essential. Practitioners need to prioritize tasks, wrap up ongoing projects, and ensure a smooth transition for the incoming social work practitioner. This involves balancing administrative responsibilities with the emotional aspects of bidding farewell.

Maintaining Professionalism and Ethical Considerations: Maintaining professionalism and upholding ethical considerations is paramount during the transition period. Practitioners are guided on the responsible handling of client information, respecting confidentiality, and ensuring a seamless transfer of responsibilities. This ensures the integrity of the social work practice.

Supervisory Support and Guidance: Supervisors play a central role in providing support and guidance during the transition. Through supervisory support, practitioners can navigate both emotional and practical aspects. Supervisors contribute to the reflective process, offering insights and helping practitioners frame their experiences for future professional growth.

Closure Rituals and Symbolic Gestures: Exploring closure rituals and symbolic gestures provides a structured way to bring closure to the fieldwork experience. Whether through team gatherings, reflective sessions, or symbolic activities, these rituals acknowledge the shared journey, fostering a positive ending to the placement.

Transition Back to Academic Settings or Other Roles: Addressing the transition back to academic settings or other professional roles is crucial. Practitioners need guidance on managing this shift, including re-entering academic environments or adapting to new workplace cultures. Support is provided to navigate these transitions successfully.

Personal Reflection and Learning Integration: Encouraging personal reflection is integral to the transition process. Practitioners are guided to reflect on the entirety of their fieldwork experience, integrating the lessons learned into their professional identity. This reflective practice contributes to ongoing personal and professional development.

Creating a Future Professional Development Plan: Looking ahead, practitioners are guided to create a future professional development plan. This involves setting goals, identifying areas for growth, and planning for ongoing learning opportunities. This assists practitioners in envisioning their future in social work and preparing for continued success and impact.

16.2 Celebrating Achievements and Drawing Lessons from Fieldwork Experience

Defining Professional Milestones: Take a moment to list and describe the specific professional achievements you attained during your fieldwork. This could include successful interventions, positive outcomes for clients, or the completion of significant projects that showcase your growth and impact.

Team Accomplishments and Collaborative Success: Reflect on the collective achievements of your team during the fieldwork experience. Recognize the collaborative efforts that contributed to shared success, fostering a sense of accomplishment within the team.

Reflecting on Challenges as Opportunities: Approach challenges faced during fieldwork as opportunities for personal and professional growth. Consider how overcoming obstacles has shaped your resilience, adaptability, and problem-solving skills.

Resilience and Problem-Solving Skills: Recall instances where you demonstrated resilience and effectively employed problem-solving skills to overcome challenges. Reflect on how these experiences have enhanced your capacity to navigate complex situations.

Learning from Setbacks: Acknowledge setbacks encountered during fieldwork as valuable learning experiences. Consider the lessons learned from these situations and how they contribute to your ongoing development as a social work professional.

Enhanced Decision-Making Confidence: Reflect on moments where your confidence in decision-making was strengthened. Identify the factors that contributed to this growth, such as increased knowledge, experience, or successful outcomes.

Skill Development and Acquisition: Detail the new skills and competencies you developed and acquired during your fieldwork. Reflect on how these skills have contributed to your effectiveness as a social work practitioner.

Deepened Understanding of Social Work Practice: Explore how the fieldwork experience has deepened your understanding of social work principles and practices. Consider the insights gained into the complexities of client interactions, systemic issues, and the broader context of social work.

These reflections on achievements and lessons learned will contribute to a comprehensive understanding of your fieldwork experience, facilitating ongoing personal and professional growth.

16.3 Embracing Technological Advancements in Social Work

As social work evolves, the integration of technology becomes integral to the profession's efficacy and responsiveness. Embracing technological advancements in social work involves understanding and leveraging digital tools to enhance service delivery, communication, and overall effectiveness.

Digital Tools for Client Engagement: Explore how digital platforms and communication tools can be harnessed to engage clients effectively. This includes virtual sessions, telehealth options, and online resources that enhance accessibility and convenience for clients.

Data Management and Analysis: Delve into the use of technology for efficient data management and analysis. Discuss digital systems for record-keeping, data visualization, and analytics that empower social workers to make informed decisions and track client progress.

Telehealth and Remote Services: Discuss the increasing relevance of telehealth and remote services, especially in reaching clients in geographically distant or underserved areas. Explore the benefits and challenges of providing social work services through digital platforms.

Digital Literacy and Inclusivity: Address the importance of digital literacy among social work practitioners and clients. Explore strategies to ensure inclusivity, considering the digital divide and how to bridge gaps to ensure equitable access to services.

Online Advocacy and Awareness: Examine the role of technology in amplifying advocacy efforts and raising awareness about social issues. Discuss the use of social media, online campaigns, and digital storytelling as powerful tools for social work advocacy.

Ethical Considerations in the Digital Realm: Navigate the ethical considerations associated with the use of technology in social work. Discuss issues related to privacy, confidentiality, and the responsible use of data, emphasizing the importance of maintaining ethical standards in the digital realm.

Professional Development in the Digital Age: Encourage social work practitioners to embrace continuous learning in the digital age. Discuss online resources, webinars, and digital platforms that facilitate professional development, keeping practitioners updated on the latest advancements.

Collaboration and Networking Platforms: Explore how collaboration and networking platforms contribute to a connected social work community. Discuss the benefits of online forums, professional networks, and collaborative tools that foster knowledge-sharing and support among practitioners.

Embracing technological advancements in social work is not just about adopting new tools but understanding the transformative potential of technology to enhance the profession's impact and reach. This exploration encourages social workers to leverage the digital frontier ethically, inclusively, and innovatively.

16.4 Adapting to Evolving Societal Needs and Challenges

In the ever-changing landscape of society, social work practitioners must continuously adapt to address emerging needs and challenges. This involves a proactive and responsive approach to staying relevant and effective in the pursuit of social justice and well-being.

Identification of Emerging Social Issues: Discuss the importance of staying informed about evolving social issues. Explore strategies for identifying and understanding emerging challenges, ensuring that social workers are well-equipped to address current and future societal needs.

Flexibility in Service Delivery Models: Emphasize the need for flexibility in service delivery models. Discuss how social work practices can adapt to different contexts, including virtual platforms, community-based interventions, and collaborative partnerships to meet diverse needs.

Cultural Competence and Sensitivity: Explore the significance of cultural competence in adapting to diverse societal needs. Discuss how social workers can enhance their cultural sensitivity to better serve communities with varying backgrounds, values, and traditions.

Incorporating Technology for Accessibility: Discuss the integration of technology to enhance accessibility. Explore how digital tools and online platforms can be leveraged to reach populations with limited resources, ensuring inclusivity in service delivery.

Policy Advocacy and Systemic Change: Highlight the role of social work in advocating for policy changes to address evolving societal needs. Discuss strategies for engaging in systemic advocacy and contributing to the development of policies that promote social justice and equity.

Community Engagement and Empowerment: Explore approaches to community engagement that empower individuals and communities to address their unique challenges. Discuss the importance of building partnerships, amplifying community voices, and fostering sustainable initiatives.

Education and Skill Development: Encourage social workers to engage in continuous education and skill development. Discuss how staying abreast of new theories, practices, and interventions equips practitioners to navigate evolving societal dynamics effectively.

Trauma-Informed Approaches: Discuss the relevance of trauma-informed approaches in adapting to evolving societal challenges. Explore how understanding and addressing trauma can enhance the effectiveness of social work interventions in various settings.

Adapting to evolving societal needs and challenges is not just a professional duty but also a commitment to the foundational principles of social work. This dynamic approach ensures that practitioners remain responsive, empathetic, and equipped to create positive change in an ever-changing world.

Review Questions

1. How does the process of transitioning out-of-field placement contribute to professional development and growth in social work practice?
2. Reflect on your own achievements during fieldwork. What lessons can be drawn from these experiences, and how can they inform future practice?
3. In what ways have technological advancements influenced the field of social work, and how can practitioners adapt to leverage these advancements for societal benefit?

Multiple-Choice Questions

1. What is the primary purpose of celebrating achievements in the context of fieldwork?
   (a) Boosting personal ego
   (b) Drawing lessons for future practice
   (c) Meeting organizational requirements
   (d) Documenting individual accomplishments
2. How can social workers embrace technological advancements in their practice?
   (a) Ignore technological changes
   (b) Resist incorporating technology
   (c) Adapt and leverage technology for societal benefit
   (d) Delegate all technological tasks to support staff
3. Why is it important for social workers to adapt to evolving societal needs and challenges?
   (a) To conform to popular trends
   (b) To maintain a static approach to practice
   (c) To avoid change and remain traditional in practice
   (d) To address emerging issues and provide relevant services

References

Chilvers, D. J. (2017). *Social work field educator practice: Expanding the vision*. https://ir.canterbury.ac.nz/items/81ee35c4-ce13-42e9-9ef9-f9c30f0d15f9

Homonoff, E. (2008). The heart of social work: Best practitioners rise to challenges in field instruction. *The Clinical Supervisor, 27*(2), 135–169.

Appendix: Answers to Review Questions and Multiple-Choice Questions

Chapter 1

Review Questions

1. The key meanings associated with social work include service, social justice, dignity and worth of the person, importance of human relationships, and integrity. These meanings contribute to the profession's identity by guiding social workers in their mission to enhance the well-being of individuals and communities, promote social justice, respect the dignity of all individuals, value human relationships, and uphold ethical standards.
2. The scope of social work extends across micro, mezzo, and macro levels of practice. At the micro level, social workers focus on individual and family support, addressing personal challenges and providing direct services to clients. Mezzo-level practice involves working with groups and communities to address issues that affect larger segments of the population, such as community development and advocacy. Macro-level practice involves working on a broader scale to address systemic issues and promote social change, such as policy analysis and development.
3. Ethical considerations and principles are fundamental to social work practice. Examples of their application include maintaining client confidentiality, respecting client autonomy and self-determination, promoting social justice and equity, avoiding conflicts of interest, and adhering to professional boundaries. Social workers must navigate complex ethical dilemmas and make decisions that prioritize the well-being and rights of their clients.
4. Social work encompasses diverse divisions and specializations, including areas such as child welfare, healthcare and medical social work, gerontology and aging services, crisis intervention, and international social work. Each specialized

M. R. Islam, *Fieldwork in Social Work*,
https://doi.org/10.1007/978-3-031-56683-7

area addresses unique challenges and populations, requiring specific knowledge, skills, and approaches to practice effectively.

5. Major social work theories contribute to understanding and addressing various social issues and challenges by providing frameworks for assessment, intervention, and advocacy. For example, systems theory helps social workers analyze the interconnectedness of individuals and their environments, while cognitive-behavioral theory informs interventions aimed at modifying negative thought patterns. Person-centered theory emphasizes the importance of the therapeutic relationship, while feminist theory critiques social inequalities and advocates for gender equality.
6. Social work is recognized as a vital profession due to its impact on individuals and communities. Social workers play essential roles in addressing social injustices, advocating for marginalized populations, providing support and resources to those in need, and promoting positive social change. The profession's commitment to social justice, human rights, and empowerment contributes to its significance and relevance in addressing contemporary social issues.
7. Micro-level social work practice involves providing direct services to individuals and families, such as counseling, case management, and advocacy. Mezzo-level practice focuses on working with groups and communities, such as facilitating support groups, organizing community events, and advocating for policy changes. Macro-level practice addresses systemic issues and social change efforts, such as conducting research, developing policies, and lobbying for legislative reforms.
8. Theoretical concepts in social work can be translated into practical applications to address real-world challenges by informing assessment, intervention, and advocacy strategies. For example, systems theory may guide social workers in assessing the interplay of individual, family, and community factors in a client's life, while empowerment theory may inform interventions aimed at promoting self-determination and resilience. By applying theoretical frameworks to practice, social workers can better understand the root causes of social issues and develop effective strategies for intervention and change.

Multiple-Choice Questions

1. (a) Individual clients
2. (b) Respecting clients' autonomy and choices
3. (c) Facilitating support groups for families
4. (c) They guide understanding and intervention in social issues
5. (c) It integrates theoretical knowledge into practical interventions

Chapter 2

Review Questions

1. The significance of social and mental preparation before engaging in fieldwork lies in ensuring that students are emotionally and mentally prepared to handle the challenges and complexities of real-world social work practice. It helps them develop resilience, self-awareness, and coping strategies necessary for effective engagement with clients and situations they may encounter in the field.
2. The EARIS formula, which stands for Exploration, Action, Reflection, Integration, and Supervision, can benefit social work students in preparing for field practice by providing a structured framework for their learning and development. It encourages students to explore their motivations, values, and expectations, take proactive actions to acquire necessary skills and knowledge, reflect on their experiences to gain insights and learning, integrate their learning into practice, and seek supervision and guidance from mentors or supervisors.
3. Setting clear objectives is essential for effective fieldwork because it provides students with a clear sense of direction and purpose. Clear objectives help students identify what they aim to achieve during their field placement, whether it is developing specific skills, gaining experience in a particular area of practice, or achieving learning outcomes outlined by their academic program. By setting clear objectives, students can focus their efforts, track their progress, and evaluate their achievements effectively.
4. Fieldwork contributes to the overall development of social work students in several ways. First, it provides students with hands-on experience in applying theoretical knowledge to real-world situations, thereby enhancing their practical skills and competence. Second, fieldwork exposes students to diverse client populations, social issues, and practice settings, broadening their understanding of the complexities of social work practice. Third, fieldwork offers opportunities for personal and professional growth, including the development of empathy, cultural competence, self-reflection, and resilience. Finally, fieldwork facilitates the integration of classroom learning with real-world practice, bridging the gap between theory and application.
5. Ethical considerations and principles are crucial in the preparation phase of fieldwork as they guide students in navigating ethical dilemmas, maintaining professional boundaries, and upholding the values and ethics of the social work profession. By emphasizing ethical awareness and responsibility, students learn to prioritize the well-being and rights of clients, adhere to professional standards of conduct, and practice with integrity and accountability. Ethical preparation also involves understanding the ethical codes and guidelines relevant to social work practice, seeking supervision and guidance when facing ethical challenges, and engaging in ongoing reflection and self-assessment to ensure ethical practice.

Multiple-Choice Questions

1. (c) It is crucial for gaining practical experience and skills
2. (a) It guides social work students in preparing for fieldwork
3. (a) It contributes to effective engagement and coping in fieldwork
4. (d) They provide a roadmap for effective fieldwork
5. (c) It provides practical experience, skill development, and professional growth

Chapter 3

Review Questions

1. Setting clear objectives in social work fieldwork preparation is important because it provides a roadmap for what needs to be achieved during the placement. It helps in focusing efforts, measuring progress, and ensuring that the learning goals are met effectively.
2. Personal learning goals contribute to a meaningful fieldwork experience by aligning the student's interests, aspirations, and areas of growth with the objectives of the placement. They provide direction, motivation, and a sense of purpose, enhancing engagement and fostering a deeper understanding of social work practice.
3. Ethical considerations and principles guide social work practice in fieldwork settings by providing a framework for ethical decision-making, ensuring that the well-being and rights of clients are prioritized, maintaining professional boundaries, and upholding the values of integrity, respect, and social justice.
4. Socioeconomic, cultural, and psychological factors impact the challenges addressed by fieldwork agencies in various ways. Socioeconomic factors such as poverty, unemployment, and lack of access to resources can exacerbate social issues and increase the demand for social services. Cultural factors influence the norms, beliefs, and practices of diverse populations, requiring culturally competent approaches in service delivery. Psychological factors such as trauma, mental health issues, and interpersonal dynamics affect the well-being and functioning of individuals and families, necessitating tailored interventions and support.
5. Understanding the introduction, function, and challenges faced by social work agencies is significant in preparing for fieldwork as it provides insight into the organizational context, goals, and dynamics within which social work practice occurs. It helps students navigate agency structures, roles, and expectations, anticipate potential challenges, and develop strategies for effective collaboration and service delivery.

Multiple-Choice Questions

1. (a) To guide and direct the fieldwork experience
2. (c) By fostering a more purposeful learning journey
3. (d) Adhering to ethical standards and principles
4. (d) To navigate and address agency-specific issues
5. (c) They provide insights into agency dynamics and structures

Chapter 4

Review Questions

1. The key foundational principles of field assignments in social work practice include adherence to ethical guidelines, maintaining client confidentiality, fostering cultural competence, promoting client autonomy and self-determination, and ensuring professional boundaries.
2. Roles and responsibilities in fieldwork contribute to client-centered approaches by ensuring that interventions are tailored to meet the unique needs and preferences of clients. Social workers collaborate with clients to develop treatment plans, empower them to make informed decisions, and advocate for their rights within the context of their communities.
3. Effective fieldwork documentation is crucial for maintaining accurate records of client interactions, assessments, interventions, and progress. Social workers must adhere to ethical standards such as confidentiality, accuracy, objectivity, and integrity when documenting client information to ensure privacy, confidentiality, and accountability.
4. Ethical challenges in field practice can be navigated by adhering to ethical principles such as beneficence, non-maleficence, autonomy, justice, and fidelity. Social workers should engage in ethical decision-making processes, seek supervision and consultation when faced with dilemmas, and prioritize the well-being and rights of clients.
5. Supervision contributes to the professional development of social work practitioners by providing guidance, support, feedback, and opportunities for reflection on practice. Supervisors help social workers enhance their clinical skills, develop self-awareness, address ethical dilemmas, and promote personal and professional growth.
6. Adaptability is essential in responding to dynamic situations during field assignments as social workers encounter diverse client populations, complex issues, and changing environments. Being adaptable allows social workers to adjust their approaches, interventions, and strategies based on the unique needs and circumstances of clients, ensuring effective and responsive service delivery.

Multiple-Choice Questions

1. (d) To ensure client-centered approaches
2. (c) By responding to dynamic situations
3. (b) It provides constructive feedback
4. (c) To tailor interventions to client needs
5. (c) They guide professional conduct and decision-making
6. (a) To tailor interventions to meet client needs

Chapter 5

Review Questions

1. Cultural sensitivity enhances effective fieldwork practice in social work by promoting understanding, respect, and responsiveness to the cultural backgrounds, beliefs, and values of clients. It helps social workers avoid misunderstandings, misinterpretations, and unintentional harm while fostering trust and rapport with clients from diverse cultural backgrounds.
2. Evaluating personal biases and cultural assumptions is important for social work practitioners to ensure that they provide fair, unbiased, and culturally competent services to clients. By acknowledging and addressing their own biases, social workers can prevent discriminatory practices, promote inclusivity, and deliver more effective interventions that respect the dignity and autonomy of all individuals.
3. Key elements of anti-oppressive practices include recognizing and challenging power imbalances, promoting social justice and equity, advocating for marginalized populations, and actively opposing discrimination and oppression in all forms. These elements can be integrated into fieldwork by adopting inclusive and participatory approaches, advocating for systemic changes, and centering the voices and experiences of marginalized communities in decision-making processes.
4. Enhancing cross-cultural communication skills in social work is significant because it enables practitioners to effectively engage with clients from diverse cultural backgrounds, facilitate mutual understanding, and overcome language and cultural barriers. Strong cross-cultural communication skills also promote trust, respect, and collaboration, ultimately leading to more meaningful and successful social work interventions.
5. Collaboration with diverse stakeholders positively impacts the outcomes of social work interventions by bringing together different perspectives, expertise, and resources to address complex social issues comprehensively. By collaborating with diverse stakeholders such as community organizations, government agencies, and other service providers, social workers can leverage collective

strengths, coordinate services more effectively, and develop sustainable solutions that meet the diverse needs of clients and communities.

Multiple-Choice Questions

1. (c) To enhance understanding and respect for diverse cultures
2. (d) To provide equitable and unbiased services
3. (c) Promoting fairness and challenging oppression
4. (c) By fostering understanding and cooperation
5. (a) Positive impacts on intervention outcomes

Chapter 6

Review Questions

1. Key components of foundational skills in social work practice include active listening, empathy, professionalism, ethical decision-making, self-awareness, and boundary setting.
2. Effective communication fosters trust, understanding, and collaboration between social workers and clients. It enables the exchange of information, emotions, and needs, leading to more accurate assessments and tailored interventions.
3. Evidence-based approaches in assessment and intervention planning ensure that social work practices are informed by research and proven methodologies. By relying on empirical evidence, social workers can enhance the effectiveness and efficiency of their interventions, leading to better outcomes for clients.
4. Crisis intervention skills enable social workers to respond promptly and effectively to individuals or communities facing acute distress or emergencies. Conflict resolution skills help in managing interpersonal conflicts and facilitating constructive dialogue to resolve disputes and restore harmony.
5. Cultural competence is essential for providing inclusive and diverse social work interventions as it allows social workers to understand, respect, and effectively engage with individuals from diverse cultural backgrounds. It enables them to tailor interventions to meet the unique needs, preferences, and values of clients while promoting cultural humility and sensitivity.

Multiple-Choice Questions

1. (a) Fundamental abilities
2. (a) It facilitates strong relationships
3. (c) It ensures inclusivity

4. (d) To resolve immediate issues
5. (c) It fosters continuous improvement

Chapter 7

Review Questions

1. Agency assessment and analysis are crucial in social work field practice because they help social workers understand the organizational structure, resources, challenges, and opportunities within the agency. This understanding is essential for effective intervention planning and service delivery.
2. Needs assessment contributes to effective social work planning at the agency level by identifying the specific needs and priorities of the target population or community. This information guides the development of tailored interventions and resource allocation to address identified needs effectively.
3. The key principles of strategic planning for social impact in agency settings include goal alignment with the organization's mission and vision, stakeholder engagement, data-driven decision-making, resource optimization, and sustainability. The goals include maximizing positive outcomes for clients, enhancing organizational effectiveness, and promoting social justice and equity.
4. Client-centered approaches enhance the success of agency planning in social work by ensuring that the needs, preferences, and strengths of clients are central to the planning process. This approach promotes empowerment, autonomy, and collaboration between clients and service providers, resulting in more relevant and effective interventions.
5. Cultural competence and diversity integration are important in the context of agency-level field practice to ensure that services are accessible, responsive, and inclusive for diverse populations. By recognizing and respecting cultural differences, social workers can build trust, mitigate barriers to service access, and deliver culturally competent care that meets the unique needs of clients.
6. Evaluation plays a crucial role in ensuring continuous improvement in agency planning in social work by providing feedback on the effectiveness, efficiency, and impact of interventions and programs. Through ongoing evaluation, agencies can identify areas for improvement, measure progress toward goals, and make informed decisions to enhance service delivery and outcomes.
7. Social workers can effectively engage with stakeholders during the agency planning process by fostering open communication, building collaborative relationships, and soliciting input from diverse perspectives. Engaging stakeholders ensures that planning efforts are informed by community needs, priorities, and feedback, leading to more relevant and sustainable interventions.

Multiple-Choice Questions

1. (b) Evaluating continuous improvement
2. (b) By prioritizing client needs
3. (c) Goal setting and clarity
4. (b) To foster inclusivity and flexibility
5. (c) By fostering inclusivity and collaborative partnerships
6. (d) Involving clients and communities in feedback processes

Chapter 8

Review Questions

1. Tailoring interventions to client needs ensures that interventions are relevant and suitable for addressing the specific challenges and circumstances faced by each client. This personalized approach increases the likelihood of positive outcomes by addressing the root causes of issues and empowering clients to actively engage in the intervention process.
2. Collaborative goal setting fosters a sense of ownership and empowerment for clients as they actively participate in defining their goals and objectives. This collaborative process enhances intervention outcomes by ensuring that goals are meaningful, achievable, and aligned with the client's values and priorities. Additionally, it strengthens the client–worker relationship by promoting trust, mutual respect, and shared decision-making.
3. Utilizing evidence-based practices (EBPs) in social work interventions offers several advantages, including increased effectiveness, efficiency, and accountability. EBPs are informed by rigorous research and proven to produce positive outcomes for clients. Social work practitioners can stay updated on relevant research by engaging in ongoing professional development, attending training workshops, participating in peer-reviewed journals, and accessing online databases and resources dedicated to evidence-based practice in social work.
4. Addressing systemic factors in interventions involves recognizing and addressing the broader social, economic, and political structures that contribute to clients' challenges and inequalities. By addressing systemic factors such as institutional discrimination, socioeconomic disparities, and systemic barriers to accessing resources and opportunities, social workers can create more sustainable and impactful interventions. For example, advocating for policy changes to improve access to affordable housing can positively impact clients experiencing homelessness by addressing underlying structural issues contributing to housing instability.
5. The Case Management Model typically includes several key components, such as assessment, planning, linking, monitoring, and advocacy. In social work

practice, this model can be applied to enhance client support by providing comprehensive and coordinated services tailored to the individual needs of clients. Through systematic assessment, case managers identify clients' strengths, challenges, and service needs. They then develop personalized care plans in collaboration with clients and other stakeholders. By linking clients to appropriate resources and services, monitoring their progress, and advocating for their rights and interests, case managers facilitate access to necessary support systems and promote clients' overall well-being and self-sufficiency.

Multiple-Choice Questions

1. (b) Enhanced effectiveness
2. (c) Enhance the client–worker relationship
3. (b) Latest research and empirical evidence
4. (c) It considers broader influences on clients
5. (a) Tailoring interventions to client needs

Chapter 9

Review Questions

1. The primary purpose of data collection in social work field practice is to gather relevant information and insights that inform decision-making, assessment, and intervention strategies.
2. Two qualitative data collection techniques discussed in this chapter are:
   - Interviews: This involves conducting structured or semi-structured interviews with participants to gather in-depth information about their experiences, perspectives, and needs.
   - Focus groups: Focus groups bring together a small group of participants to discuss specific topics or issues in a facilitated group setting. It allows for the exploration of diverse viewpoints and group dynamics.
3. Ethical considerations related to participant autonomy and privacy in data collection include:
   - Informed consent: Ensuring that participants are fully informed about the purpose, risks, and benefits of the research and voluntarily consent to participate.
   - Confidentiality: Protecting the privacy of participants by safeguarding their personal information and ensuring that data are anonymized or de-identified where necessary.
4. Integrating mixed-methods approaches in social work field research is beneficial because it allows researchers to triangulate data from different sources, provid-

ing a more comprehensive understanding of complex phenomena. By combining qualitative and quantitative methods, researchers can complement each other's strengths and compensate for their respective weaknesses, enhancing the validity and reliability of the findings.

5. The role of technology in data collection for social work field practices offers several advantages, including:
   - Increased efficiency: Technology enables researchers to collect, manage, and analyze data more efficiently, saving time and resources.
   - Accessibility: Digital tools make it easier to reach a diverse range of participants, including those in remote or underserved areas.
   - Enhanced data quality: Technology allows for standardized data collection procedures, reducing errors and improving data quality.

   However, there are also potential ethical considerations associated with technology in data collection, such as:

   - Privacy and security concerns: Safeguarding participants' sensitive information from unauthorized access or breaches.
   - Digital divide: Ensuring equitable access to technology among all participants, especially those from marginalized or disadvantaged backgrounds.
   - Data ownership and consent: Clarifying participants' rights regarding their data and obtaining informed consent for its use, storage, and sharing.
   - Technological competency: Ensuring that both researchers and participants have the necessary skills to effectively use digital tools and platforms without bias or discrimination.

Multiple-Choice Questions

1. (b) Increased depth and breadth of understanding
2. (c) Content analysis
3. (c) Informed consent
4. (c) Surveys and questionnaires
5. (a) It protects participants' rights and choices

Chapter 10

Review Questions

1. Exploring diverse agency environments enhances social work practice by exposing practitioners to different organizational cultures, resources, and approaches. This exposure fosters adaptability, cultural competence, and the ability to tailor interventions to specific contexts and client populations.

2. Understanding unique agency dynamics and structures is essential for navigating and effectively engaging within different organizational settings. It allows social workers to grasp the hierarchies, communication channels, decision-making processes, and organizational cultures, which are critical for building relationships, advocating for clients, and implementing interventions.
3. SWOT analysis, which stands for Strengths, Weaknesses, Opportunities, and Threats, can be applied as a strategic tool in social work fieldwork situations by systematically assessing an agency's internal strengths and weaknesses, as well as external opportunities and threats. This analysis helps identify areas of improvement, potential growth opportunities, and challenges that need to be addressed.
4. The integration of SWOT analysis is crucial for adapting to and addressing challenges within agencies because it provides a comprehensive understanding of the agency's internal and external landscape. By identifying strengths to leverage, weaknesses to mitigate, opportunities to pursue, and threats to navigate, social workers can develop strategic plans, allocate resources effectively, and maximize the agency's capacity to meet client needs.
5. For example, during a SWOT analysis conducted in a social work agency, it was identified that one of the strengths was a dedicated and experienced staff with diverse skill sets. This finding influenced decision-making by highlighting the potential for internal capacity-building through peer learning and mentorship programs. Additionally, a weakness identified was outdated technology infrastructure, which led to interventions focused on securing funding for technological upgrades to improve service delivery and efficiency.

Multiple-Choice Questions

1. (c) To enhance the effectiveness of social work practice
2. (b) It contributes to the success of fieldwork experiences
3. (a) By assessing internal and external factors influencing practice
4. (c) It provides a systematic approach to decision-making

Chapter 11

Review Questions

1. Effective engagement with clients and their families builds trust, rapport, and a deeper understanding of their needs, which are essential for tailoring interventions and achieving positive outcomes in social work practice.
2. Community engagement fosters collaboration, empowers community members, and ensures that interventions address local needs effectively. It promotes own-

ership of solutions, increases social capital, and facilitates sustainable change by leveraging community strengths and resources.

3. Understanding political systems equips social workers with knowledge of policymaking processes, power structures, and stakeholders involved. This understanding enables social workers to navigate bureaucracies, advocate for policy changes that benefit clients and communities, and effectively influence decision-makers.
4. Maintaining a comprehensive case record is crucial for documenting client information, interventions, progress, and outcomes. It ensures continuity of care, facilitates communication among team members, supports evidence-based practice, and provides legal and ethical accountability.
5. Social workers collaborating within multi-disciplinary teams may face challenges such as communication barriers, differing professional cultures, power differentials, and conflicts over goals or approaches. These challenges can be addressed through clear communication, mutual respect, role clarification, interdisciplinary training, regular team meetings, and conflict resolution strategies.
6. Policy assessment allows social workers to analyze existing policies' impact on clients and communities, identify gaps or barriers to services, and advocate for necessary changes. It ensures that interventions align with broader policy goals, promote social justice, and address systemic issues contributing to clients' challenges.

Multiple-Choice Questions

1. (b) Establishing rapport and understanding client needs
2. (a) To promote positive change and address social issues
3. (d) By informing advocacy strategies and policy change initiatives
4. (b) To track intervention outcomes and client progress
5. (c) Communication barriers and conflicts

Chapter 12

Review Questions

1. Theoretical foundations provide a framework for understanding social work practice, guiding supervisors in providing relevant guidance and support to fieldwork students.
2. Cultural competence enables supervisors to understand and respect the diverse backgrounds of fieldwork students, fostering trust and effective communication in the supervisory relationship.

3. Supervisors have responsibilities such as providing feedback, facilitating learning opportunities, advocating for students, and ensuring adherence to ethical standards.
4. A structured template for supervision sessions ensures consistency, facilitates goal setting and progress tracking, and provides a framework for discussing challenging cases, ultimately enhancing the effectiveness of supervision.
5. Challenges in the supervisory relationship may include communication barriers, differing expectations, or conflicts. These challenges can be addressed through open communication, clarifying expectations, and fostering a supportive and collaborative environment.
6. Ongoing professional development and continuing education for supervisors are essential to stay updated on best practices, new research, and evolving ethical standards, ensuring that they can effectively support and guide fieldwork students in their learning and development.

Multiple-Choice Questions

1. (b) To provide structure and guidance
2. (b) It fosters a positive supervisory relationship
3. (c) Providing guidance and support
4. (d) By addressing them effectively
5. (c) It ensures supervisors stay updated and informed

Chapter 13

Review Questions

1. The key considerations when navigating ethical dilemmas in social work fieldwork include upholding ethical principles, considering the best interests of clients, seeking supervision or consultation when needed, and being transparent about decisions and actions.
2. Social work practitioners can effectively manage personal boundaries and prioritize emotional well-being by setting clear boundaries with clients, engaging in self-care practices, seeking support from colleagues or supervisors, and regularly reflecting on their emotional experiences.
3. Cultural competence is crucial in addressing diversity challenges during fieldwork as it involves understanding and respecting cultural differences, being aware of one's own biases, adapting interventions to meet the needs of diverse populations, and engaging in continuous learning about different cultures.
4. Strategies for overcoming systemic barriers in social work fieldwork practice may include advocating for policy changes, collaborating with community orga-

nizations, empowering clients to advocate for themselves, and challenging oppressive systems through social justice initiatives.
5. Practitioners can handle client resistance and navigate difficult situations in a client-centered manner by actively listening to clients' concerns, validating their experiences, exploring underlying reasons for resistance, offering support and alternatives, and maintaining a collaborative approach to problem-solving.
6. Supervision can contribute to addressing challenges and fostering professional growth in fieldwork by providing support and guidance, offering opportunities for reflection and self-awareness, facilitating skill development, and promoting ethical practice.
7. Opportunities for students in fieldwork practice include gaining hands-on experience, applying theoretical knowledge in real-world settings, developing professional skills and competencies, building relationships with clients and colleagues, receiving feedback and support from supervisors, and contributing to positive change in communities.
8. Ethical considerations associated with technology use in social work fieldwork include ensuring client privacy and confidentiality, obtaining informed consent for using technology, maintaining professional boundaries in online interactions, addressing disparities in access to technology, and staying updated on relevant laws and regulations regarding digital communication and data security.

Multiple-Choice Questions

1. (a) Seeking guidance from colleagues
2. (b) Establishing flexible boundaries
3. (a) It enhances effective communication and interventions
4. (b) Advocating for policy change
5. (c) By embracing a client-centered approach
6. (d) To address challenges and foster professional growth
7. (c) Opportunities for both personal and professional development

Chapter 14

Review Questions

1. Having clear objectives in a fieldwork report is significant because they provide a framework for the report's content, guiding the writer in presenting relevant information and ensuring that the report addresses specific goals and expectations.
2. The characteristics of a good fieldwork report, such as clarity, conciseness, organization, and accuracy, contribute to effective communication by making the information accessible, understandable, and engaging to the intended audience.

Clear and well-structured reports facilitate comprehension and interpretation, fostering communication between the writer and the readers.

3. Potential challenges in compiling the contents of a fieldwork report may include:
   - Gathering comprehensive and relevant data: Addressing this challenge involves conducting thorough research, utilizing various sources of information, and ensuring data accuracy and completeness.
   - Organizing and synthesizing information: This challenge can be addressed by developing an outline or structure for the report, categorizing information logically, and using clear headings and subheadings.
   - Ensuring objectivity and avoiding bias: To address this challenge, it is essential to critically evaluate sources, acknowledge any limitations or biases, and strive for balanced and impartial reporting.
   - Managing time constraints: Planning and scheduling tasks, setting priorities, and allocating sufficient time for each stage of report writing can help address this challenge effectively.
4. A well-structured fieldwork report benefits the social work practitioner, the client, and other stakeholders in several ways:
   - For the practitioner: It serves as a documentation of their work, providing a record of interventions, outcomes, and reflections. It can also support professional development by facilitating self-assessment and learning.
   - For the client: It offers insights into the services provided, progress made, and areas for improvement. It can enhance transparency, accountability, and trust in the practitioner-client relationship.
   - For other stakeholders (e.g., supervisors, policymakers, and funding agencies): It provides valuable information for decision-making, program evaluation, and quality assurance. It can also contribute to knowledge sharing, collaboration, and continuous improvement in social work practice.

Multiple-Choice Questions

1. (d) To communicate professional observations and interventions
2. (b) They help guide the report's content and focus
3. (c) They contribute to a thorough and accurate assessment
4. (a) Relevant and significant information

Chapter 15

Review Questions

1. Reflective practice in social work agencies involves critically examining one's experiences, actions, and decisions to gain insight into strengths, weaknesses, and areas for improvement. It contributes to professional development by foster-

ing self-awareness, enhancing learning from experiences, improving decision-making skills, and promoting continuous growth and adaptation.
2. Integrating reflective practices into the organizational culture of social work agencies requires commitment from leadership, creating safe and supportive environments for reflection, incorporating reflection into regular activities and processes, providing training and resources on reflective techniques, and valuing and recognizing reflective efforts.
3. Establishing structural mechanisms to support reflective learning within social work organizations involves developing formal policies or guidelines for reflective practice, allocating dedicated time and resources for reflection, fostering peer support and learning networks, integrating reflective supervision into supervisory practices, and promoting a culture of openness and learning from mistakes.
4. Key challenges associated with implementing reflective practices in social work include time constraints, resistance to change or self-reflection, perceived lack of value or relevance, fear of judgment or blame, and organizational barriers. Strategies to overcome these challenges may include providing training and support to build reflective skills, addressing organizational barriers and promoting buy-in from leadership, fostering a supportive and non-judgmental culture, and integrating reflection into existing workflows and processes gradually.

Multiple-Choice Questions

1. (a) Promote ongoing learning and professional development
2. (c) By fostering an environment that encourages self-reflection
3. (c) An established system that supports reflective practices
4. (d) Developing strategies to address and overcome challenges

Chapter 16

Review Questions

1. Transitioning out-of-field placement in social work contributes to professional development and growth by providing opportunities for reflection, consolidation of learning, and integration of theory into practice. It allows students to assess their strengths, areas for improvement, and career goals, fostering self-awareness and confidence as they transition into professional roles.
2. Reflecting on personal achievements during fieldwork offers valuable insights into one's strengths, challenges, and professional growth. These experiences can highlight effective strategies, interventions, and interpersonal skills while also identifying areas for further development. Lessons drawn from fieldwork experiences inform future practice by informing decision-making, enhancing critical thinking, and guiding professional development goals.

3. Technological advancements have significantly impacted the field of social work by transforming service delivery, data management, communication, and advocacy efforts. Practitioners can adapt to leverage these advancements by staying informed about emerging technologies, receiving training on relevant tools and platforms, and integrating technology into practice to enhance efficiency, accessibility, and client engagement. Additionally, practitioners must remain mindful of ethical considerations related to technology use, such as privacy, confidentiality, and digital equity, to ensure responsible and equitable service provision.

Multiple-Choice Questions

1. (b) Drawing lessons for future practice
2. (c) Adapt and leverage technology for societal benefit
3. (d) To address emerging issues and provide relevant services

Index

M. R. Islam, *Fieldwork in Social Work*,
https://doi.org/10.1007/978-3-031-56683-7